Apocalyptic Faith and Political Violence

Prophets of Terror

James F. Rinehart

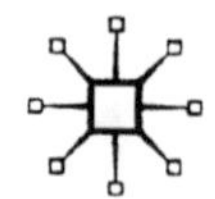

APOCALYPTIC FAITH AND POLITICAL VIOLENCE

First published in 2006 by
PALGRAVE MACMILLAN™
175 Fifth Avenue, New York, N.Y. 10010 and
Houndmills, Basingstoke, Hampshire, England RG21 6XS
Companies and representatives throughout the world.

PALGRAVE MACMILLAN is the global academic imprint of the Palgrave Macmillan division of St. Martin's Press, LLC and of Palgrave Macmillan Ltd. Macmillan® is a registered trademark in the United States, United Kingdom and other countries. Palgrave is a registered trademark in the European Union and other countries.

ISBN-13: 978–1–4039–7461–7
ISBN-10: 1–4039–7461–6

Library of Congress Cataloging-in-Publication Data

Rinehart, James F., 1950–
Apocalyptic faith and political violence : prophets of terror / James F. Rinehart.
p. cm.
Includes bibliographical references and index.
Contents: Terrorism and prophecy—The rise of millenarian terror—The mediating role of the prophet—Alienation and the quest for renewal—Identity and apocalyptic violence.
ISBN 1–4039–7461–6
1. Terrorism—Religious aspects—Christianity. 2. Violence—Religious aspects—Christianity. 3. Religion and politics. 4. End of the world. 5. Armageddon. I. Title.

BL65.T47R56 2006
303.6′25—dc22 2006041584

A catalogue record for this book is available from the British Library.

Design by Newgen Imaging Systems (P) Ltd., Chennai, India.

First edition: September 2006

10 9 8 7 6 5 4 3 2 1

Printed in the United States of America.

For Betty
My wife, my companion, my best friend

Contents

Introduction

Questions surrounding the "end times" have haunted cultures and societies from the very beginning of human existence. The possibility of the demise of one's society—one's way of life—conjures up questions that are outside the human capacity to answer in a satisfactory manner. Can there be an end time? Can we prepare for such an event? What will be the outcome? As evidence of the immense power of apocalyptic faith, these questions stand at the foundation of religions worldwide.

Despite the fact that it was virtually ignored during the Cold War, recent events have brought religion back to the forefront of scholarship on world politics. In particular, we must now confront the complex relationship between apocalyptic faith and the phenomenon of political violence; however, scant material exists on the subject.

This study seeks to fill a modest portion of this void by investigating the functional relationship between millenarian-inspired terrorism and the process of political change. Specifically, it examines three cases that emerged in the late twentieth century—Aum Shinrikyo, Sendero Luminoso, and Hezbollah—and their political impact on the global community. Although its appearance has been episodic, becoming most explicit during periods of general restiveness and in response to conditions of pervasive alienation, millenarianism has been an ever-present mechanism for engendering limited political change in all three societies.

The advent of Western imperialism impinging on their traditional life created the most significant challenge these societies had faced. An important response was the evolution of a paradigm of millenarian expectations usually involving political violence. I argue that this paradigm remains fully intact and is exemplified by these late-twentieth-century movements that utilized terror to achieve their political goals.

At first glance it would appear that the societies that gave birth to these movements would have little in common and thus would be poor candidates for a comparative study of political violence. After all, Japan is one of the most advanced industrialized democracies, possessing one of the highest standards of living in the world. Peru and Lebanon, on the other hand, exhibit a rather inchoate form of democratic system and, economically, must be included in the category of the "developing" world. Japan is ethnically homogeneous with virtually no racial diversity. Peru, much like the rest of Latin America, can only be described as a heterogeneous mixture of races. Japan possesses a unitary culture, whereas Peru is a diverse convergence of many different cultures including a distinctly and sociopolitically dominant Spanish, and thus European, system, and a majority of its population is American Indian. Although seemingly falling under the rubric of an Arab state, Lebanon possesses a diversity of religions, races, and cultures.

Nonetheless, these seemingly different societies have much in common that make them fertile ground for cross-cultural research about political violence. First, all three societies possess a lengthy and durable history of pervasive, religiously inspired millenarian beliefs. These beliefs frequently manifest themselves, since the ancient period, as protest movements, which tend to emerge following episodes of extreme social stress, associated with the challenges of massive cultural transformation.

Second, the indigenous peoples of each society have traditionally been imbued with a powerful sense of historical destiny and an equally well-defined identity. For example, according to traditional legend, the people of Japan are descended from the sun goddess, Amaterasu, and the land itself is considered to be divine by its inhabitants.[1] Indeed, the oldest written records of Shinto, the *Kojiki* (AD 712) and the *Nihon Shoki* (AD 720), primarily focus on the ancient, supernatural origins of the Japanese imperial family and its divine mission on earth.[2] In Peru, Andean Indians trace their roots to the Inca Empire, an advanced political and economic social system that thrived in the pre-Columbian era. Their sacred emperors were considered to be sons of the sun and, thus, gods.[3] Shi'a Muslims of Lebanon see themselves as the inheritors of the infallible teachings of Prophet Muhammad.

Third, the intrusion of Western ideas of modernity introduced new socioeconomic and political ideas in each of these societies that challenged and in many ways threatened not only their traditional way of life but also their collective sense of identity. Indeed, each have had to succumb, to no small extent, to European ways that disrupted traditional systems and forced peoples to reframe their identities in such a way as to seek compatibility and conformity with Western norms.

Our first task is to define the notion of millenarianism. It is the belief that at the end of time some sort of rescuer or savior will return to the culture and save the faithful from the wrath of an anti-god, and deliver them into a Promised Land or utopian existence.

As one might expect, in its earliest form, millenarianism was perceived of as an explicitly religious phenomenon. Indeed, it stood at the foundation of traditional Chinese folklore,[4] ancient Zoroastrianism,[5] early Judaism,[6] African animism,[7] Christianity,[8] and Islam;[9] it survives in these forms to the modern age.

The concept of millenarianism is both significant and pervasive. It is noteworthy in both its capacity to mobilize a culture for action, generally in the presence of perceived danger, and its relationship to the necessity of collective identity that establishes the foundation of cultural unity. Its pervasiveness is equally incredible. Millenarianism permeates virtually every culture around the world largely due to its capacity to adapt to the wants and needs of the people, even in the most modern societies. As a result, it is both a traditional and modern phenomenon.

The Christian faith has always anticipated the end time, and its teachings reflect this expectation. Originally, millenarianism referred to the belief held by many Christians that after his Second Coming, Jesus Christ will create a messianic kingdom on earth and will reign over it, with the help of a select or chosen people, for a thousand years preceding the Final Judgment.[10]

More recently, social scientists have sought to understand millenarianism well beyond that of its original religious foundations. Supported by an ever-growing body of research about non-Christian movements that, nonetheless, exhibit the characteristics of millenarianism, researchers have come to view the phenomenon in increasingly secular as well as behavioral terms—as a response to massive upheaval such as that engendered by natural disasters, socioeconomic disturbance, or the disorientation resulting from the collision of highly different cultures.[11]

Outbreaks of millenarian fervor are not exclusively dependent upon Jewish or Christian traditions of religious prophecy or, for that matter, on a traditional worldview. Over the past century, scholars have uncovered remarkably similar movements, led by a prophet leader, claiming divine revelation, outside of the traditional realm of Judeo-Christianity in remote regions of Africa, Asia, the Americas, and Melanesia.[12] Despite their diverse cultural sources, the conditions present at the time of their eruption are notably alike. Society is undergoing rapid change. In addition, long-standing cultural traditions are systematically invalidated by seemingly more powerful forces generally delivered by the invasion of Western culture into the region. As a result, the peoples of these communities are experiencing mass alienation and insecurity. Under such disruptive circumstances, powerful modern messiahs have emerged around the world.[13]

Millenarian movements are powerfully emotional social movements whose members anticipate a unique type of social salvationism—an immediate, collective, total, this worldly, supernatural rescue, and subsequent transformation of society.[14]

It is important to point out at this early juncture that most millenarian movements are nonviolent. There are numerous examples of millenarian movements that are quite passive and doctrinally committed to peaceful reconciliation of conflict.

Indeed, among those millenarian movements that have exhibited a bent toward violent action, more often than not it has been aimed inward, at the self, not at society at large. As a result, self-destruction is a common characteristic of millenarian sects, possibly seen as yet another tool of hastening the end time.[15]

Nonetheless, political violence and the spread of "terror" have been frequent tools of millenarian movements as in the cases under present investigation.

Methodology

The study of millenarianism and its relationship to terrorism presents us with some rather significant methodological difficulties.

For example, both phenomena restrict the potential for field studies. As a result, empirical data is rare. Such movements are quite difficult and often dangerous to penetrate, rendering first-hand accounts and independent observations limited, thorny, and challenging. In addition, those who survive such movements tend to selectively limit their recall of events, reconstructing a narrative account only within certain boundaries of their experiences.[16]

Research studies on terrorism or millenarianism are often not placed within an impartial analytical structure. Unfortunately, many of those who write about terrorism, for example, tend to possess a preconceived bias of a "problem–solution" orientation in which he or she is simply attempting to justify a set of counterterrorist prescriptives.[17] Such an orientation is frequently presented in an emotional manner and laden with personal preferences/biases.[18]

An additional major methodological hurdle to be overcome in any analysis of millenarian-inspired political violence involves the nature and difficulty of accounting for human perceptions of events. In other words, what we or anyone else "sees" in any episode occurring in time and space depends very much on the "lens" through which we view it.

The processes of perception formation and social cognition involve thinking that is focused on social stimuli—mainly persons and groups. We know that the perceptions of individuals are based on a cognitive process and that people are actively organizing perceivers, not merely passive receptacles of information.[19] Such a process has four important aspects. Each of these has relevance to the study of both millenarianism and political violence.

First, the processing of information about people and their surroundings involves perceiving some coherent and discernable meaning in the stimulus object. For example, we can't observe the phenomenon of millenarianism without conjuring up our own personal questions about the end time. It is within that context that we perceive of such movements. Equally so, terrorist acts are most effective when they provoke the audience to ask some critical questions: Who did this? Why did it happen? Will it happen again?

Second, as perceivers of sociopolitical events, individuals tend to pay special attention to the more salient features of the perceptual field around them rather than giving equal attention to everything. This provides the terrorist with an ideal environment to make maximum use of the demonstration of his or her acts. Death, physical destruction, violence: these are the tools of the terrorist. They have a capacity like no other to elicit emotional responses from the audience they are intended to reach.

Third, we organize our personal perceptual view of the world by categorizing or grouping stimuli. This invites stereotypes, the bane of good research on social phenomena. When asked, for example, to describe a "terrorist," Americans will overwhelmingly respond with (1) they are male and (2) they are Muslims of Middle East origins.[20] These stereotypes were pervasive long before the attacks of September 11, 2001 (9/11).

Fourth, individuals perceive stimuli as part of some kind of structure. Each separate stimulus tends to be related to others in time, space, and a causal flow. In other words, on impulse, we insert the individual stimulus in a broader structure of knowledge. Millenarian movements and the actions of terrorists are among the more salient of stimuli available in a modern media–active world of twenty-four hour news channels and the demand for fresh and evermore compelling "news breaks." We find it impossible to understand terrorist attacks as isolated events. Rather we perceive of them in a far broader context of meaning and structure, for example, religion, ethnicity, poverty, hatred, bigotry, imperialism, modernization, among others.

All of these characteristics of perception and the problems they create are exemplified in a persistent image that became widely broadcast in the aftermath of the 9/11 attacks on the World Trade Center (WTC) and the Pentagon in the United States in 2001.

The night before the attacks, Mohammed Atta, one of the "pilots" of the first airliner that crashed into the WTC, drove a rental car to Portland, Maine, in order to take advantage of the more lax security in a smaller airport, at the beginning of the operation. Early the next morning, Atta and his colleagues were caught on a security camera passing through a metal detector at the Portland International Airport along with everyone else who boarded the plane headed for Boston.

This videotape was shown repeatedly on American and international TV news networks in the aftermath of the attacks. It shows a well-dressed, young, thirty-three-year-old man, brief-bag over his shoulder, calmly headed to his gate. He could very well have been a salesmen or accountant on his way to a business meeting; headed out of town for a few vacation days of rest and relaxation; or, on his way to visit relatives in another part of the country. His lack of emotion and his demeanor provided little evidence of the tragic events that would unfold before the morning was over. Eventually, the reality would become all too plain.

It is an image that I cannot forget because, on the one hand, it is embedded in a highly complex set of events that developed quite rapidly and, on the other hand, there is the hauntingly cool and emotionless look on Atta's face.

Yet, there are many complex perceptions at work here. What is "seen" depends on where one "sits" and through what lens they are looking.

From an American and generally Western perspective, what is seen is a crazed terrorist bent on massive destruction of life and property, including his own ritual suicide.

In contrast, among some in the Islamic world, these images of Atta and his colleagues offer a perception of martyrdom and unprecedented heroism.[21]

And, finally, Atta's perception of self that Tuesday morning must have seemed that the day was of enormous spiritual significance. He would worship God in the most personal and ultimate of ways: self-sacrifice for a sacred cause in which he truly believed.

In a poem later found in the rental car at the airport, Rawil al-Sheri, one of Atta's colleagues, had expressed that they were heading into the "face of death with our heads held high." In addition, seemingly providing instructions to himself for the morning, Atta had scribbled his own words: "be calm," he assured himself, "you are carrying out an action—God loves you."[22]

So, perception presents a significant problem for the student of political violence. Relying on one exclusive point of view is a flawed and fruitless undertaking if we are to truly understand these complex events.

The terms "terrorism" and "terrorist" are among the most abused in our contemporary vocabulary. The mere utterance of these words in a political speech or the media can immediately conjure up the most egregious of mental images.[23] In turn, such images engender an emotional reaction representing a rather unique combination of fear, personal disgust, and individual anxiety. One has a difficult time turning to analysis or solutions when we are so traumatized by the problem itself. Indeed, it is this social trauma and the accompanying emotional outpouring that renders terror so politically efficacious. In a very uncomfortable way, acts of terror meet head on our fundamental system of values regarding order, stability, and predictability within society. As a result, both our personal reaction and that of society as a whole to terrorist acts can only be measured through the emotion of "aroused fears." This has a profound impact on our ability to translate, analyze, and, ultimately, clarify events.[24]

Often, our perceptions guide us to define political violence along a normative spectrum. War, for example, can be seen as normatively good in the presence of evil. In the same way, organized violence in the presence of oppression or injustice can be seen as necessary. In contrast, to many, war is never justified. Further, insurgency against any political regime is always unacceptable. Nonetheless, to define any sociopolitical phenomenon, whether it is war, insurgency, revolution, rebellion, or terrorism, in moral terms renders it "unscientific."

Normative perceptions of political violence tend to place too little focus on answering the question "why?" To some extent, this is where we find ourselves with respect to current scholarship on the subject. Much is known about the "what," "when," and "where" of terrorism, but little about the "why."

Defining political violence along a normative spectrum also involves a fatal assumption that renders objective analysis impossible. This is so because such definitions inherently assume that some forms of political violence are morally justified, whereas others are not.

For example, perhaps the single most significant act of political terror in history: the dropping of nuclear bombs on two Japanese cities by the United States in August, 1945, is generally not perceived of by

Americans as a terrorist attack. It has been historically justified in the eyes of many as moral. After all, the dropping of these bombs actually "saved" lives through the avoidance of an American invasion of the island of Japan, perceived to be necessary to end the war.[25]

On the other hand, a suicide bombing by Islamic "fundamentalists" resulting in the deaths of dozens of innocent people in a Jerusalem marketplace is perceived of by most as morally reprehensible and completely unjustified. Indeed, those who would carry out such an act are frequently considered psychopaths.

From an analytical perspective, we must come to understand that both of these sets of events are part of the same sociopolitical phenomenon and that normative questions are irrelevant to their scientific study. It is the behavior itself that establishes the framework for analysis.

The primary methodology employed in this study is a cross-cultural comparison of three non-Western communities that engendered sociopolitical movements that utilized political violence in the late twentieth century. Analytically, it attempts to identify and characterize the nature of the millenarian components in all three cases.

This study is not an attempt to recount the entire history of these three movements. As you proceed, you will notice that the approach is quite focused. I seek an investigation that uncovers common threads of millenarian-inspired social change as well as variations of terrorism in these cases.

This is not to imply that the origins and processes of political violence may be explained exclusively in the context of millenarianism; they cannot. Many other variables were in play in these highly complex, multifaceted circumstances. Nonetheless, my goal is a narrower and modest inquiry, which seeks to highlight a significant variable—millenarianism—present in these cases: a variable that has not been fully developed analytically in previous scholarship.[26]

The task is to seek objectivity through the elimination of bias and emotionality. In my judgment, one can evaluate events only by relating ideology to action. Thus, a primary goal of this study is to understand the motivations of political actors who utilize terrorist tactics. It is only through such analysis that we can come to understand their actions.

I argue that millenarianism performed four important functions in the political violence exhibited in our three cases. First, millenarianism offers guidance about how to respond to things of which the individual has no experience, and perhaps no control over. As such it plays an important role to the individual who lacks certainty. Millenarianism provides individuals with readymade solutions to problems. It specifies choices for us and offers a structure to enable us to understand the events in our environment over which we have no experience or control—thus it reduces uncertainty.

Second, I argue that in all three cases an important mediating function was performed by a political figure who came to be perceived as a messianic leader.

Millenarianism performed a unique therapeutic function within these movements by providing a sacred justification for the use of egregious violence in the achievement of their objectives, leaving group participants free from guilt, reducing stress, and relieving a massive sense of group alienation.

Finally, millenarian beliefs established a clear, certain identity as God's chosen people among members of these three groups. This identity, in turn, augmented group members' self-esteem and satisfied fundamental motivations. This identity role served to link people along a common dimension.

Chapter 1 of this study attempts to define both terrorism and millenarianism in more detailed terms. In addition, it investigates and characterizes the unique and important relationship between the two phenomena.

Chapter 2 traces the evolution of a paradigm of apocalyptic expectations as a component of political change within these societies. It outlines the first of the functional roles of millenarianism in the three cases: as a tool of mobilization and a call for political action in the presence of perceived sociopolitical turbulence.

Chapters 3–5 focus on three additional functional roles I argue are performed by millenarianism among political groups committed to political change through the use of violence: (1) a leadership function, (2) a therapeutic function, and (3) an identity function. These chapters are organized along thematic categories, which allow for a comparative framework of an analysis of the three cases.

A resilient and omnipresent stream of millenarian expectations had become a salient component of the persistent worldview of the members of each of these societies. It was through this "lens" that they conceptualized sociopolitical change.

These apocalyptic expectations were able to bubble forth in times of social turbulence that resulted from direct challenges to their culture and way of life; challenges that engendered social, economic, and political disturbance, manifested by a widespread sense of oppression, injustice, disorientation, and alienation.

Late-twentieth-century political violence that emerged in these three cases owed much more than has been generally acknowledged to their capacity to draw this powerful millenarian tradition to the surface of society and shape it to fit the specific needs of that moment in time and space. It is the goal of this study to shed a more significant light on this important and enduring phenomenon.

CHAPTER 1

Terrorism and Prophecy

Terrorism is a worldwide phenomenon; rarely a day goes by without some mention of political violence somewhere on the globe. As a result, the phenomenon plays a not so insignificant role in international affairs and is of interest to ordinary citizens around the world. Indeed, it has been argued that political terrorism is perhaps the "most difficult problem of our time."[1]

Nonetheless, despite this ubiquity and seeming intractability, the sociopolitical spectacle of terrorism remains a dramatic, yet ambiguous, concept. This is so primarily for two important reasons.

First, is the extraordinary unconventional character of political terror.[2] As the events of September 11, 2001, clearly demonstrated, it possesses dramatic value even when such acts occur hundreds or even thousands of miles away, either here at home or in an entirely different culture.

Second, there is no consensus on what exactly constitutes terrorism. This raises some rather significant problems for all of us. For example, politicians and the media alike can and do exploit the notion of terrorism because of the sensationalism and public fear it can rouse. The instantaneous pictures of graphic and egregious violence delivered into our homes have exacerbated the problem of scientific inquiry of the phenomenon by overemphasizing its subjective and emotional character.

Society cannot begin to control terrorism without first achieving consensus on what it is. This has not yet been accomplished, either at the national or international level.[3] In the same way that the legal control of criminal murder and war on the battlefield requires workable definitions of various terminologies, eventually, terrorism will require societies around the world to classify and characterize the concept more precisely.

An example of this legal ambiguity involves the "detainees" currently being held by the U.S. government at Guantanamo Bay,

Cuba. Are they "belligerents"? Do they have the status and, thus, the rights of prisoners of war? Or, are they criminals to be tried in a court of law following due process? If so, of what specific crimes are they charged? Without a consensus on a definition of terrorism it is impossible to begin to answer these questions.

Terrorism as a tool of social and political change is nothing new. As early as AD 48 a Jewish religious faction known as the Zealots carried out a campaign of violence in an attempt to incite an insurrection against Roman imperialism in the colony of Judea. The Zealots utilized political assassins (derived from the Latin word *sicarii* or dagger men) who killed or kidnapped both high-level Roman officials as well as Jews, who were their known collaborators.[4]

Beginning in the second half of the twentieth century, the world has witnessed resurgence in the use of terrorism as a device of political change. Although such tools as political assassination remain persistent,[5] new, more high-tech tactics, such as airline hijackings, have become common.

Terrorism: A Definition

In studying terrorism one finds oneself conducting evaluations and analyzing a topic that lacks a precise and consistent definition.[6] Such a predicament merely exacerbates the analysis by creating some significant methodological hurdles. If you can't define something, it is impossible to study it scientifically. A clear example of this lack of consensus and consistency is demonstrated in table 1.1, which contains five different definitions of terrorism supplied by various branches of the U.S. and Canadian governments: the U.S. Central Intelligence Agency, the U.S. Department of State, the U.S. Department of Defense, the US Federal Bureau of Investigation, and the Canadian Security Intelligence Service. As one can see there is limited consistency among these related government agencies in their classification of the phenomenon.

Nonetheless, it is possible to conduct a brief content analysis to identify those definitional attributes that appear across all five.[7] Of a total of eleven different attributes identified in the five definitions, only two—"violence" and "politically motivated"—are shared by all five. Only three share "noncombatant targets." Remarkably, only two identify such activity as "unlawful" within the definition itself.

Such a content analysis more clearly illustrates the remarkable failure to achieve both definitional consensus and consistency among those charged with combating terrorism. Effective policy will not be

Table 1.1 Definitions of terrorism supplied by various branches of the U.S. and Canadian governments

Department	*Definition of Terrorism*
United States Department of State[a]	"Premeditated, politically motivated violence perpetuated against noncombatant targets by subnational groups or clandestine agents, usually intended to influence an audience"
United States Federal Bureau of Investigation[b]	"The unlawful use of force or violence against persons or property to intimidate or coerce a government, the civilian population, or any segment thereof, in furtherance of political or social objectives"
Canadian Security Intelligence Service[c]	". . . the deliberate and systematic threat or use of violence to achieve an objective. In the modern context, the expression is generally associated with politically motivated coercion"
United States Central Intelligence Agency[d]	". . . politically motivated violence that is carried out either by subnational groups or by clandestine agents of a government, and that involves more than one nationality when on considers who the perpetrator and the victim are, and where the attack is carried out"
United States Department of Defense[e]	"the unlawful use of—or threatened use of—force or violence against individuals or property to coerce or intimidate governments or societies, often to achieve political religious, or ideological objectives"

Sources:

[a] Office of the Coordinator for Counterterrorism, *Patterns of Global Terrorism 1996*, US Department of State Publication 10433 (Washington, DC: State Dept., April 1997), vi.

[b] Terrorist Research and Analytical Center, National Security Division, Federal Bureau Of Investigation, *Terrorism in the United States 1955* (Washington, DC: US Department of Justice, 1966), ii.

[c] Canadian Security Intelligence Service Publications, Commentary No. 13, "Terrorism and the Rule of Law: Dangerous Compromise in Colombia," October 1991.

[d] Speech by Senior Analytical Manager, DCI Counterterrorist Center, US Central Intelligence Agency to the World Affairs Council, San Antonio Texas, October 7, 1996.

[e] Department of the Army and Department of the Air Force, *Military Operations in Low Intensity Conflict*, FM 100-20/Air Force Pamphlet 3-20.

achieved so long as what is to be combated is not sufficiently defined and consistent attributes and characteristics identified.

This lack of consensus on a definition of terrorism, not only among the examples just cited, but across a much broader spectrum, is the result of a number of factors. Rather than being too broad—a problem that characterizes many social science academic pursuits—the notion of terrorism is frequently found to be unduly narrow. Rather than being perceived of as a form of political violence with application to many different scenarios including war, the notion is often used as a pejorative label to describe the activities of certain political actors for rather narrowly constructed activities usually in opposition to a legitimate state. This analytical construction seems to virtually ignore the possibility, indeed, the oft-occurring reality, that states, themselves, embark on activities that any analyst could reasonably call "terrorist." The outcome has been what is considered by many to be a trite and hackneyed phrase, namely that "one man's terrorist is another man's patriot."[8]

This presents us with an important first clue in our quest to achieve a consistent definition of terrorism. Such a definition must focus on the acts of terrorists, not simply labeling the actors.[9] Indeed, an important source of the problem surrounding an effective analysis of terrorism is the emphasis that has traditionally been placed on the identity of the actors, rather than what constitutes such acts and why they occur in the first place. Nonetheless, this is a predictable human reaction, albeit an inappropriate one. To cope with such egregious forms of violence that so violate our own cognitive maps, humans, out of necessity, must come to define such acts along a normative plane—a process that, as we have already mentioned, consistently and effectively blocks our objectivity.

Many researchers argue that this persistent, careless use of the term "terrorism" has even effectively infiltrated academic scholarship about the phenomenon. Unfortunately, the rather arbitrary use of the term not only exaggerates data about political violence, but also limits our ability to both understand and cope with its effects.[10]

In addition to a focus on the acts and not the actors, a definition of terrorism must include a political agenda: a specific set of grievances or demands that are of utmost importance to the actors willing to use terror.[11] Thus, we are attempting to understand an exclusively political concept. It cannot be otherwise. Yet, as is so often the case, when one attempts to understand political concepts, it inherently involves a debate about relationships of legitimate and illegitimate power: its acquisition, use, and consequences.[12]

Political actors that utilize terror, be they officials of states or members of a particular sociopolitical movement, are well organized and purposeful. Their goals are clearly defined, and their actions calculated. Terrorism utilizes violence as a strategic tool to bring about specific results within a target population, usually civilian; sometimes within a combination of civilians and government officials too. In either case, the utilization of terror is always designed to engender an emotional response among a target group significantly larger than the population actually victimized by the terrorist act(s). Indeed, some political organizations that employ terror seek only to destroy nonhuman targets, for example, office buildings during nonworking hours when they are unoccupied or unloaded jet aircraft sitting on the ground.

In this way, those who employ terrorism seek to place their grievance and/or their political agenda in a public forum and draw attention to it in a dramatic way.[13] Terrorism, therefore, is a tool of communication, conveying a message from the group carrying out such acts of violence to the larger population as a whole.

Another significant difficulty in defining terrorism is differentiating it from other forms of violent behavior. For example, some consider the use of terrorist tactics as merely criminal behavior. After all, it generally involves assault, destruction of property, and even murder, among other commonly defined criminal acts. It is difficult to refute such arguments especially when one considers that crime is defined in the general (nonlegal) sense as a serious offense against another or against humanity as a whole.

Nonetheless, we must acknowledge that terrorism is more than just mere criminal activity. Although it is true that terrorism involves either physical and/or psychological abuse in some form, to exclusively identify it as criminal behavior is an incomplete characterization of the phenomenon.[14] This becomes evident as one comes to understand the relationship between terrorists and their victims.

The victims of terrorism fall into two distinct categories: direct and indirect targets.[15] Direct targets are those who, in some way, come into physical contact with those utilizing terror. This group may include hostages, abductees, the injured, or the dead victims of a physically violent act.

At the same time, indirect targets are those members of a much larger target population who, although not in direct contact with terrorists or physically affected by their actions, are, nonetheless, psychologically abused by events. Perhaps their only contact was through media reports. The key in terms of direct victims is their innocence. "Innocence is the quintessential condition of terrorist victimology, for the terrorist victim is not the ultimate target. When political terrorists strike out at innocent third parties, their real intent is the destabilization of governments and a demoralization or even panic among the public-at-large," not to carry out an exclusively criminal act.[16]

Terrorism is a group phenomenon. "Terrorist organizations are not just collections of separate individuals; they are functioning units that exert strong pressures on their members and hold out powerful rewards."[17] In addition, Robert Jay Lifton argues, "social and historical forces cannot be reduced to individual psychopathology or clinical concepts."[18]

So, where does this leave us regarding an effective definition of terrorism, a task we must confront in the context of this study? In the end, our need for definition is satisfied by the notion that *terrorism is limited, organized, premeditated violence, carried out by both state and non-state actors, that is calculated to instill a sense of instability, disorder, and, most importantly, a fear of future, greater violence, in an attempt to achieve specific and, purposeful political goals.*

This study focuses on terrorism carried out by three non-state actors. This, by no means, should diminish the equally significant use of terror by state actors. As such, this definition is not unduly restrictive and is sufficient to include both terrorism "from below"—that is, terrorism stemming from discontent or ideologies aimed at the existing state and originating from subnational groups, and, also, state-sponsored terrorism where the state carries out forms of systematic violence against a specific target(s) in order to achieve/sustain political legitimacy.

Theories of Terrorism and Political Violence

To understand terrorism requires us to look at the topic of political violence writ large. We may categorize such an investigation into three broad theoretical schools of thought: (1) the structural school, (2) the organizational school, and (3) what we may call the psychological school. Within each of these theoretical schools a number of sub-schools have emerged over time.

Prior to the twentieth century it was widely believed that political violence was both irrational and random. Angry crowds, street mobs, rioters and protestors against public policies, social conditions, and economic circumstances were perceived of as composed of nothing more than malcontents, misfits, and otherwise irrational individuals who simply wanted to stir up trouble.[19] It was generally accepted that such violence could not be studied in a systematic and scientific manner.

Structural School

In the mid-nineteenth century, Karl Marx challenged these conceptions by arguing that episodes of political violence (1) were nonrandom in nature, (2) could be studied in a systematic way, and (3) rather than being a function of the characteristics of the crowd, mob, or the individuals who composed them was largely a function of the overall framework of society.

Here we see the origins of the structural school. According to Marx, political violence is likely to occur at a point when existing social and political structures and leadership interfere with economic development. Marx traces such development through various stages from feudalism to capitalism to socialism and eventually, he predicts, to communism. As technological and economic change takes place during the period of capitalist industrialization, a conflict develops between the new urban industrial working class—the proletariat—and the ruling capitalist class.[20]

Marx predicted that the importance of the working class (the actual profit producers) in an advanced industrialized economic system would eventually exceed that of the class of capitalist elites who merely owned the means of production. As their importance weakened, Marx predicted, economic elites would attempt to hold onto their power through political repression thus setting up an inevitable clash, which becomes violent. What Marx referred to as "the dictatorship of the Proletariat" would follow, enabling the working class to take control of the structure and process of government.[21]

In the late nineteenth century, Emile Durkheim and Gustave LeBon, among others, argued that societies in the midst of turbulent political violence had actually "broken down." Under such conditions of breakdown, political authorities must rely on the use of government coercion at critical points to ensure the continued existence of the system. Nonetheless, coercion alone cannot maintain the system.[22]

The use of government coercion, although accepted as legitimate by a majority of the population, nonetheless engenders dissident movements, which are opposed to some or all forms of government policy. Under such pressure, the structural capacity for the government to coerce is eventually broken down and collapses.

In his Resource Mobilization Theory, Charles Tilly[23] argues that collective action stems not from the decay of society but rather from the competition between rival political groups for position and advantage within a system. As such it focuses on organizational structure within a society and the relationships between the components of that structure.

Organizational School

Some scholars of political violence pursue an organizational approach. They argue that the phenomenon of terrorism and our notion of it rely greatly on historical context. Here we must take into consideration political, social, and economic conditions of the time as major variables accounting for participation in and actions of terrorist movements. In other words, terrorism and political violence in general are cause and effect phenomena; they are rather predictable responses to social, political, and economic conditions.

Martha Crenshaw perceives of political violence as a rational, tactical choice of action, planned and executed in an organized group environment.[24] Those who use violence as a political tool, she argues, have already exhausted all other available and conventional possibilities to achieve their objectives. The only tool left is that of violence, which is utilized to enlist support for their cause and achieve their political goals.[25] In this process, terrorist movements become purposeful political units, goals are established, a structure begins to form, an ideology is crafted, and the movement becomes "organized" for action. In contrast to the image of the "deranged," isolated individual carrying out random acts that are seemingly without purpose and simply requiring forceful elimination by state institutions, the organizational school asserts that modern terrorists are sophisticated, well organized, and capable of achieving their stated goals with impunity.[26] Crenshaw concludes that terrorism is a well-organized, rational, purposeful process carried out by structured groups who reach "collective decisions based on commonly held beliefs." Nonetheless, the degree of commitment to these beliefs can vary from member to member.[27]

One of the factors that tend to limit terrorist organization membership is their usually rigid recruiting techniques. Highly centralized, efficient organizations screen out potential members who could be dangerous to the survival of the group. Those individuals who seek to join terrorist groups merely to fulfill their personal desires for placing themselves in harm's way, thrill seeking, and excitement are systematically filtered out through the rigorous recruit and selection process employed by even the most violent of political groups that employ terrorism. The result, Crenshaw argues, is that "the outstanding common characteristic of terrorists is their normality."[28]

Organizational theorists emphasize that terrorism tends to emerge in the presence of very specific conditions and contexts that exist within a society. For example, Donatella della Porta, in her analysis of modern terror movements in Italy, concludes that terrorism emerges in the presence of a unique convergence of ideology, resources, and thoughtful, appropriate tactics.

First, a portion of the society must come to believe that their collective interests are not being satisfied. In addition, a political culture that justifies the use of violence as a tool of conflict management is required. In turn, the group makes a strategic choice of violent tactics, as opposed to nonviolent ones. This, she argues, is a political decision, not an emotional one: a decision that occurs in an organized, rational environment and includes such resource considerations as appropriate use of the media and logistical and financial support from the outside world.[29]

Finally, the organizational school argues that scholarship about political violence should not exclusively focus on the causes of violence, but also on its consequences, which they assert creates new conditions and new contexts for potential further violence or conflict resolution.[30]

Psychological School

Terrorism is a psychological process of intimidation much more than it is a physical process of destruction of property or abuse, injury, and murder of individuals. The tactic of the terrorist is not so much to destroy, maim, or kill, as much as it is to incite widespread panic and horror in the minds of a designated audience. As a result, political violence has often been explained in a sort of cause and effect relationship through the application of conventional behavioral theories that first focus on such phenomena as frustration/aggression,[31] relative deprivation,[32] or fanaticism[33] and second, their influence on the target population. Indeed, much of this theoretical debate has centered on reactions to perceived inequities—uneven distribution of power, rights, and resources—that exist within or across society between repressed minorities and the mainstream of the population.[34]

Ted Robert Gurr has been an important figure in the development of psychological theories of political violence since the publication of his book *Why Men Rebel* in 1970. In direct contrast to the structural and organizational schools, Gurr argues that the mind of the individual represents the most critical factor in political violence—that is, public violence occurs because people purposely decide to make it happen. To Gurr, the necessary precondition for violent civil conflict is the perception of relative deprivation (RD), which he defines as "a perceived discrepancy between people's value expectations and their value capabilities." Value expectations are the goods and conditions of life to which people believe they are rightfully entitled. Value capabilities are the goods and conditions that they think they are capable of attaining or maintaining, given the social means available to them. The widespread perception of relative deprivation leads to discontent, which tends to lead to politicization of discontent, which leads to political violence.[35]

Another theory that possesses enormous resonance among members of the public at large is the notion that those who pursue political violence, in particular those that we might call terrorists, are psychopathological.[36] This is a predictable response on the part of the public when one considers that the acts of violence prosecuted by terrorists are perceived to be outside of the realm of rational human behavior. After all, no "normal" human, many assume, is capable of carrying out such heinous acts.

Psychiatrist Jerrold Post is one of the leading proponents of the notion that terrorism involves acts carried out by individuals who are mentally ill. On the one hand, he argues, terrorism is a logical endeavor, ostensibly purposeful, planned, and executed in a reasoned manner. Nonetheless, Post asserts, terrorists possess a form of what he refers to as "psycho-logic." Terrorists do not freely choose to utilize egregious public violence as a political tool. Instead, they feel compelled to carry out acts of violence in response to internal psychological drives as a consequence of psychological forces. This phenomenon of psycho-logic forms as a tool of personal rationalization of the deeds they commit.[37]

In contrast to Post, there appears to be an extensive body of evidence that terrorists are not insane. Ken Heskin, in his analysis of political violence in Northern Ireland, found that members of the Irish Republican Army (IRA) are not emotionally disturbed. He concludes that terrorism does not seem to result from individual psychopathologies among the members of the organization.[38] In their study of juvenile offenders found guilty of offenses utilizing terrorist tactics in Northern Ireland, Elliott and Lockhart have demonstrated that, in spite of their similar socioeconomic characteristics, such offenders were more intelligent, possessed a higher level of educational achievement, exhibited less evidence of early childhood developmental problems, and had a smaller number of prior appearances in court when compared to "ordinary" juvenile offenders.[39]

Irish psychologist Maxwell Taylor takes a multivariable approach to the study of political violence by seemingly accounting for a convergence of ideological, behavioral, and structural forces. He argues that many different forces impinge on terrorist behavior: psychological, cultural, social, legal, and ideological, among others. He concludes that although terrorists are political fanatics they are not mentally ill.

Taylor defines fanaticism as "behavior which is excessive and inappropriately enthusiastic and/or inappropriately concerned with significant life purpose, implying a focused and highly personalized interpretation of the world." Fanaticism appears not to be the end result of any particular attribute of behavior but, rather, an expression of the extent of commitment of the individual and the degree of energy he or she is willing to put forth in pursuit of that commitment.[40]

As a result, the fanatic is one who is genuinely focused, in an extraordinary way, on the achievement of a particular objective. The achievement of this goal takes priority over all other considerations. He or she is exclusively concerned with their own cognitive perception of the world and excludes all alternative perspectives. Fanatics do not seem to possess a consistency of logic in their thoughts and actions that is in general present in the population as a whole. This may be derived largely from his or her highly focused and personalized worldview.[41] For example, the anti-abortion activist who fanatically supports "the sanctity of life" but will blow up abortion clinics and kill people in the interests of his cause does not perceive of the moral inconsistency of the argument.

The fanatic, Taylor asserts, is one operating under the enormous pressure of ideology. As such, he or she is highly organized and directed toward particular ends. In other words, political fanaticism is not an exhibition of irrationality but, rather, a display of deep commitment influenced by a powerful ideology.

Structural, organizational, and psychological theories have been offered as explanations of the origins, nature, and process of terrorism. Whereas each of these theoretical schools contributes to the body of knowledge on the subject, they do not, by themselves, adequately explain political violence. To describe it as a form of simple antisocial or psychopathic behavior places an excessive emphasis on the individual and an inadequate amount of attention on the political, economic, or social setting in which political violence occurs. On the other hand, to account for political violence strictly as a function of structural factors would be equally invalid because it ignores the role of ideology or characteristics of the individuals involved.[42]

One is forced to conclude that uni-causal explanations are an inappropriate response to a phenomenon as complex as political terrorism, where interpersonal psychological factors converge with structural forces operating both external to and outside the control of the individual.

Terrorism and Millenarian Prophecy: Toward an Alternative Theory of Political Violence

Terrorists purposely choose acts of violence that will be perceived by large numbers of people as outrageous specifically because they stand in contrast to reasonable "civilized" behavior. Here we see the very essence of terrorism—the deliberate disruption of the social, political, economic, and legal fabric of society, through the use of or threatened use of violence in an effort to draw attention to one's cause and intimidate some targeted group in order to achieve political goals.[43] This process involves political choices that are both calculated and purposeful, not mere random acts of violence.[44] Yet our understanding need not end with this conclusion. A further investigation of how and why otherwise rational and often deeply religious peoples can justify acts involving egregious violence is required.

The specific relationship between the intervention of foreign power in a society and how that may engender sociopolitical transformation, the emergence of apocalyptic beliefs, and political violence has received limited attention from social and political analysts. Indeed, when one considers the durability, saliency, and pervasiveness of millenarian ideas in the world it is a remarkably understudied sociopolitical phenomenon. Nonetheless, the existing literature can provide us with some insight into both its nature and process.

Norman Cohn produced what many consider to be the first and what remains the classic text on millenarianism as a political behavior phenomenon and a factor in the process of political violence. Writing in the 1950s, Cohn was the first to thoroughly investigate exclusively Western and Central European apocalyptic movements. Focusing historical attention on the period from the sixth century onward to the fifteenth century, Cohn argues that the groups he investigated represented the repeating cycle of a revolutionary millenarian paradigm that frequently utilized violence to achieve their political goals.

He argues that perceptions and conceptualizations of the idealized notion of human progress can play an important role in the process of political violence. Such notions began in antiquity as a sacred context involving a supernatural force (e.g., Messiah, Mahdi, or Maitreya) and have gradually evolved into a substantive component of modern, secular, ideological expression.

From its beginnings, Cohn asserts, millenarianism appeared as a response to foreign domination, perceived corruption, and cultural imperialism injected into a society and manifesting an abrupt change in the existing social order. Additionally, it exhibited a profound potential for political violence.

Cohn's historical analysis allows us to begin to piece together the basic components of the millenarian paradigm: a community composed of deeply ethnocentric people, disrupted by a perceptibly wicked, evil, and alienating power of seemingly demonic dimension that upsets and menaces their traditional way of life. In the presence of such danger, the community comes to be convinced that their role and purpose must be defended to the death largely because they are God's chosen Elect, destined to ensure that righteousness overcomes evil. Triumph, which is viewed as inexorable and according to God's plan, represents the true finale of history, which reveals itself as heaven on earth.[45]

Later millenarian movements that emerged concurrently with religious dissent in Western Europe in the medieval era demonstrated a similar character. Prompted by a growing dissatisfaction with an increasingly corrupt and unresponsive church,[46] peasant movements led by charismatic prophets began to appear, demanding moral reform.[47]

Eventually, these wandering preachers attracted particularly devoted followings and often came to be perceived as living saints or the returned Messiah. In some cases, these groups developed into a full-fledged social movement that was distinctly millenarian. These movements found their most receptive audience in those areas that were undergoing rapid social and economic change.[48] Such change brought cultural shock and disorientation, disrupted the existing socioeconomic order, and had a powerful impact on traditional life.[49]

Social change has always created social dislocation and normative disturbance; dislocated groups and individuals who feel the impact of profound change eventually need to be effectively blended into the new social structures that emerge as a result of such change. At the same time, these groups and individuals may also demand that they be included in the emerging new political system. Political movements that inevitably appear on the scene to meet these demands have often been a major contributing factor in the occurrence of political violence. Millenarianism evolved as a mechanism for the peoples of these societies to deal with profound socioeconomic change and as a channel for their reintegration into new forms of societal community.[50]

The identifiable position or place of these peoples within society had been lost. Kinship relationships and the traditional structure of their rural village and its complementary social network were deteriorating. A durable history of religious-inspired millenarian doctrines was pervasive in these societies, as was the availability of potential charismatic leadership.[51]

Life, as these people had known it for generations, with its ancillary system of customary norms and rules of behavior, was disintegrating. In short, they must have believed that their functional world was coming to an end, causing both deep stress and indignation. It cannot be surprising that such a belief would serve to substantiate the pervasive religious-inspired eschatological prophecy existing in these societies.

The adherents of these movements possessed a persistent sense of tension and anxiety over how to cope with the catastrophe of abrupt socioeconomic change and the introduction of new cultural norms, perceived as both alien and corrupt. This distress appears to have manifested itself as moral outrage and righteous indignation. Such indignation, in response to social injustice, is recognized as a necessary and sufficient catalyst of political violence.[52]

Indignation calls for an individual or a group to construe the events that are happening around them within the context of their personal normative system. In order to label an action as "immoral" or "an injustice," one must compare that action to one's personal values. Indeed, what one individual may consider being immoral, another may find fully acceptable as an appropriate action. In other words, indignation is a concept grounded in one's culture. It dictates that one compare what has happened to one's expectation of what "ought" to have happened and "depends upon a learned standard of what is right and wrong." Defined as "the attitude and behavioral manifestations of wrathfulness because of unworthy or unjust treatment,"[53] indignation is a source of political violence and appears to have some relationship with the expression of millenarian expectations.[54]

To many millenarians, paradise is viewed as an egalitarian community. In the eyes of God, many chiliasts argue, all humans are the same. Thus, the utopia promised by the advent of the millennium will most certainly be a classless society in which there will be no rich and poor: no haves and have-nots.

As a result, the injection of a new order or hierarchy into a society—one that divides humans into unequal classes through profound socioeconomic change—has frequently engendered millenarian expectations. For example, as the modern world began to take shape in Western Europe, particularly in the late eighteenth and early nineteenth centuries, when the class divisions engendered by industrialization came to be an important source of conflict, one sees an increase in indignation of the lower classes toward the growing wealth of the emerging middle class: the bourgeoisie. Concurrently, there was an increase in both explicitly religious and secular millenarianism within these areas.

Michael Adas has demonstrated that participants in political violence can be stirred by millenarian expectations when confronted by the changes and dislocations engendered by European imperialism, colonization, and cultural conquest of diverse societies in Africa, Asia, and the South Pacific. He argues that traditional religious ritual and apocalyptic myth may be utilized in an attempt by indigenous peoples to offset European technological superiority. Adas confirms the importance of a prophet figure who performed central roles in violent, apocalyptic movements and the significance of their millenarian visions as catalysts of protests and violence.[55]

In addition, Eric Hobsbawm has analyzed millenarian insurgencies in early-twentieth-century Mediterranean Europe, where capitalism and modernity had recently "irrupted" into peasant society and people were being subjected to pervasive government control. He argues that millenarian movements tend to arise in complex and rapidly modernizing societies with the accompanying developing capitalist system and increasing government intervention in people's everyday lives. In response, people seek simplicity of life and a new moral order. They come to see themselves as the alienated objects of insidious socioeconomic and political forces that are beyond their control. Land reforms, including the abolition of common forest and pasture lands, increased taxes, rapid industrialization, the development of a national market, and the introduction of capitalist legal and social relationships all had "cataclysmic effects" on these societies. According to Hobsbawm, the participants in the movements he investigated did not grow with or into modern society; instead, they were "broken into it." Their principal problem was "how to adapt themselves to its life and struggles."[56]

Finally, Michael Barkun has identified that an important external factor resulting in social disorder and disaster is the consequence that follows the contact between more complex and less complex cultures, a notion that he labels the "colonial hypothesis." This literature contends that millenarianism emerges in an inferior or colonial society in response to intervention or invasion by a superior foreign power that attempts to impose its cultural values on the life of the lesser society. Subjection to a foreign power is a particularly grievous experience when a society is profoundly ethnocentric and when the political leader is also a religious leader or, at the least, is perceived as one who is divinely inspired. Perhaps not surprisingly, millenarian expectations tend to emerge as a specific response to the suppression of, or serious interference with, the traditional religious practices of the native peoples by the intervening power. Barkun argues that "the colonial hypothesis, in effect, holds that there is a causal sequence at work: culture contact—social change—mental disturbance—millenarian movements."[57]

Millenarian behavior is controlled by a limited set of rules, which are relatively constrained in extent and are closely related. This contrasts with the relative multiplicity of rules that might otherwise control social behavior, and the extent of control exercised by immediate circumstances. Millenarianism gains coherence through expression, which relates idealized consequences to immediate activity.

Millenarianism and the "Clash of Civilizations"

Samuel Huntington has argued that the future of international conflict will be largely determined by cultural factors or as the result of what he terms the "Clash of Civilizations."[58] If Professor Huntington is correct then we must attempt to determine the nature of these intercultural conflicts. It is an important thesis of this study that a significant form of the "Clash of Civilizations" will be political violence engendered by apocalyptic belief systems. More specifically, the clash of civilizations will frequently manifest itself in what we will call millenarian terrorism—a modern ideology of political violence that traces its roots to traditional religious beliefs.

Not all millenarians are terrorists. Indeed, most groups anticipating the end time exhibit rather passive characteristics and remain nonviolent in nature. At the same time, all terrorists are not millenarians. General Sherman's "March to the Sea," an overt act designed to terrorize American Southerners to realize that their cause was fruitless, was not convinced that his actions would engender Armageddon or the onset of a paradise on earth. His goal was to utilize what he considered to be effective tactics that could end a violent and relentless war.

Nonetheless, the convergence of millenarian expectations and terrorist violence is not only possible, it is more common than previously acknowledged.[59] The comparative cases that are the subject of this present study are clear examples of the power and complexity of such a combination.

A desire to achieve justice or what the individual perceives as justice motivates all violence. War, murder, torture, genocide, and capital punishment, as examples, are each attempts to achieve what the perpetrator—the state, the freedom fighter, the soldier, the alienated of society, or others—perceive of as justice.[60] Thus to become a terrorist one must possess two congruent cognitions: (1) a worldview that clarifies one's conceptualization of what is just and unjust in some highly satisfactory way, and (2) the establishment and sustainment of an identity consistent with that worldview. Indeed, one cannot possess a worldview without a lucid identity that unmistakably grounds the individual within his or her context.

Religion has always occupied a central and generally positive force in the development of human civilizations. Nonetheless, religious thought, conceptualizations of the sacred, and messianic expectations surrounding beliefs about the end time can also have negative consequences for intergroup (nee intercultural) relations. Such consequences can include aggressive ideas and violent behavior, to include war, rebellion, and the use of terror, in response to other identity constructions, perceived of as alien.[61] Yet the relationship between religion and political violence is not limited to historical accounts of trained armies and military operations. A parallel relationship exists within the lay public in the form of millenarian organizations that can possess both social and political characteristics.

In recent years such organizations have risen in a variety of forms. Some of these have led to spectacular episodes of serious aggression, to include violent homicidal and suicidal behaviors. For example, the 900 deaths that occurred in Jonestown, Guyana, in 1978, when the leader of the People's Temple, Jim Jones, ordered his followers to poison themselves with cyanide as a "revolutionary act" that was intertwined with Jones's apocalyptic religious ideas.[62] In 1993, David Koresh, the leader of the Branch Davidians was alleged to have ordered what amounted to the burning and killing of his followers in their compound in Waco, Texas. Koresh's messianic claims and apocalyptic worldview were based on his highly idiosyncratic interpretations of the book of Revelation.[63]

Even more recent examples of this relationship between millenarianism and violence is demonstrated in the mass suicides of members of the Solar Temple in Switzerland and Quebec (1994), and in France (1995), as well as the incredible methodical, ritual suicide of 39 members of the Heaven's Gate movement in San Diego, California, in 1997.[64] In each of these cases, mass self-destruction was the principal means of violent behavior in a complicated, not easily understood set of group and individual expectations.

Millenarian terrorism is no less complex. At perhaps an overly simplistic level, millenarian terrorists utilize violence in a perceived

sacred cause. The cause is personally created from a worldview that allows the adherent to make sense of life and death by linking him or her to some form of immortality. This is required if one is to make sense of life and achieve some degree of transcendental satisfaction—an innate human need.[65]

Millenarianism has performed a substantive role in all premodern as well as modern liberation movements. This is a clear indication that there is a relationship between millenarianism and the desire and decision by political groups to seek political freedom, however it may be defined, as well as to exert a greater say in public policy. In addition, this study seeks to demonstrate that in such processes millenarianism also performs a significant role in the utilization of public violence in the pursuit of these goals.

Millenarian terrorists are fanatics, which is not to imply that they are mentally disturbed or psychopathological. Rather, they are extraordinarily and exclusively focused on and committed to their political cause and are willing to exert enormous energy in its achievement. Although they possess a firm loyalty to the conventions of stable and orderly daily life within their society and are obliged to ensure their longevity, under certain conditions of disorientation, disharmony, and/or foreign impingement that threatens the institutions and norms of their way of life, they are driven to invoke traditional images of cultural salience.

The emergence of overt millenarian activity becomes a feature of the group experience that gathers its energy primarily from underlying psychological and motivational characteristics. The forces that drive the powerful wishes and fantasies embedded in all forms of eschatological and apocalyptic expectations are part of the motivational structure of the paranoid process.[66]

Nonetheless, this does not, in and of itself, indicate psychopathology. Paranoid behavior is a commonplace and pervasive part of everyday life. All human beings suffer from some degree of paranoia that waxes and wanes dependent upon structural conditions. It manifests itself across a broad spectrum of action ranging from the suspicions of ordinary people to the ravaging delusions of the emotionally disturbed.[67] In addition, paranoia is structurally induced, occurring in very distinct environments under rather specific circumstances related to social stress, anxiety, shame, humiliation, a belief in conspiracies, and, often, misperceptions.[68]

Paranoid social cognitions can be seen as consequences of the interaction between information about specific events processed through the cognitive maps of the individual and the social circumstances in which they are perceived to have occurred. They comprise those attempts by the individual to make some sense of, deal with, and adapt to disturbing, threatening, and frightening social situations.[69] Paranoid social cognitions can be widespread in a society and affect those in the extreme of the political spectrum.[70]

Millenarianism demonstrates the human capacity for episodic group interludes of delusional paranoid thought in the presence of situational stress. As such it is a component of a much greater adaptive process in which not only the individual but society as a whole must change in order to meet the needs of a new and different sociopolitical reality.

Anthony F. C. Wallace, who studied primarily non-Western millenarian movements, asserted that under conditions of severe collective stress and potential cultural disintegration, societies come to realize that they must either initiate a process of "revitalization" or "face extinction." Their reaction is quite rational. According to Wallace, millenarian movements are, in reality, instruments of social renewal. They present a new and potent ideology offering an imminent and efficacious solution for what appears to be an especially grim period of social difficulty. In this way, the "revitalization" or millenarian movement is a rational process with very purposeful goals. They seek a cultural adaptation to a new sociopolitical paradigm that is filled with perceived danger, yet is nonetheless very real.[71]

I argue that the millenarian-inspired violence exhibited by these three cases is a manifestation of the modern revitalization movement. Such seemingly unconventional behavior is a firmly entrenched component of the cognitive maps of these societies, offering therapeutic beliefs that have historically acted to reduce the enormous stress of sociopolitical change.

Although the actions of millenarian terrorists are usually well planned and purposeful, their doctrines can be both ambiguous and logically inconsistent. Leaders and adherents must make continuous choices about tactics, strategies, aims, and objectives. They may abandon some of these for others that appear to be more valuable yet equally valid. Nonetheless, in every case millenarian terrorists demonstrate a powerful belief in a world that must be destroyed in order to achieve their ultimate goals. This belief defines the character of both the participants and the organization. They are carrying out God's will. Terror is attractive in and of itself simply because it represents activity that is outside the conventional range of violence. For that reason it symbolizes complete liberation from the wickedness and injustice of the past.[72]

Millenarian terrorists operate under the effective rule control of an apocalyptic ideology that successfully links three ideas: (1) a recognition of sociopolitical and/or economic disturbance manifested as injustice, a violation of sacred cultural norms, and a sense of indignation. This recognition demands (2) rule following behavior, perceived as having the therapeutic capacity to (3) achieve an idealized outcome.

Ideology involves the identification of specific objectives toward which the political actor aims his/her sights. It comes to relate certain political behavior to the achievement of those specific objectives. In this sense, ideology clearly defines an end point toward which a political actor strives, but also a set of rules, which, if followed, will ensure that the actor will safely arrive at some utopian destination—an idealized world free from the difficulties, hardships, and problems surrounding the actor's current status and, indeed, are the factors that have contributed to his/her mobilization in the first place. Ideology provides both the context and the content of political behavior. Some have argued that we can characterize religious enthusiasm in much the same way.[73]

Millenarianism is the intellectual mother of all political ideologies. It is the ultimate belief system. No other set of ideas offers such a compelling message and provides such a powerful tool for influencing the popular mind. It is the definitive articulation of discontent and a powerful unifying force that provides the most effective meaning to popular grievances. Millenarian expectations are inherently normative. As a result they lead to action—to change. It is a guide to action—something all humans require.[74]

Millenarianism, as is true of all ideological constructions, are sourced and sustained by the material and structural conditions of life. Millenarianism is a viable and working ideology only to the extent that it accounts for real conditions, however distorted, disguised, and exaggerated they may be. In this way, the emergence of millenarianism is directly related and explained by the conditions the individual or the group finds itself in at that particular moment in time and space.[75] For example, as we shall see, Aum Shinrikyo doctrine held that murder could help both victim and murderer to salvation.

Millenarians seek to advance history toward the promise of paradise. In the process they tend toward a form of violence that they perceive of as a part of the process of the last days. From such beliefs and values it is not a large step to engaging in acts of terrorism to expedite the process.

Millenarianism is a socially integrative phenomenon. Its ideological attraction offers significant shelter against despair, and its adherents are inspired with a durable form of the human emotion of hope. Members of millenarian movements come to believe that ultimate victory against the forces of darkness and injustice will be theirs. It engenders a profound sensation of collective identity and a sense of purpose. Indeed, members of society frequently form their identities in millenarian motifs.

At the group level, millenarianism is a liberating, galvanizing, and unifying power in the process of broad-based sociopolitical mobilization. This is particularly so in traditional societies that have previously exhibited lengthy and durable patterns of political dormancy, passivity, and isolation.

It is an important objective of this study to demonstrate the functional role performed by millenarianism in three cases of late-twentieth-century political movements that utilized terror as a tactic of goal achievement. Logically, such an analysis must begin with a detailed comparative examination of the origins of millenarian beliefs in each case.

CHAPTER 2

The Rise of Millenarian Terror

Terrorism is never the result of any single causal factor. It is frequently in response to multiple and long-festering socioeconomic and political problems. Indeed, terrorist attacks exemplify the presence of serious, unresolved conflicts within a society. Of course, all parties to a conflict will seek a resolution that is advantageous to their cause. They pursue such a resolution through the unique vernacular of the "cognitive maps" of their society. Such maps have been defined as "the set of shared symbols describing the collective environment and prescribing the organized behaviors appropriate to preserving social stability in that environment."[1] Here we can classify society as a type of organism and its cognitive maps are conceptualized as consisting of those models of learned behavior that the organism displays in a repeating pattern, confirmed over a long period of time.[2]

Society, as an organism, represents the convergence of the individual cognitive maps that exist within it. These unite to create a much larger, comprehensive, and far more complex map, which functions at many different levels. In this way, the much broader social cognitive map is sustained by many different ways of thinking and acting in concert with one another, and any one of these contains only a small portion of the larger cultural map.

Cognitive maps carry out a significantly influential task in the lives of those who constitute a culture. It creates for each member of that culture a social reality—a point of view, an outlook, a "lens," if you will—through which they see events unfolding every day in "their" world. In this way, each member of a culture comes to hold a "unique reality" of what constitutes right and wrong, good and evil, or what is just and unjust.

In addition, cognitive maps provide members of a society with a guide to social behavior and how to manage the inevitable conflicts that life presents to them. It is the cognitive maps of a society that both define morality, often in the form of persistent myths, and those behaviors and rituals that are required to sustain it. In addition, they define both the identity and the social roles of the people. They create "value symbols" that impose certain behaviors. In turn, those behaviors engender certain social and cultural structures that institutionalize behavior. Future generations are socialized and prodded to imitate certain behaviors that are considered moral and righteous. In contrast, they are taught to avoid certain behaviors that are considered evil. In such a process, as succeeding generations teach themselves the same narratives, practice the same rituals, confirm the same legends, "a complex society comes into being."[3]

Not surprisingly, the founding myth and the rituals that surround it are firmly entrenched in the cognitive maps of all societies.[4] For example, in the Judeo-Christian culture of the Western world the paternalistic character of the culture writ large is, to no small degree, fixed in the Biblical relationship between Adam and Eve. In this way, cognitive maps are an instrumental device in upholding the recollections of the world going back to the very beginning of that culture.

An important component of any society's cognitive map deals with accepted responses to challenge, conflict, struggle, and perceptions of catastrophic events. In the presence of perceived disaster or in response to challenges from other competitive cultures (and thus, competitive cognitive maps), how does a society react? What is the vernacular of their reaction?

I argue that millenarianism is an important component of the cognitive maps of the three societies under examination. As such, it is a substantial component of the reaction to such challenges. In addition, understanding the millenarian stream that pervades these cognitive maps provides us with the opportunity to more fully explain the viability of violence as an agent of political change in these cultures. This is so for three reasons.

First, millenarianism sets up the possibility that the present circumstances can, in fact, be transcended. In the absence of such a faith, every succeeding generation of the members of these societies would continue a static view of the world, possessing no comprehension of the notion of progress beyond the material conditions of the moment. Thus, millenarianism is a group phenomenon and embodies the most intense form of mystical cognitive experience.[5] In addition, it is pervasive, which implies that rather commonplace mental occurrences can be experienced as a type of spiritual or religious incident involving the sense that contact has been made with a supernatural force. It also implies that many people within a given society can have such an experience.[6]

Second, millenarianism is the agent that comes to provide the terrorist with his or her view of an idealized future. Apocalyptic expectations characterize what the future has in store in rather specific terms, once the evils of the present have been successfully transcended. Indeed, it is from millenarian beliefs that the capacity to establish a drastic contrast between the ideal and present conditions is developed. In the process, millenarianism creates an extraordinary sense of tension between a vision of what the world should be and what it actually is.

Finally, millenarian expectations serve to direct human behavior to transform or "revitalize"[7] society consistent with the future ideal it portrays. These beliefs mobilize sociopolitical movements to prepare themselves for the changes that are believed to be imminent. In short, millenarianism comes to characterize the violent response to conflict and struggle within a society.

Political movements utilize terror as a tactic of both communication and transformation. Frequently, terrorist violence emerges out of a failure of more conventional, nonviolent grievance processes in which the movement has sought and fell far short of achieving their sociopolitical objectives. They come to perceive that violence is the only remaining course of action in their quest for justice. Terrorists are not content to simply repair the sources of problems and evils of today. They seek to transform the sociopolitical institutions of society and, in particular, their rightful place within it.

Millenarianism in Traditional Andean Culture

The region that now comprises the state of Peru has a durable and significant history. Placed between high mountains and volcanoes at an altitude of well over 12,000 ft. lies a huge plain, the Altiplano, which is about the size of the state of Colorado. In this region, some of the more advanced civilizations that have ever existed in the western hemisphere—the Tiahuanaco, the Aymara, and the Inca—created empires through a process of conquering the rather distinct, independent tribes that have historically populated the area. Only extremely well-organized and powerful societies and governments, such as that of the Incas, have been able to rule over the people that inhabit the Altiplano with any degree of success.

In the modern day, the Altiplano continues to form the cultural core of the region. The ruggedness of the high Andean terrain, which has always been more densely populated than the surrounding tropical jungles and hot coastal regions, made communication and transportation to the outside world difficult—this gave rise to powerful regional jealousies and rivalries and accounts for the relative difficulty rulers have had over the centuries in governing over the peoples of the region.

Two characteristics appear to stand out when one evaluates the nature of the peoples of the Altiplano: they are isolated geographically and, perhaps as a result, they live on the margin of society in Peru. As a result, the state remains significantly divided along ethnic and racial lines. This promotes a divided sociopolitical and economic system that, on the one hand, is dominated by a minority White community composed of peoples of Spanish ancestry living in the metropolitan Lima area. On the other hand, there is a majority non-White population, composed of the descendants of various indigenous tribes, who largely inhabit the rural regions of the country. This majority is generally characterized by poverty and political and ethnic repression that began during the colonial era.

When the Spaniards, under Juan Pizarro, captured the Incan Empire in the early sixteenth century by destroying the royal family and its power, in a process that took four decades to complete, they proceeded to assault the culture of the natives and created a complex, multilayered caste system—which lasted for four centuries—in which Indians provided what amounted to slave labor for White European masters (Criollos). As a result, today, in spite of great economic and social strides made during the past three decades, Indians, comprising a large proportion of the population, have not yet successfully been integrated into the mainstream of so-called modern Peruvian life. They remain alienated from a society designed by and for the minority Criollo population, who control the levers of power in the state.

The indigenous population of the Andes is composed of many different cultural and ethnic groupings possessing numerous diverse myths and religions. The practice of ancestral worship pervaded all aspects of life. Religious ideologies and associations provided the peoples of the region with an important confirmation of their identity and unique culture. Millenarian myth and the institutions that it sustained provided an illuminating vision of the nature of their world and what the future held for them. It was a vision that they easily understood and was capable of clarifying their life experiences in a simple and satisfying manner.[8]

There is some suggestion that in the precolonial period the peoples of the region worshipped multiple gods. Remnants of this remain true today. For example, the ritual of sprinkling holy water onto the soil as a way of worshipping *Pacchamama* or Mother Earth, remains common.[9]

In many ways, and following a path not dissimilar from other regions of the world, Andean sacred belief systems have evolved as syncretic mixtures of various dogma, narrative, and ritual brought to the region (almost always in the form of a conquering culture) and heaped onto previous sacred constructions with their own versions of the divine truth. What emerged was a complex yet functioning web of doctrinal and spiritual notions. This demonstrates that, early on, the societies were able to incorporate new ideas into their culture with relative ease.[10]

Nonetheless, what evolved out of this theological entanglement have been significant and often durable New Religions that come to supplant previous beliefs in an enduring, evolutionary process. A systematic study of these New Religions is far beyond the scope of the present research project. Nonetheless, a durable component of these New Religions is their millenarian or apocalyptic character.

We know that millenarianism was present in what is now Peru following the Inca conquest of the region.[11] Indeed, its significance in the life of the region can be traced to the prehistoric period. Thus, it was an ever-present force that at times lingered just below the surface of society. Yet, we can discern certain factors that contributed to its bursting forth with incredible energy under particular circumstances and in response to specific structural factors. Not the least among these was the response to contact and struggle with alien cultures.

For example, through contact with the Inca in the immediate pre-Columbian period, the Shipibo peoples, who populated the region along the banks of the Ucayali River in what is now eastern Peru, formulated a set of richly dichotomized beliefs regarding the sources and nature of good and evil in their world. The "Good" Inca was cognitively mapped onto the Sun—"the benevolent 'culture donor' who gave the secrets of cultural existence, like fire and cultigens, to humankind, thereby making life easier."[12] In contrast, the Evil Inca was mapped onto the Moon: "a 'stingy' culture withholding custodian who sought to keep humans in a state of nature and who . . . remains the origin of all difficulties in this life and, ultimately, of mortality itself."[13] Following the arrival of the Spanish in the early sixteenth century, the Shipibo came to believe that the

> . . . Good Inca fled and the withholding aliens, who are assimilated with the evil Inca, kidnapped him or took his buried wealth and now rule. Their god, either God the Father or Jesus, becomes the "Good Inca" and the Sun. But the Shipibo are not fooled and await the millennium, the return of the "real" Good Inca, who will bring with

> him the White Men's wealth and power while expunging their obnoxious physical presence. A new "Golden Age" will dawn, recapitulating the "beginning time" of mythic origins when the Good Inca first gave the people fire. The doomed Whitemen and their ilk will be melted in "world floods" and or "cooked = civilized" to death in world fires.[14]

Over time, the Shipibo elaborated the Inca mythic tales into their religious beliefs and practices. They provide us with a striking example of syncretism by giving cultural form to a number of alien-derived social practices and products: the Christian conceptualization of Good versus Evil, inequitable commercial relations between the Indians and the White Man, and the significant difference in technological development and how it came to be used (principally in firearms) as a tool of domination by the Spaniards over the indigenous culture. It was their millenarian expectations that drove the Shipibo to seek a violent overthrow "of the switch of time, to return White Men and Black Men to the past from whence they came." In the end, the only "true humans, the Shipibo, will prevail, but with the material wealth of the White Men."[15]

Among all of the Indian nations of the Andean region, none were more religious than the Inca. By far, they were the most weighed down with a wide variety of sacred ceremonies. Their adherence to these rituals was so careful and detailed that they were able to perpetuate the notion that their practices were inviolable laws, never to be questioned.[16]

For example, the Inca myth of creation centered on the figure of Viracocha Pachayachachi, who, it was believed, was the creator of life. In addition, Viracocha was perceived to have created the norms and morals of the Inca peoples and had admonished them to follow the rules without exception. If they did not they would be severely punished. This was the basis of the people's covenant with their creator.

Eventually, the people fell from the grace of Viracocha, it was believed, because they had violated his rules. In response, Viracocha followed through with his threat by destroying mankind, with the exception of three men. These were saved in order to assist him in creating the humans of the Second Age. According to the myth, Viracocha produced an enormous, destructive flood following 60 days and nights of rain.[17] Afterward, Viracocha created the sun, the moon, and the stars and began work on a new race of humans who would constitute the new nations of the earth.[18]

Following this re-creation of humankind, Viracocha disappeared from earth by walking toward the West, across the ocean. Nonetheless, it is widely believed that he will one day return to his creation.[19] On frequent occasions, in times of difficulties or severe social stress, the expectation of Viracocha's return has resurfaced among various groups within the region in an outburst of millenarian enthusiasm.[20]

Other millenarian expectations were widespread among the Inca at the time of the Spanish conquest. One of the Inca leaders, known as Inkarri, was beheaded by Spanish forces in a violent show of strength. Nonetheless, a myth immediately began to circulate among the Indians that the head of Inkarri was kept by the Spanish as a trophy and returned to Spain where it remains alive. Eventually, many believed, the body of Inkarri will return to Spain and be physically rejoined to its head. Then, Inkarri will battle the Spanish, overthrow their government, and reestablish the rule of the Incas. Nonetheless, only those who possess the true faith will be allowed to participate in this renaissance of Indian power.[21]

In another example, in 1549, approximately 300 members of the Tupi society from coastal Brazil, completed a ten-year journey that had taken them across the entire South American continent to Chachapoyas, in the Andes, in search of "land of immortality and eternal rest" and a "land without evil," that is, a paradise.[22]

Historical evidence indicates that similar journeys of the Tupi-Gurani tribes continued for more than three centuries. They appear to have been stirred by prophet figures within the society known as *carais* or *caraibas.* These prophets were considered by the community to be man-gods, a tradition deep in the ancient history of the indigenous peoples of the Americas,[23] who held extraordinary powers. Under certain conditions they could take control of one or more villages and prepare them for a sort of supernatural trek that would guide them to a promised land. "By leaving sedentary life behind, the Tupi abandoned the prevailing social structure in search of a place beyond secular space and time."[24] In the aftermath of the Spanish conquest, within a short period the Tupis had assimilated symbols of Christian figures into their messianic practices.[25]

Many of the creation myths of the Andean region possess a common thread. In addition to the transition from one age to the next, most contain a Third Age yet to come. This Third Age is usually portrayed as a paradise. In one version, the First Age is one of "Dios and the moon." Their destruction will engender the present age of Jesucristo, the saints, and the sun. It is widely believed that this age was set in motion at the time of the appearance of the first human, Inka Manko Qhapaq, and will end with a great day of judgment. The end of the Second Age is frequently depicted as a great flood, which will open the door to the Third and Final Age, "that of Espirtu Santo, Holy Ghost." In this period, the people will no longer "suffer hunger or want or pain."[26]

These myths demonstrate how the peoples of the region in many instances successfully merged ancient, indigenous sacred traditions with Christian ritual in order to create a satisfying new religion. An excellent example of this persistent phenomenon is the story of "Jesus Christ and the Supay-Chullpas," a message that survives among Aymara-speaking peoples to the modern day. The narrative relates how the present age emerged out of the destruction of the previous one as a result of the good works of a messianic figure who personally defeats the forces of the evils of the past.

In the story, Christ arrives in a community dominated by evil and darkness. On two separate occasions he is murdered by evil men. Yet, in both instances he successfully overcomes death and emerges from his tomb. After his second resurrection he rose into the sky and became the sun. As the sun, he orders the day and the night, which allows the people to grow abundant crops and usher in a new age of wealth and happiness; one in which evil has been destroyed.[27]

In this way, millenarianism was a device utilized by the indigenous cultures of the region as a tool of resistance to and coping with Western conquest and oppression.

Following the military conquest by the Spanish, it was the Church, more than any other institution that led the sociopolitical and even economic domination of the Indian community in Peru. Large-scale religious conversion of the Indians was commonplace. This engendered effective political control through Church authority. In the process, the Indians' icons, such as ceramic symbols of the sun, moon, and animals, were demolished, their sacred rites degraded, and their former religious men were either jailed or cast out of the community altogether.[28]

Yet, in an ambitious attempt to keep their ancient beliefs alive, Indian communities were able to successfully conceal age-old rituals from European Catholicism. On the one hand, Indians would act out a dramatic facade of conversion to their conquerors' religion. On the other, they would secretly continue to worship their ancient gods. This fact was later confirmed when sacrificial mounds purposefully constructed directly behind Christian altars were discovered by historians. The Indians were surreptitiously reburying their dead, in accordance with ancient ritual, only after they had received the rites of a Christian funeral.[29]

Eventually, under the assault of Christianity, the Indians came to idealize the way of life that they had enjoyed before the arrival of the

White man. New generations came to glorify the Inca Empire as a form of a "Golden Age." In the process, the historical account of colonization was revised in distinctly mythological terms that offered the Indians hope that their independent way of life could be restored. The prophesied return of the Inca became connected to a future Indian utopia.[30]

Taki Onqoy

In 1564, Spanish missionaries observed what they described as a "subversive heresy" that quickly captured the imagination of the Indians living in the region of Parinacochas. The Indians had come to believe that the *Taquiongos*, the native Andean Gods, were preaching that, quite soon, a "pan-Andean alliance" of their Gods would rise up and overcome the Christian God in a massive "cosmic violence." Eventually, this new alliance, flush with power, would destroy the Spanish conquerors through disease and other disasters. Members of the Indian community were warned not to cooperate with the Spanish and to renew the worship of their traditional gods.[31]

This radical millenarian uprising, known as the Taki Onqoy, grew to be a rather significant and violent protest movement.[32] Indeed, it spread rather quickly to the north toward Jauja and Lima, and to the East toward Cuzco and Cahrcas.[33] Contemporary estimates contend that out of a total population of approximately 150,000 Indians, perhaps as many as 8,000 were actively involved in the movement. This immense size helps to explain the enormous fear that the uprising provoked among the Spanish.[34]

Taki Onqoy literally translates as "dancing sickness" and much of its ceremony centered on singing and dancing by those who came to be possessed by its spiritual powers. The ritual of singing and dancing was seen by the Indian believers as a tool of collective purification that would prepare the way for the return of their gods who would free them from the domination of the Spanish. The Spaniards would die in a great flood, they prophesied, and under those catastrophic conditions a new age of peace and freedom would unfold.[35] In the process, adherents were ordered to renounce any belief that they may have had in Christianity and were compelled to renew their sacred beliefs in traditional gods.

The movement was led by a deeply spiritual and mystical figure, based in Huamanga, named Juan Chocne. He was accompanied by two women who took the names Santa Maria and Santa Maria Magdelena, obviously influenced by the Christian stories brought by the Spanish priests.

Chocne preached that he was a true messenger sent by the ancient Andean gods. He declared that now was the time for the complete rejection of Spanish dominance in the region and the reemergence of traditional Incan culture and authority.

Eyewitness accounts by Spanish observers observed that the Indians were defiant in their belief that massive change was imminent.

> When the Marques [Francisco Pizarro] entered this land, [his] God defeated the [Huacas] [Andean gods] and the Spaniards defeated the Indians. However, now the world has turned about, and this time God and the Spaniards [will be] defeated and all the Spaniards killed and their cities drowned; and the sea will rise and overwhelm them, so that there will remain no memory of them.[36]

The end result was to be a "new world." An Andean paradise populated by the chosen people of the gods "free of colonizers, materially abundant, [and] unplagued by disease."[37]

The millenarian prophecy of the Taki Onqoy, focusing on first, the destruction of the old world, and second, to be followed by the creation of a new Indian paradise, coincides with the recurring view of history symbolized by traditional religious beliefs among the peoples of the region.[38] It represented yet another turn in the durable and persistent cycle through which the Andean spirits created another new awakening.[39]

Anthropologists have concluded that the Taki Onqoy represented the beginning of a millenarian ideological model in which the conquered Indians of the region came to expect a savior, symbolized by both Inca and Christian imagery and rituals, that would ultimately restore what the Indians perceived to be their traditional natural order.[40]

In response to the Taki Onqoy, Spanish colonial leadership launched what they termed the "anti-idolatry campaign." This lasted for over two years and, eventually, led to the death of over 8,000 Indians and the suppression of the uprising.[41]

The eighteenth century was a time of difficulty and despair for the Indian communities living in Colonial Peru. Increasingly, indigenous peoples of the Meso America and Andean regions found themselves beleaguered and burdened by the nature and structure of Spanish colonial institutions. They literally were forced to restructure themselves in order to meet the needs of their masters and ultimately to survive.[42] After the War of Spanish Succession ended in 1713, and the peace that followed, the Spanish royal Bourbon family sought to reform their state, including their colonial holdings in the New World. Under the notion of "enlightened despotism," the Bourbon kings sought to complete a total reorganization of the existing economic and political framework of Spain in an attempt to close the gap of power between what had been a once great empire and the rapidly developing newer imperialist states of Europe. Included in these efforts was a revamping of Spanish colonial policies. The Bourbons centralized colonial administration in an attempt to make it more efficient and their colonial commercial operations more productive. The result was increased pressure on both colonial authorities and the Indians who worked for them. Eventually the whole system was fraught with crisis.[43]

Colonial Peru was a "patrimonial society."[44] At the very top of the sociopolitical and economic order was, of course, the king of Spain, whose authority was grounded in unquestioned, royal prerogative that was virtually guaranteed by a symbiotic relationship with the Church. The territory of the colony was separated into *curatos* or parishes, *corregimientos* or magistries, and *curacazgos* or chieftainships. As a result, Indians were ruled by three distinct levels of Spanish political power—a *cura* or priest, a *corregidor* or magistrate, and a *curaca* or chief.[45]

As a result of the Bourbon Reforms, the viceroyalty of Peru was expected to increase its production, particularly in mining and agricultural operations, the two most important activities in the colony. For example, the silver ore quotas that the *mitayos* or drafted workers were required to produce were doubled in the years between 1740 and 1790. They were forced to work much longer hours per week for the same wages. In addition, the quotas could only be met if they enlisted the assistance of their wives and children to work the mines along side them. The results were achieved, but they came at a very burdensome social cost.[46]

Sales taxes were increased and their collection was tightened up in an attempt to reduce corruption, which had been rampant. These measures made life difficult for both the workers and their native *curacas*, who were responsible for collecting the taxes and tribute to the king.[47]

Partially in response to these increasing pressures on the Indian community, powerful eruptions of millenarian expectations began to rock Peru in the middle of the eighteenth century. In 1742, Juan Santos Atahualpa, a rather well-educated Quechua, emerged as a prophet figure among the Asháninkas. He successfully persuaded his tribe as well as the nearby Arawakan and Panoan tribes, to abandon the religious practices of the Franciscan clerics who had been working in the area since the 1630s and to follow his teachings.[48]

Santos aggressively declared that the Spanish must be expelled from Peru, the Inca Empire must be restored with himself as the emperor, and Indian clerics take the place of Spanish priests, who would regain their rightful control of religious life in the community. His millenarian vision seems to have been formed out of a syncretic mixture of ancient Inca belief in the Inkarri, the Christian concept of the Messiah as taught by the Franciscans, as well as messianic constructions derived from African sources. His movement became both widespread and violent. For example, the forces of Santos achieved a sweeping victory over the Spanish in a number of battles and were able to shut off the southern region of Peru to further settlement by the Spanish for almost a century.[49]

Tupac Amaru Rebellion

Beginning in 1780, the most powerful rebellion to hit the Andean region during the colonial era unfolded in the highlands of Peru. A further reaction to the burdensome requirements engendered by the Bourbon Reforms,[50] the indigenous rebellion aimed its violence primarily on the Spanish *corregidor*.

Its beginnings may be traced to the city of Cuzco. However, before it had run its course, the rebellion had a profound impact on a region that stretched from modern-day Argentina to Colombia. Its immediate goal was to relieve the Indians of the extraordinary burdens recently placed on the community. Its greater goal was to eventually drive the Europeans out of the region and restore the Inca emperor.[51] Quite remarkably, the rebels came very close to overthrowing Spanish colonial power in the Andes.

The leader of what became known as the Tupac Amaru Rebellion was a native mestizo elite named José Gabriel Condorcanqui. Well-educated and prosperous, he claimed to be a direct descendant of the last Inca ruling family in the sixteenth century.[52] Following the attack of his forces on the Corregidor, in November 1780, he took the name of Tupac Amaru II. Eventually he came to fashion himself as the new king of Peru and established a government for the territory that was now under his direct control.[53] Such an identity effectively capitalized on a yearning for the resurrection and revival of Inca life that was sweeping the region in the late eighteenth century. Neo-Incan nationalism was emerging among the Indians of the area and it possessed enormous power. By the middle of the eighteenth century, descendants of the Inca elites sought to regain as well as to authenticate the cultural traditions of the region, exemplified by a reflective and idealized confirmation of Inca power, magnificence, and success in the past. This was manifested as a genuine cult that prospered in the ancient Inca capital of Cuzco.[54]

This revival among Indian elites was accompanied by the mass of the Indian community yearning for the miraculous return of the Inca to rescue them from the pain of their present conditions. Gradually they fleshed out their own unique interpretation of the Inca Empire and the possibility of its reemergence—one that they characterized as:

> An egalitarian society, a homogenous world consisting only of *runas* [Andean peasants] in which there would be no great merchants, no colonial authorities, no haciendas, no mines, and those who were then pariahs and wretched would again determine their own destiny . . . the world upside down.[55]

Condorcanqui was able to utilize his lineage to effectively tap into this millenarian force. Nonetheless, the movement he led was not merely a romanticized look back at the past. It was fixed in the sociopolitical needs of the present.[56] It was much more than a simple anachronism that sought to merely recapture an Andean utopia.[57] Rather, it utilized modern political ideologies emerging from the Enlightenment. These were always linked to traditional Indian millenarianism to effectively mobilize a widespread terror force of significant proportion.

Over time, Condorcanqui had worked diligently to achieve some form of relief for the Indians through legal mechanisms. Yet, these efforts came to naught. Frustrated, he turned to violence to achieve the movement's objectives. In November 1780, he led a force into the province of Quispicanchis, where they easily defeated a Spanish force. Casualties from the battle included not only the Spanish, but also a number of Creole women, who had sought to hide in a church, which was set afire by the rebels. News of this atrocity was utilized by the Spanish authorities as propaganda to denounce the rebel cause as well as to characterize the war as a clash of Indians versus Whites (Creoles plus Europeans).[58]

Later the rebellion moved south into the Lake Titicaca region spreading additional terror among Whites along the way. Yet, the rebels failed to gain their ancient capital at Cuzco. On April 6, 1781, Condorcanqui and his wife were captured. Despite their trial and execution that spring, followers of the Tupac Amaru continued their violence. Eventually, the rebellion was put down by colonial authorities in 1783. Nonetheless, the horrific punishments inflicted on the leaders of the movement, including Condorcanqui, his wife, and family members, was a clear indication of the scale of the terror and the panic it had created among the ruling Spanish elites.[59]

The Tupac Amaru Rebellion was a messianic-inspired violent event that ultimately weakened the hold of the Spanish in the region and contributed in a significant way to Peru's Independence in the early years of the nineteenth century.

Millenarianism and the Modern Peruvian State

Despite the theoretical liberalism of the new Peruvian constitution and the practical necessities of the development of a modern market-based economy, postcolonialism in the region created little more than a revamping of the antiquated and inefficient feudal system that the region had already known. This system served the exclusive needs of and was dominated by Creole Peruvians, particularly the old land-owning families of the colonial period.

As a result, many indigenous inhabitants of the new state did not perceive that what had happened in throwing off the yoke of Spanish imperialism was of value to them at all. The burdens that they had known throughout the colonial era would continue with little improvement.

In the early nineteenth century, a modest peasant movement in the village of Huancavelica came to embrace the figure of Santiago, the patron saint of the community. Many believed that Santiago would usher in a new, more prosperous age. According to contemporary accounts:

> Santiago told the Indians that if they followed him, he would lead them in a return to the past in which there would be produce in abundance and no one would die of hunger.[60]

In the 1890s, some accounts emerge that Carlos Fitzcarrald, a businessman who operated rubber plantations in the region dominated by the Asháninkas, was considered by many to be a supernatural figure, the Son of the Sun or *Itomi Pavá*.[61]

In 1908, Frederick A. Stahl, a Seventh Day Adventist missionary established a school for the Aymara Indians living in the region of Lake Titicaca. Later, he established a health clinic and preached the religion of Adventism to the community. By the 1920s, a broad-based crisis cult emerged within the community created by Stahl. It expected the end of the world to be imminent.[62]

Beginning in the early twentieth century, Peru began to move increasingly into the mainstream of international life in the western hemisphere. Largely as the result of British and American investment in copper mining, cotton and sugar production, a growing network of railroads, and hastened by the opening of the Panama Canal in 1914, Peru became increasingly integrated into a growing modern world economy. Nonetheless, this rapid economic change, in turn, roused unexpected social and political turbulence.[63]

To many Peruvians, especially among those in the middle and lower classes—the vast majority of the population—life became increasingly confusing and unpredictable. There was a persistent anxiety over their diminishing socioeconomic and political status within a society that was undergoing profound change.

For example, between 1920 and 1973 the population of Peru more than tripled.[64] Yet, during this same period, many traditional Indian communities in the rural regions of Peru were destroyed in order to make land available for modern industrial and mining use. The combination of these two variables—rapid population growth and the redirection of traditional lands—forced large numbers of the peasant Indian class to forsake their traditional village life and move to new mining, industrial, or agricultural centers or to the larger, urbanized areas closer to the coast. Traditional kinship relationships were disrupted. In addition, many Indians found themselves victimized by an alienating world that increased their awareness and exposure to racism, relative deprivation, and sociopolitical discrimination at the hands of the minority, yet powerful, non-Indian elite class. Many members of the peasant class found themselves to be isolated, culturally estranged, and marginalized from an increasingly prosperous center of Peruvian life.[65] As a result, "Peru was accumulating an undermass made up of people partially adrift, no longer fully integrated into community or manorial life."[66]

Racism has been a persistent problem in the history of Latin America and this is no less true in Peru.[67] The Criollos (Peruvians of White, European ancestry) perceive of the majority Native American population as an inferior race to be relegated, automatically, to a lower socioeconomic status. The result is a massive chasm between upper-class Whites and lower-class Indians. The process of economic development beginning in the early twentieth century exacerbated this problem. By the 1960s, as the economy of Peru continued to get bigger, class differences worsened as the uneven growth expanded the socioeconomic gap between the races.[68] Perhaps not surprisingly, the Indian communities came to fear the process of modernity.

In recent years, religious movements have emerged in the Andean region that carry on the millenarian traditions of the past. The congregation of Jehovah or the Mision Israelita del Nuevo Pacto Universal del Peru (Israelite Mission of the New Universal Pact) believe that their founder, Ezequiel Ataucusi Gamonal, is a prophet and son of God. Created in 1955, the movement now claims a following of over three million.[69] Gamonal preached that the world would end before the year 2000 and that all who joined the congregation must strictly follow his teachings. The organization's headquarters is located near the city of Huarochiri.[70]

Los Israelitas, as it is commonly known, possesses symbols and theology uniquely crafted from both Judeo-Christian and pre-Columbian Indian sources. Nonetheless it appears to be "explicitly Peruvian and implicitly Andean in its use of symbols and sacrifice." As new members join the movement they must submit to rigorous indoctrination that informs them "of the absolute literal truth contained within the Old Testament." Nonetheless, the message of the death and resurrection of Jesus Christ is entirely omitted from their teachings. Rather than a worship of Christ, Israelitas worship Israel as the "personified place of the Old Testament."[71]

Israelitas embrace two important components of their faith. First is "sacrifice, awaiting the apocalyptic return of Israel to Peru." Second, it is perceived that the coming of the apocalypse will be preceded by seven years of famine and it is their assignment, as the followers of the new Savior, Gamonal, to prepare the world for the end. They conceive of themselves as the chosen Peruvians. "When the time comes, governments from all the nations of the world," they believe, "will come in planes and beg the Israelitas to send representatives to their countries to instruct them in the righteous way to live."[72]

In 1965, Guillermo Lobáton, a regional commander of the Movement of the Revolutionary Left (MIR) and a well-educated Black from the coastal region of Peru, was considered by the native Asháninkas to be the Son of the Sun, who would guide the Indians "in militant appropriation of whites' material wealth."[73] Operating in Satipo Province, Lobáton was considered to have modeled himself after Fidel Castro.

In the 1970s, a wandering preacher and visionary named José Francisco da Cruz, a Brazilian by birth, began to spread his message in the villages along the Amazon River and its tributaries in Peru. He declared that the destruction of the world was imminent and on the direct instructions of Jesus Christ he was forming the "Third Universal Reform of Christianity" to assist people in preparing for the approaching end time. In its aftermath, the world would be one of abundant wealth and universal peace.

Over time, da Cruz's movement, known as the Orden Cruzada, has attracted over 10,000 followers in Brazil and Peru. Despite its overtly Christian foundation and character, some argue that its doctrines can be connected to the ancient Tupian search for the "Land without Evil."[74]

The Emergence of Indian Radicalism

Twentieth-century radicalism in Peru was closely identified with the *indigenismo* movement among primarily coastal Peruvian intellectuals seeking to address the grievances and alleviate the deplorable conditions of the Indian population.

Intellectuals on both the Left and the Right began to speak of the need to break the back of the Peruvian oligarchy and Western imperialism that seemingly now dominated the life of the country. Of particular importance were the writings of Carlos Mariategui. His efforts ultimately led to the formation of the Communist Party of Peru (PCP) in the 1930s.[75]

Mariategui stressed the political importance of the Peruvian Indian community in the future of the state. His evaluation of the communal character of the indigenous Andean society combined with his scathing criticism of Peru's oligarchic political and economic system, dominated by Criollos, laid the foundation of the political Left in Peru in the 1960s and 1970s.[76]

Mariategui was deeply distrustful of the traditional political process in Peru and, probably as a result, never worked out a broad-based ideology grounded in Western-style Leftist thought. Rather, his Marxism was based on the reality of the experience of the Peruvian indigenous peasant and the urban poor. In his most significant work, *Seven Interpretive Essays on Peruvian Reality*, he argued that all of Peru's problems of class, poverty, race, and social conflict could be traced to two factors: a semifeudal economic system and neocolonialism.

> Peruvian unity is still to be accomplished . . . what has to be solved is a dualism of race, language and sentiment born of the invasion and conquest of indigenous Peru by a race that has not managed to merge with the Indian race, eliminate it, or absorb it.[77]

Mariategui argued that the problem of the Indian was a socioeconomic problem, tied up in the ownership and use of land. As he put it:

> The problem of the Indian is rooted in the land tenure system of our economy. Any attempt to solve it with administrative or police measures, through education or by a road building program, is superficial and secondary as long as the feudalism of the large landowners (gamonales) continues to exist.[78]

Mariategui viewed revolution as the only means to achieve true national integration in Peru and to overcome the effects of feudalism. At the heart of his ideology was the incorporation of the Indian into the Peruvian nation. At the vanguard of his revolution would be the intellectuals who were prepared to establish a new economic system based on the combination of indigenous traditional values and Marxist principles—a significant alteration of the Marxist revolutionary model.

Mariategui died in 1930 at the young age of thirty-five. As a result he was never allowed to complete the full development of this potentially powerful Marxist-indigenous synthesis. Nonetheless, the idea did not die with him. As we shall see, this notion would stand at the intellectual foundation of Sendero Luminoso.

Millenarianism in Traditional Japanese Culture

Much like the case of what is now Peru, historians and social theorists are unsure of exactly when millenarian beliefs sprang up among the Japanese. Nonetheless, it can be concluded that the convergence of Buddhism and Japanese folklore provided a powerful catalyst for the inculcation of millennial faith into the traditional Japanese societal cognitive map. By the sixth century AD, Buddhism had made its way from its origins in India, through China and Korea, to Japan. In each of these regions it had added devoted believers.

Interestingly, for centuries, Japanese Buddhists quietly lived side by side with the adherents of Shinto, the nation's animistic nature religion. In some interpretations, Buddhism, in a manner somewhat similar to Christianity, offers the hope of a future savior or messiah figure. Called Miroku (Bodhisattva Maitreya) by Japanese Buddhists, this character is expected to descend from his home in the *Tsuita* Heaven[79] and reestablish Buddhist law on earth at the end of the latter days of the Mappo.[80] In response to different scriptural interpretations, the character of Miroku advanced over time. In contrast to the second coming of Jesus Christ, which is considered by many Christians as imminent, the greater part of Japanese Buddhists do not expect Miroku to return as savior until far into the future. Nonetheless, at certain times in both Chinese and Japanese history, the arrival of Maitreya or Miroku, has exploded on the scene as an imminent possibility.[81]

Perhaps the most influential Buddhist text to ever arrive in Japan was the *Lotus Sutra*, which revealed the essential characteristics of the Mayahana or "Great Vehicle" aspect of the philosophy. Just as its appearance had greatly influenced the spread of Buddhism in China, Tibet, Mongolia, and Korea, the Lotus Sutra became widely known among the Japanese.

According to the eschatology of the Lotus Sutra, Shakyamuni, the historical Buddha, was only one in a series of Buddha figures who had actually made an appearance on earth and initiated a new Buddha age. Such an age consists of three distinct phases. The first is characterized by the appearance of the "true law." Nonetheless, the true law eventually decays and becomes only a shell of its former self. This decay represents the second phase. Finally, there is a complete corruption and the "true law" disappears, initiating the third phase. At the end of each phase, a new Buddha appears to bring back the "true law" and enforce it with authority. The next Buddha, whose appearance is prophesied in the Lotus Sutra, is Maitreya.[82]

Despite having been brought to Japan in the sixth century, the idea of the Maitreya or Miroku received very little attention until the Heian Period (794–1133) when it began to develop into an increasingly powerful spiritual force that provoked a great deal of interest and popularity among members of the Japanese aristocratic class.[83]

It was during the Tokugawa Period (1600–1867) that millennial beliefs and practices associated with the notion of Miroku became a common feature of Japanese folk religion among the mass of the population.[84] Its acceptance was actively promoted primarily by priests (yamabushi) who organized numerous cults that worshipped, among other things, sacred mountains and other natural objects. Nonetheless, the specific spiritual focus of their attention was the expected appearance of a number of Miroku. Their purpose, it was believed, was the rescue of the weak and the helpless of Japanese society; it was this group that many assumed would be among the first to enter into Heaven.[85]

Such apocalyptic beliefs were most pronounced during periods of perceived difficulties in Japanese life, such as famine or epidemic diseases. People widely believed that such problems were signs that the Miroku-no-yo (the world of Miroku) was about to begin.[86]

By the middle of the eighteenth century, the feudal system that had historically characterized the Tokugawa Period was beginning to crumble. In its place, a new, more modern social structure that centered on a class of merchants, financiers, and business interests was emerging. From that time forward, as the Industrial Age unfolded, social crises that largely affected the common people and the lower classes became endemic in Japan. By what must have appeared to many as Satanic forces of evil, traditional life was being inexorably disturbed.[87] Political and economic power in the state was realigning and this manifested as a burden on the mass of the people. Such problems were exacerbated by the forced opening of Japan to international trade in 1854. This event dramatically and abruptly increased Japan's potential for and responsiveness to outside influences on its traditional way of life. During the Tokugawa period, more than 1,000 peasant uprisings were documented. In the period 1752–1867, there was an average of six violent, sporadic disturbances per year and many of these may be described as messianic in form.[88]

For example, a common form of public protest in the first half of the nineteenth century was the notion of *okage mairi* or sponsored pilgrimage in which representatives of an entire village or community would march to a distant temple in order to worship the sun goddess, Amaterasu, as a statement of nationalism as well as a public rejection of government policy.[89]

In addition, in the 1850s, an outbreak of unexplained and tumultuous dancing accompanied by continuous chanting was observed in many areas including the major city of Nagoya. Participants claimed that they had seen religious charms and symbols falling out of the sky. This phenomenon spread rapidly to nearby communities where other apocalyptic "signs" were said to have been observed. In many cases the dancing and chanting eventually led to riots and antigovernment protests.[90]

In the Chichibu Rebellion of 1884, adherents claimed to be agents of Miroku who were committed to bringing about the renewal of the world. They saw it as their divine task to alter the world and engender a truly egalitarian state.[91]

Millenarianism in Modern Japan: The "New" Religions

During the latter years of the Tokugawa era, Japan was beginning an age of extended sociopolitical and economic transition; a process that, to this day, has not been fully completed.[92] This is because the traditional and the modern have never achieved any degree of unity in Japan.

We begin to see evidence of the chasm between the two at the onset of the Meiji Restoration. From the perspective of everyday Japanese life, the people saw themselves as the victims of this process of transition, not as its vanguard. Modernization was not a popular notion among the mass of Japanese people. It was not initiated as the result of some popular swell of enthusiasm, "but because the government willed that it should be so."[93]

Throughout the past century and a half, rather than being a proactive force in the life of the country and society, the common people of Japan have been merely reactive to economic, political, and social forces that usually seem far more threatening than encouraging. During most of this period they have been powerless to exert any type of meaningful control over the structure and nature of their society and largely incapable of fully understanding either the sources or the longer-term implications of the sociopolitical transition impinging on them. These problems—powerlessness, poverty, disruption, anomie, moral stress—have led to the rapid rise of new millenarian religions during the period.[94] For this reason, the study of the rise of New Religions in modern Japan—their sources, processes, and functional role—attract comparisons with other millenarian cults of traditional societies going through profound yet inexorable change.

The aspirations of the New Religions not only articulated the imminent advent of Miroku, but also the very popular notion of *yonaoshi* (world renewal), which called for a radical transformation in the Japanese social order. Most sought to rectify corrupt and moral abuse within the system and to "set the world right again." Yonaoshi provided divine sanction to Japanese social protests in response to the modernization policies of the Meiji.[95]

Millenarian themes and symbols were prevalent among these New Religions. One of the first was Tenrikyo, founded by Nakayama Miki in 1863, which is today one of the larger and more powerful of the older "new" religions in Japan.

Miki had suffered a series of personal tragedies in her life, which, according to contemporary accounts, had a significant influence on her. In 1838, during a series of traditional folk medicine treatments of her young son for relief of severe and enduring pain in his legs, she experienced a religious conversion. These treatments involved extensive use of mystical ritual, a common healing device in early-nineteenth-century Japanese life. Nonetheless, Miki herself became caught up in the mystical, ritual powers and took on the persona of the medium able to communicate with spirits.[96]

> As the spells began to get under way Miki's face suddenly changed and she fell into a violent state of trance. To the question of what deity was possessing her she answered, "I am Ten-no Shogun." "What manner of god might Ten-no Shogun be?" they asked. "The true god and the original god, who was descended from heaven to save all mankind," the deity answered through Miki's mouth. It then demanded that Miki's body should be given over as a shrine for its own use. Miki's husband, much taken aback, replied that such a request was impossible to grant, since Miki was the mother of four children, the youngest only a few months old. The god thereupon threatened that if its orders were disobeyed it would blast the whole family with curses.[97]

Over time, Miki gained a reputation among those around her for possessing miraculous healing powers.[98] In particular, she made a name for herself by seemingly granting painless childbirth. As her fame grew, a movement began to form around her remarkable spiritual force.

Miki predicted that at some moment in the not too distant future a "heavenly dew" or *kanro* would fall from the sky and cover the earth. This event would be the sign that a new age of perfect bliss or *yokigurashi* had begun. She declared that at that moment all of the misery and difficulties surrounding present conditions in Japan would vanish and the world would be born again. All those who drank of the dew would live in "effortless and perfect wisdom and virtue for 115 years."[99]

Remarkably, Miki's revelation indicated that the coming of the new age of *yokigurashi* depends not on god's efforts but the efforts of humankind itself. The more people begin immediately to purify and cleanse themselves of sin and rid their minds of the "eight dusts," she preached, the closer the time of the falling of the heavenly dew and the beginning of the new age.[100]

Miki and her movement were harassed by state authorities throughout the Meiji period. Miki, herself, was jailed by the government. Nonetheless, one year after her death, in 1888, the Tenrikyo movement was given official status by the Japanese government as a "Shinto sect."[101] It continued to expand and by 1937 its membership was between 4.5 and 5 million.[102]

In 1892, Deguchi Nao, a middle-aged seamstress from the Ayabe district of Japan, declared that she had received divine revelations from God. Remarkably akin to the experiences of Nakayama Miki, Nao was said to have had a rather dramatic dream in which she was wandering around in the world of spirits. A couple of days later she suddenly fell into an intense trance-like state. Eventually, her body went into a seizure, gyrating and moving up and down from sitting to a standing position and her stomach made loud noises. In the course of this seizure, the following conversation is said to have taken place between her voice and the beast-like "stomach" voice of the spirit inside of her.

> I am Ushitora no Konjin . . .
>
> You cannot be. You only say such things to deceive me . . .
>
> I am not a fox or a badger. I am the god come to rebuild and renew the world and make it into the Three Thousand World. The Three Thousand World, the world of Ushitora no Konjin, will open up like a plum blossom in spring. Now that I have appeared I will roll the Three Thousand World into one and make a divine world which will last for all eternity.[103]

Like Nakayama Miki, Deguchi Nao was believed to possess enormous powers of healing the sick. Those afflicted and for whom she prayed recovered almost immediately. Not surprisingly, she soon had a rather large following that surrounded her and eventually her movement included hundreds of thousands. Nonetheless, she prophesied that not her but, rather one who would follow her, would be the true savior of Japan.[104]

In 1898, her prophecy of a savior yet to come seemingly came to pass when she met a twenty-eight-year-old man, Ueda Kisaburo, who would later become known as Deguchi Onisaburo. Kisaburo also believed that he had received divine revelations. He claimed that he had been instructed to climb Mount Takakuma in order to achieve a divine state following a period of fasting and ascetic exercises. During this experience, he believed that his soul had physically left his body and embarked on a journey among the spirits. It was here that he was informed of his mission to free the world of injustice by saving it. Following his introduction to Nao, he declared her writings and preachings to be in complete accordance with those he had produced while on Mt. Takakuma. Eventually, Onisaburo was adopted into the family of Nao and was married to one of her daughters. It would be Onisaburo who would come to promote the Omoto movement into a national cult and be perceived by many to be its cofounder.[105]

The Omoto movement reached its peak in the 1920s as a paramilitary organization espousing ultranationalist ideas. Nonetheless, it was increasingly perceived by government officials as an insurgent movement bent on overturning the position of the royal family and installing Onisaburo as the emperor of Japan. Following years of harassment and closely monitoring the activities of the sect, in 1935, the government forcibly disbanded the movement.[106] Its headquarters in Ayabe and Kameoka were destroyed. All of the senior leadership were arrested, tried, convicted, and sent to prison. Eventually, these convictions were overturned on appeal. Nonetheless, the damage had been done. The movement was severely weakened only to reemerge as a much smaller organization in the aftermath of World War II.[107]

Deguchi Onisaburo of Omoto Kyo organized paramilitary groups from within the movement's membership. At the core of the Omoto Kyo belief system was an imminent apocalyptic war with the United States, which would result in the complete destruction of Japan with the exception of the sect's compounds and its adherents.[108] Onisaburo claimed to be the Bodhisattva Miroku and prophesied that the end of the world would occur in 1922.[109]

Following World War I, the state of Japan was now counted among the great powers of the world. In the 1920s, liberal politicians were able to control the forces of militant nationalism. Nonetheless, with the onset of the Great Depression, liberalism waned and Japan was overcome in a wave of ultranationalist fervor. Beginning with the Manchurian "incident" in 1931, followed by a full-scale war with China in 1937, Japan initiated a plan of conquering east and southeast Asia. This led to conflict with the United States and the onset of World War II in the Pacific.[110]

Any religious faith operating in the country during this time was under enormous pressure to actively take part in the ritual of State Shinto and support Japanese military imperialism. Those faiths that did not comply or directly challenged these ideas were quickly crushed.[111] For example, both Roman Catholic and Protestant Christian churches operating at the time slowly adapted themselves to this ardent ideological atmosphere by developing revised theologies that legitimized the actions of the state. On the other hand, those religious sects that refused to cooperate with government purposes were openly punished. Their leaders and members were arrested and many died in prison.[112]

In 1945, with much of their nation in sociopolitical, economic, and physical ruin, Japan surrendered to the Allied Forces, led by the United States. General Douglas MacArthur headed a government of occupation. Almost immediately, executive orders were issued by MacArthur that would engender significant changes in the political, economic, social, and religious life of Japan.

State Shinto was disbanded and Emperor Hirohito was forced to renounce his divine status. For the first time, freedom of religion in Japan was guaranteed as a right of the people. As a result, a wave of new fringe faiths quickly emerged. Between 1945 and 1947 the number of New Religions in Japan grew from 43 to 207. And, by 1951, the number had exploded to a total of 720. Of these, 258 were identified as Shinto, 260 were Buddhist, and 46 were Christian. The other 156 were not classified. Among these New Religions were a number of organizations that had been simply resurrected from a previous existence, having been banned by the government before the war. Nonetheless, the vast majority were truly New Religions.[113]

Many of these New Religions were remarkably successful to the point that they stood in stark contrast to the older religions, which seemed increasingly stale and lifeless to many Japanese. Some constructed huge modern cathedrals and marketed themselves aggressively to the public. As a result, their membership continued to grow and they flourished financially.[114]

These new, postwar religions in Japan were distinctive in their consistent millenarian quality. For example, Jikosan, who founded Jiukyo in 1947,[115] declared that it had been revealed to her that the present hopeless conditions that existed in Japan would soon come to an end through discernable spasms and tremors of nature itself. The country would be destroyed. However, emerging from the devastation would be a new "divine" land, "abounding in peace and happiness."[116]

One of the largest of the New Religions was *Soka Gakkai*, which, though founded in 1937, prospered in the postwar period.[117] The entire nature of the movement is profoundly millenarian. It anticipates the advent of not only a new age in Japan but also a spiritual transformation around the world through the application of the teachings of a thirteenth-century Japanese Buddhist monk, Nichiren.[118]

Nichiren is perceived of as the messiah who would appear during the age of Mappo foretold by Shakyamuni.[119] Nichiren taught that Japan, in his day, had actually already entered the evil and immoral period known as Mappo when law and justice would begin to disappear. The concept of Mappo had been a fundamental teaching of Buddhism for quite some time. And, the difficulties that now engulfed Japan were evidence to Nichiren that Mappo had arrived.[120]

The followers of Soka Gakkai are convinced that the problems of post–World War II Japan are clear evidence that the age of Mappo has arrived and the writings of Nichiren are of value once again. They cling to his notion that the difficult period of Mappo would be followed by a Golden Age of justice and harmony.

> The wonderful Law will spread throughout all the peoples of the world, and all will with one voice chant Namu Myoho Rengekyo. Behold how the world will enter the golden age of the sages. Disasters and calamities will cease, and the principles of perpetual youth and everlasting life will be revealed to me. Here are the signs of *gensei annon*—peace and joy on this earth.[121]

Soka Gakkai asserts that no state in the world currently bases its secular laws on the True Law of the universe. As a result, world society is in chaos and individuals everywhere are suffering. Though any individual can achieve substantive and immediate benefits through a personal commitment to Soka Gakkai and the principles of Nichiren, total happiness and justice on earth will not be achieved until all societies are converted to the movement.[122]

Soka Gakkai is highly critical of the Japanese government. It asserts that it does not live up to the expectations of the people and the constitution that created it. As a result, it is corrupt and the needs of the people are largely ignored in order to achieve the goals of the state and politicians.[123]

In 1951, under the leadership of Toda Josei, Soka Gakkai began a massive and controversial national recruiting campaign. Many Japanese were offended by the heavy-handed techniques employed by the movement, including the use of considerable propaganda, speeches promoting intolerance and denouncing other religions,[124] and generally aggressive behavior. There were frequent accusations of intimidation, coercion, terrorism, and blackmail lodged against the movement and the tactics it employed. Nonetheless, the membership effort was quite effective. By 1957, Soka Gakkai claimed a legitimate membership body in excess of 750,000 families.[125]

Today, Soka Gakkai is the most powerful popular organization in Japan. It is a unique blend of what is old and what is new; a modern lay organization composed of broad-based membership, yet still worshiping the traditional writings of the 700-year-old Buddhist prophet Nichiren.[126]

The Millenarian Nature of Shi'a Islam

As is true of the previous two cases in Peru and Japan, the Muslim tradition contains an overt and durable millenarian "stream." Its teachings and rituals possess a complicated instrument of learning with respect to how eschatological events will unfold on earth. For example, all Muslims believe that human and cosmic history has both a beginning and an end and it is widely accepted that the last days of history will be characterized by great difficulty, injustice, and despair within the community culminating in the return of a savior figure that all Muslims refer to as the Mahdi. It will crush all forms of oppression, overcome the enemies of the faith, and restore peace and justice on earth.

Although there is no direct or indirect reference to the concept of a deliverer or savior contained in the Qura'n, Muslims are routinely reminded and warned of the coming Day of Judgment. "They are told that they would be judged in the light of their deeds and misdeeds, and they are promised abundant rewards for good deeds and horrible doom for all acts of dereliction."[127]

Early in their evolution as a faith, Muslims conceived of a powerful and durable ritual of millenarianism and messianic beliefs. Over time these became central to both their religious and political thought. This ritual was borrowed from the earlier Judaic-Christian tradition. Nonetheless, it was greatly modified to fit the specific needs of the Islamic community.[128]

More specifically, Twelver Shi'a Muslims believe in a tradition that Muhammad told Ali:

> There will be twelve Guides (Imams) after me, the first of whom is you 'Ali, and the last one will be the "support" (al-Qa'im), who with the grace of Allah, will gain victory over the whole east and west of the world.[129]

Following the death of Mohammed, early Shi'a theologians introduced the notion of the Imamate. At the foundation of this concept is the occultation of the Twelfth Imam. Shi'ite adherents are expected to practice *Intizar*, or waiting, for his promised reappearance.[130]

In its most fundamental construct, the doctrine of the Occultation or *Ghayba* holds that Muhammad ibn Hasan, the Twelfth Imam, never died. Rather he has been concealed by God and may not be seen by mortal men. In a miraculous and mysterious way his life has been extended until that day when he will make himself evident once again, through the will of God.[131]

Shi'ites believe that without the Imam as their protector and would-be redeemer, the universe would quickly collapse. He is considered "the Proof, the Manifestation, and the Organ of God, and he is the Means by which human beings can attain, if not knowledge of God, at least what is knowable in God." He is the "perfect man" and the "sacred guide." As such, the concept plays a significant mediating role between the people and God. Without such a figure, there can be no way into the world of the divine. In this way, the Imam is a medium through which Allah and the people of the faith communicate. He achieves both a reason for the religion to exist and the order that it establishes within the community.[132]

There are obvious similarities between the concept of the Judeo-Christian Messiah and the notion of the Twelfth Imam among the Twelver Shi'a. Nonetheless, for the purposes of this study there is an important difference. In the Christian eschatological tradition, the role of violence is unclear,[133] but the Shi'a theology is unmistakably clear that the rise of the Mahdi will be accompanied by a *Jihad*, or Holy War, in which the forces of evil on earth will be defeated and the world will enter an age of unprecedented universal peace and happiness.[134]

Over a lengthy period of time, Shi'a theological scholars have identified a broad base of characteristics associated specifically with the notion of the Imamate. Central to these attributes is the idea that sovereignty within the community rests exclusively with the Imam. All law within the community must be implemented only by a legitimate descendent of the Holy Prophet. Otherwise they have no validity. The esoteric knowledge possessed by the historical Imams is an inherited trait and its power is unquestionable.[135]

The notion of the Imamate, which began as a simple messianic concept following the death of Muhammad, has evolved into a complex theological and political construction. It is from this construction that all other aspects of Shi'ism, such as ethics, law, politics, and mysticism, find their origins.[136]

Obviously, eschatology performs a salient role in Twelver Shi'ism. Nonetheless, under what conditions will the Twelfth Imam reappear? In the customs associated with the return of the Imam Mahdi, there are a number of "signs" that Shi'ites point to that they believe foretell his return. Many of these are directly connected to worldly conditions. Probably the most widely known of these signs and one that can be linked to both Sunni and Shi'a literature asserts that the Mahdi will "fill the earth with justice after it has been filled with injustice and tyranny."[137]

Other prophecies of the return of the Mahdi are linked to moral decline in the world and are interpreted by many to assume that such an advent will occur concurrent with growing secularization, the expanded political power of women, and an increasingly liberal culture around the world.[138]

Shi'ism is believed, by its adherents, to be a comprehensive guide to a life of righteousness, and one that is subordinate to no other set of principles: secular or theological. Shi'as have always believed that as long as the hidden Imam remains in occultation then there is no real foundation for political, social, or theological power in the world. As a result, the ulama have generally adopted a subdued attitude toward secular affairs. For example, they have tended to tolerate the temporal rule of secular monarchical governments, as long as these governments did not infringe upon or seemingly violate Shi'a doctrine and Islamic law (Sharia).[139]

Traditional Shi'ites do not believe that humans have the power to create a paradise on earth through their own efforts. Such a paradise was only to be ushered in through the return of the hidden Imam. As a result, traditional Shi'ism became a faith grounded in a profound sense of helplessness: a religion of mourning, with institutionalized manifestations of grief and suffering. This sense of helplessness is best symbolized in Shi'ite ritual by the martyrdom of Imam Husayn (the third Imam, a grandson of Muhammad, who died while fighting for the cause of Shi'ism at Karbala in AD 680).[140]

Shi'ism possesses an intricate and frustrating history of hope combined with disappointment. This unique mix of what is both the best and the worst of a powerful sacred notion stems from, on the one hand, the deep and sacred eschatological tradition that pervades every aspect of the faith—that ultimately a just society will emerge among the community that will free the oppressed and the suffering. On the other hand, frustration emerges out of the repeated letdown of the faith to live up to such lofty, utopian expectations.[141]

As this study demonstrates, the cultural tradition of the expectation of the Imam Mahdi remains one of the most important components of the reality of Islam in today's world.[142]

The modern Islamic world is divided into two primary theological groupings: the Sunnis and the Shi'as. This schism traces its roots to the period following the death of Muhammad in AD 637, when a dispute broke out over who was to become the prophet's rightful successor. On the one hand, Shi'a Islam, and specifically, its largest sect, the Twelvers, put their faith in the divine nature of a hereditary line of perfect Imams who are direct descendants of the prophet Muhammad through the marriage of his daughter Fatima (Muhammad's only child) and his cousin Ali. Shi'ites believe that Ali was chosen personally by Muhammad to assume the leadership of the Islamic movement.[143] Only a leader who matched the qualities of Muhammad could lead the community to its ultimate destiny as the creator of the ideal Islamic community. After all, who could be better qualified for such a significant mission than his own family members, who would have naturally inherited his aura and ability?[144] As a result, leadership succession in the nascent movement assumed utmost importance.[145]

Nonetheless, the split in Islam over the issue of who should succeed to the leadership of the faith was much more than a debate over personality. It was equally so a debate over the proper role and function of that individual who would lead the faith. The Sunni faction asserted that the leader should be responsible for the protection of divine law and govern over the community, in the process keeping public order and protecting the frontiers of the Islamic world. On the other hand, the Shi'ites asserted that the rightful successor to the Prophet possessed special knowledge and, as a result, was capable of interpreting the Qur'an and the law. It was required that he be chosen by God, not by members of the community. The leader was to be referred to as the Imam.[146]

The early Islamic period was dominated by the Sunni–Shi'a split, which often became violent. Indeed, a number of messianic-inspired revolts broke out over the issue of political control of the Islamic state. These revolts were frequently carried out in the name of the Islamic martyrs, primarily Hasayn and Husayn, but also later Imams. The rebels who participated in these movements believed that the leader they were following was the Mahdi, who would destroy the present sociopolitical system and replace it with one based on Shi'a values and justice.[147] As a result, in its earliest stage, the concept of the Imamate in Shi'a Islam came into being largely as a consequence of social anxiety and political dissent.[148]

Gradually, this drive for a new society that was just and, at the same time, free from oppression from outside forces transformed Shi'ism from a political movement into a distinctly millenarian religious sect.[149] This religio-political ideology of Twelver Shi'ism is both innovative and utopian. Its final goal is the fulfillment of the human dream of a paradise on earth. Only as a result of the rule of the Imams will the anticipated utopia be realized.[150]

According to Twelver Shi'a doctrine, the first Imam was Ali, succeeded by his two sons, Hasan and later Husayn. They were followed by a succession of nine others, ending with the disappearance of the Twelfth (or hidden) Imam, while he was still a youth, in AD 873–874. All eleven of the previous Imams, according to Shi'a custom, had died in battle, or had been killed by evil and unmerited tyrants who sought only power. As a result, at its foundation, Shi'a theology was a message of dispossession. In the aftermath of the death of Husayn at Karbala, the Imams and the Sh'ite community withdrew into an extended period of quietism and repudiated military or political violence against the caliphate led by the Sunnis. Indeed, they chose to live on the margins of political life in the community. In particular, the Imams and the Shi'a clerics accepted a simple role as spiritual guides and teachers in the community.[151]

Nonetheless, many Shi'ites were unwilling to accept the quietism and passivity fostered by the leaders of the faith; from time to time, small political movements who openly asserted their allegiance to 'Ali and Husayn and claimed lineage to Muhammad, would emerge in response to what they perceived of as injustice and oppression precipitated by Sunni leaders.

One of the more intense and well known of these revolts occurred in the mid-eighth century. Led by the grandson of Husayn, Zayd ibn Ali, and half-brother of the Fifth Imam, Muhammad al-Baqir, a violent revolt was initiated against the practices and policies of the ruling Umayyad government in Kufa. Though the revolt failed and Zayd was killed, his political notion of the use of violence in response to oppression and injustice survived. His followers became known as the Zaydis and asserted that the power of the Imamate can be assumed by any descendant of Fatima and 'Ali, not just those in the line of the Twelver Imams. Nonetheless, to assume such millenarian power, one must reject the passiveness taught by the faith. Indeed, passivity in the face of injustice automatically disqualifies the claim to Imam. Although a tiny minority within Shi'ism, the Zaydis have survived and live predominately in the highlands of Yemen, in the southern portion of the Arabian peninsula.[152]

The narrative of the martyrdom or *al maqatil* of the sacred Imams connects how it was that the righteous and worthy descendants of the Prophet Muhammad were prevented from assuming their rightful position as rulers of the community.[153] Nonetheless, the hidden Twelfth Imam is expected by Twelvers to return as Mahdi at the end of time.[154]

Here we see a common element among Jewish, Christian, and Islamic eschatology—the Messiah (hidden Imam) returns as a great retaliator, a *Mahdi*, a savior. In each of the great traditions, such an expectation emerged in a period of great social and political difficulty. In the case of the Shi'a, the notion was confirmed by the authority of Muhammad, who had personally promised the Mahdi's return.[155]

Theological conflicts created by differing interpretations of basic texts and sacred writings are common to all religions. Nonetheless, the Sunni–Shi'a division in Islam is far more explosive than a mere theoretical debate or scriptural dispute. This is because in addition to a religious debate, the issues surrounding the split are fundamentally a political debate over leadership and law.[156] Islam is not only an apocalyptic faith that brings comfort to the weary and soothes the pain of those who suffer; its distinctive characteristic is the fact that it represents a model for how to live one's life, not simply a collection of doctrines on how to worship God. As a result, different explanations of the teachings of Islam immediately manifest themselves in political conflict. In no small way, this accounts for the enduring nature of the conflict between Shi'as and Sunnis.[157]

The Shi'a and Sunni sects of Islam have much in common from a theological and ideological perspective. Both are millennial in orientation. Nonetheless, there are some notable differences in who will be the principal actor as the end times unfold.

All Sunnis, for example, accept the concept of a promised deliverer. Yet, many do so with reservation and some degree of skepticism. Some Sunni religious scholars have gone so far as to reject the notion of a savior and have argued that belief in the concept of the Mahdi is a *Bida* or an irreligious innovation. In reality, a very large segment of the Sunni community accepts the emergence of the Mahdi as an inexorable fact of history. As we have already seen, in times of difficulty, when one has stepped forward and declared himself to be the Mahdi he has always been able to garner some degree of legitimacy and support.[158]

Both Sunnis and Shi'ites point to many different sayings of sacred figures, along with numerous specific versus of the Qur'an, to support the authenticity of the concept of the Imam Mahdi. For example, there is widespread agreement among all Muslims that Muhammad has confirmed the return of a deliverer in times of difficulty and injustice:

> Even if the entire duration of the world's existence has already been exhausted and only one day is left before Doomsday (Day of Judgment), Allah will expand that day to such a length of time, as to accommodate the kingdom of a person out of my Ahul-Bayt who will be called by my name. He will then fill out the earth with peace and justice as it will have been full of injustice and tyranny before then.[159]

There is some disagreement over the identity and nature of this deliverer among the dominant branches of the faith. The larger Sunni community believes that the Mahdi will be a direct descendent of the Prophet and will have the name Muhammad. In contrast, the smaller Shi'ite community asserts that the Mahdi is the hidden Twelfth Imam.[160] In either circumstance, the faith in the return of the expected Mahdi is so powerful that throughout its history, particularly during periods of oppression and great difficulty, it has led to a number of millenarian-inspired sociopolitical movements.[161]

Following the death in 1577 of the Safavid Shah Isma'il II, whose father had established Shi'ism as the state religion in Persia, a set of rebellions occurred that were triggered by rumors that he had, in fact, not died but gone into "concealment" and would soon reappear. Over time, a number of "pseudo-Isma'ils" appeared—first in Sabsavr, and later in Hamadar. However, the most important appeared in Kuh Giluyeh and was able to build a following of over 10,000 men. Also known as Shah-e Qalandar and Shah Isma'il-e Qatil, he was able to actually capture a substantial amount of territory, create a modest, yet functioning regime of power and ruled for over a decade until he was finally captured and beheaded in 1592.[162]

In 1844, and almost precisely 1,000 years following the occultation of the Twelfth Imam, Shi'ite millenarianism, after centuries of relative inactivity, erupted in one of the more significant insurrections of the traditional era: the Babi movement.[163] Babism arose during a period of social and religious stress and embodied an offshoot sect of the eighteenth-century Shaykhi movement.

Concentrated around the Shi'a shrine cities of Najaf and Karbala in what was at the time Ottoman-controlled Iraq, Shaykhism was founded by an Arab Shi'a cleric, Shaykh Ahmad al-Ahsa'i (1753–1826). In its formative years, Shaykhism maintained the support of most of the leadership of the ulama in the region. Nonetheless, over time and certainly by the death of the Shaykh, the movement came to be considered by many as a separate school of Shi'ism.

Early Shaykhism is best characterized as an attempt to explain traditional Shi'a doctrines within the context of an increasingly modern, nineteenth-century Islamic world. In a manner that corresponds somewhat with the efforts of Erasmus to rationalize Christianity in a modernizing sixteenth-century western Europe, it seems that Shaykh Ahmad sought to combine Shi'a theology with contemporary philosophy and to reconcile religious dogma with scientific reason.[164]

The Shaykh's teachings asserted that it was now necessary for Shi'ism to be cleansed through a return to its traditional reliance on infallible guidance: that is, the Imams. Nonetheless, this notion had to be reconciled with the idea that ordinary humans were incapable of comprehending the true teachings of Allah. As a result, intermediaries were necessary for man to gain access to divine teachings and esoteric knowledge. The Shaykhis believed that Allah's reign on earth was always present through such intermediaries, known as Babs. The Bab was the "door" between humans and the world of the Imam. It was considered a holy being, free from sin: a holy, infallible, and sinless being representing the expression of God's blessing to humankind.[165]

A particularly controversial component of Shaykhism was its eschatological teachings. Indeed, it was on the basis of these teachings that Shaykh Ahmad was eventually excommunicated by the ulama. In contrast to orthodox Shi'a beliefs, Shaykh Ahmad taught that on the Day of Judgment, creation would return not to Allah as its source but, rather, to the Primal Will (the instructor of humankind). In other words, the salvation of humankind at the end of time would take place not in the temporal body but, rather, in a "subtle body," which would come into being in the realm of *Hurqalya*', a sort of "interworld between materialism and the realm of heaven." Shaykh Ahmad taught that there were in fact two heavens and two hells, one each in this world and the next, and that the achievement of paradise in this world was possible merely through one's personal acceptance of the infallibility of the hidden Imam.[166]

Upon the death of Shaykh Ahmad, the Persian-born Sayyid Kazim Rashti, who had been designated by the Shaykh as his legitimate and authorized successor, became the one who was responsible for furthering the teachings of Shaykhism. Indeed, it was as a result of Sayyid Kazim's efforts that a truly separate congregation began to form around Shaykhism and the movement began to thrive. A considerable number of adherents were gained throughout Iran, as well as in the southern region of Iraq. Nonetheless, Sayyid Kazim's eventual death in 1843, without his naming a successor, left the movement and its disciples in a state of turmoil and confusion. Over the following months, numerous claims of successorship were advanced by several of the Sayyid's leading disciples, and several rivalries emerged.[167]

Among those claiming to be the successor to Sayyid Kazim was a young merchant from Shiraz named Sayyid Muhammad Ali. Ali had been a devoted student of Kazim for just a few months at Karbala, but in 1840 he returned to Shiraz, where he married and appeared to resettle back into the family business. Nonetheless, in 1844, Ali experienced a number of religious-inspired visions. In the most dramatic of these he saw the severed head of the Imam Husayn, "drops of whose blood he drank and from the grace of which," as he later wrote, "my breast was filled with convincing verses and mighty prayers [and, the spirit of God having] permeated and taken possession of my soul . . . the mysteries of His revelation were unfolded before my eyes in all their glory."[168]

Perhaps the most complete account surrounding the claims of Sayyid Muhammad Ali comes from the writings of E. G. Browne.[169]

> By dint of dwelling on these ideas, and concentrating all his thoughts on the Imams, the unseen dispensers of God's will, Mirza' Ali' Muhammad

[Sayyid Muhammad Ali] becomes convinced that he enjoys the favour of a special communication with them. His teacher, Haji' Seyyid Kazim, dies, and his disciples are left in doubt as to who is to succeed him. Of the exact sequence of events it is difficult to judge, by reason of the various accounts. According to the Babi historian, Mulla' Huseyn of Bushraweyh (who afterward played so prominent a part in the Babi movement) went to Shiraz from Karbala' to be cured of a palpitation of the heart. . . . On arriving there, he enquired for the house of Mirza' Ali' Muhammad, who had been his friend and fellow student at Karbala', and finding his way there, knocked at the door, which was opened by the latter himself, who welcomed his old friend, and conducted him into the house. After the customary compliments and enquiries, Mirza' Ali Muhammad said: "Is it not the case that you Sheykhis believe that it is necessary that after the death of the departed Seyyid some one should take his place? It is now five months since he died. After him who is his successor?" Mulla' Huseyn replied, "[W]e have not yet recognized anyone." Mirza' Ali' Muhammad said, "[W]hat sort of person must he be?" After a little reflection, Mulla' Huseyn described the qualities and attributes which must be found in him. "Do you behold these signs in me?" asked the Bab. Mulla' Huseyn knew that Mirza' Ali' Muhammad had only studied at Karbala for about two months, and had not while there shown any signs of an unusual degree of knowledge, besides having received only a rudimentary education previously. He was greatly astonished at the question, and replied, "I see none of these signs in you." Shortly afterwards he finds a commentary on the Suratu'l-Bakara lying on the shelf, takes it up and reads a little, and is surprised at the new meaning it discloses. He asks Mirza' Ali' Muhammad, "Whose book is this?" but the latter only replies, "a youthful tyro has written it, and he shows forth exceeding knowledge and greatness."

Next day they have another similar conversation, and the Bab again asks Mulla' Huseyn if he sees in him the signs of spiritual leadership. The latter marvels at the persistent way he returns to this point, and determines to convince him of his deficient learning by asking him some questions. To his amazement, these are answered with surprising readiness and clearness; nay, even his inward thoughts and doubts seem to be divine and answered by the Bab. He is astonished, yet unwilling to believe in this unlettered youth, whom he has always looked on as so inferior in knowledge to himself. Finally, however, he is convinced, and accepts the doctrine of the Bab with an earnestness and sincerity to which his subsequent deeds bear ample witness. Once convinced, Mulla' Huseyn does not rest idle. He hastens to inform his fellow-disciples, who are still in doubt as to whom they should choose as a successor to their late teacher; many of these come to Shiraz, and after more or less hesitation accept a new creed. Thus was formed the first nucleus of the Babis.[170]

Ali came to be accepted as the Bab and his preaching included strong attacks on the corruption of the Shi'a clergy. He clearly promoted the traditional Islamic concept of the jihad (holy war) and called upon the Babis to prepare to "conquer the countries and their people for the pure faith of God." He chided his followers to accumulate weapons so as to prepare for the "day of slaughter when God would kill the unbelievers, and the Imams and angelic hosts would aid them in battle and their martyrs would receive their due reward." Largely in response, the Bab was imprisoned by the leading Persian ulama in 1847, and a series of Babi revolts began in 1848. Between 1848 and 1850, some 4,000–5,000 Babis died in fierce clashes with Persian state troops.[171]

The Bab and many of his prominent followers were executed in 1850, and executions and persecutions of the movement continued thereafter.[172] The Babi movement presented a clear and effective challenge to the entire religious and political order in Persia. It emerged as a new religion and, to the ulama and the state authorities, as a source of insurrection and terror.[173]

In the late eighteenth century, prior to the European exploration and colonization of Africa, a number of significant religious movements spread quickly over west Africa. Along the way, a number of Islamic states were established that were based largely on the powerful attraction of charismatic prophets. Many of these claimed to be the Mahdi. The most significant was 'Uthman dan Fadio, who was born in Gobir, in what is now Nigeria, in 1754. 'Uthman was able to quickly gain control of a rather large area of west Africa and firmly establish himself as both a religious and political leader. His claim as the Mahdi brought a unique and durable unity to many of the various tribes of the region that remains viable today.[174]

In 1881, Muhammad Ahmad, a charismatic religious figure in the Lower Nile region of East Africa, declared himself to be the Mahdi and sought to unite first the various tribes of what is now Sudan, but also the entire Islamic world, in a new religious state that stood in opposition to continued British intrusion into the region. In particular, Muslims of the area were deeply concerned over efforts by the British to Westernize their way of life. In 1885, Muhammad Ahmad defeated and killed General Charles Gordon and captured the city of Khartoum, proclaiming a new Islamic state and a religious association that remains significant in contemporary Sudan.[175]

A century later, Ayatollah Khomeini sought to connect the Shi'a past, with the Shi'a future. Like those clerics before him, who had tried to reconcile Shi'ite traditional passiveness with the need to contend and even confront injustice and oppression within the community, Khomeini wrestled with the limitations of the past, and the challenges of a modernized future. In particular, he was deeply concerned with the intervention of foreign ideas into the affairs of the Shi'a community. He feared that foreign influence would eventually result in the complete abolition of Islam, both as a religion and as a guide to life. Foreign influences, he came to believe, represented nothing less than a satanic power within Shi'a society and culture—one that must be destroyed.[176]

Nonetheless, in the presence of God's continued silence on the issue of confrontation and contention with the temporal world, Khomeini decided to pursue what he rightfully could, within the prescriptions of the faith, to seek out a divine solution. It was in this pursuit that he came to believe that God had inspired and guided him to a moral answer to the perceived dilemma that faced the entire Shi'a community in the 1960s and 1970s.

Everywhere in the sermons and speeches of Khomeini, beginning in the early 1960s, one finds not only his attacks on the Shah's regime, but also his concern over the continuing expansion of Western neocolonialism in Iran and among the *umma* or community of believers. In developing his argument, he went back into the long history of imperialism in the region. For example, he argued, "the conspiracy worked out by the imperialist government of Britain at the beginning of the constitutional movement had two purposes." "The first, which was already known at that time, was to eliminate the influence of Tsarist Russia in Iran, and the second was to take the laws of Islam out of force and operation by introducing Western laws."[177]

In addition to the British, Khomeini saw Iran's more recent problems as the result of American intervention.

> All the problems facing Iran . . . are the work of America. Until recently, the British enslaved the Moslem nations; now they are under American bondage . . . The Americans appoint Majles deputies, and attempt to eliminate Islam and the Quran because they find the ulama to be a hindrance to colonialism.[178]

From Khomeini's perspective, foreign influence in the umma, from the very beginning, was part of a massive conspiracy. The Russians, British, French, and later the Americans sought to control the region, including its natural resources, its people, and their culture. He saw

Western thought and values as dangerous mechanisms that could sap the energy and vitality out of the Shi'a people.[179]

In 1963, Khomeini was arrested and deported for his political activities in Iran. The Shah believed that by getting Khomeini out of the country he could destroy his ideological authority and be rid of him forever. Khomeini went first to Turkey but spent most of his 16 years in exile within the large Shi'a community in Iraq. It was during this period that Khomeini was able to more fully develop his ideas regarding the role of religio-political authority among the Shi'a in a modern world. What he came to develop was the idea of successfully merging clerical populism with legitimate constitutional authority within the state.[180]

Since the rise of the Safavid Dynasty in Persia in 1501, the Shi'a clergy had endured the power of monarchy in a rather symbiotic relationship. Over this period, they came to be convinced that tolerating the royal family was much preferable to the possibility of anarchy. Khomeini sought to end this tradition of monarchical tolerance because, he argued, Shi'ism and the idea of monarchy were completely incompatible.[181]

In making this assertion, Khomeini began with the fundamental notion of the Imamate as not only a religious doctrine, but also as a political concept. He asserted that the policy of the ulama, to grant legitimacy to the royal family's political authority, so long as it was limited by a constitution, was not only a violation of religious law, it had been a complete failure from a practical perspective. Instead, beginning in the 1970s, Khomeini began to call for the overthrow of the Pahlavi regime in Iran. He instructed the community to then fully incorporate the political machinery of the state into the religious structure of the community based on the doctrine of the Imamate.[182] He was advancing a new theory of political Islam that promoted direct clerical rule whose task it was to act as representatives of the hidden Imam. Khomeini argued,

> Now that we are in the time of the Occultation of the Imam, it is still necessary that the ordinances of Islam relating to government be preserved and maintained, and that anarchy be prevented. Therefore, the establishment of government is still a necessity. . . . Now that no particular individual has been appointed by God, Exalted and Almighty, to assume the function of government in the time of Occultation, what must be done? Are we to abandon Islam? Do we no longer need it? Was Islam valid for only two hundred years? Or is it that Islam has clarified our duties in other respects but not with respect to government?[183]

Nonetheless, an important question remained. Who would act in the capacity as the representative of the hidden Imam? This was critical because it would be this individual or individuals who possessed the authority for interpreting Islamic law. It was in answer to this question that Khomeini introduced his most radical political concept.

> The two qualities of knowledge of the law and justice are present in countless *fuqaha* [the religious scholars] of the present age. If they would come together, they could establish a government of universal justice in the world. . . . If a worthy individual possessing these two qualities arises and establishes a government, he will possess the same authority as the Most Noble Messenger in the administration of society, and it will be the duty of all people to obey him.[184]

Khomeini asserted that the power of such a "worthy individual" should rest in the position of the *velayat-e faqih* or mandate of the clergy.[185] This concept represents the most significant innovation in Shi'a political theory in a century.[186] In a modern Islamic government, Khomeini declared, "the Mandate [of the Clergy] means governing and administering the country and administering the provisions of the sacred law."[187]

Since the hidden Imam remains in occultation, the legal and spiritual sovereignty that rests with him cannot be fully exercised.[188] As result, he requires the assistance of representatives in the temporal world to deal with the practical and spiritual matter of guiding the community. The logical choice for these representatives is the ulama who have traditionally interpreted Islamic law for centuries. From among the ulama, one can emerge who is the most enlightened and venerated cleric within the community. Ultimate authority of interpretation rests in his hands: the *velayat-e faqih*.[189]

Khomeini argued that Allah did not limit the legitimacy of his law that was interpreted by the Imams to a period of only two centuries, from the rule of Muhammad to the beginning of the lesser occultation. Rather, he intended for an Islamic state that incorporated his law to exist forever. Such a government was necessary to ensure justice, to teach the rule of God, to guarantee order, and to eliminate sin.[190]

Khomeini was very clear in identifying both the qualifications and the nature of the *faqih*. Such an individual, he argued, must possess enormous skills, demonstrated over a long period of study and service to the community. He is the legitimate intellectual and theological heir to the Prophet and the Imams, acting in their stead until such time as the hidden Imam shall return. He is considered to be a figure and a person who is incorruptible. As such, the *velayat-e faqih* is an explicitly messianic political concept.[191] At its core is the concept of divine, not human, selection.[192]

The political theory introduced by Khomeini represented a radical new approach when compared to previous interpretations of the role of religious law in government. Khomeini's ideas aimed at complete political and cultural revolution within the Shi'a community.[193] It represents a new explanation of the relationship between political authority and the authority of the faith. Nonetheless, the salience and the character of the hidden Imam remain unchanged.[194]

The Shi'a Community in Lebanon

The Shi'a community is one of eighteen different religious groups that comprise the "Confessional"-based political system in Lebanon. These include Sunni Muslims, Christian Maronites, Greek Orthodox, and Druze Muslims. Just as the Druze and Maronites, the Shi'a are a minority sect within their respective religions.[195]

During the latter years of the Ottoman Empire, the area surrounding Mount Lebanon in the Levant had been an autonomous region dominated by the Christian Maronites. Following World War I, the Maronites were successful in increasing the territory under their control to include the Bekaa Valley in what is now the southern part of Lebanon. This expansion of the control of the Maronites was supported by the French government, which had received the mandate over both Syria and Lebanon following the collapse of the Ottoman Empire in 1918.[196]

The new lands that came under the expanded control of the Maronites contained large numbers of both Sunni and Shi'a Muslims. The Sunni, in particular, strongly objected to Maronite rule over what they considered to be their lands. In response, and in an attempt to maintain control, the Maronites eventually struck a deal with Shi'a leaders. In return for a large degree of their own freedom of political action in the south, the Shi'a agreed to accept Maronite control. The Shi'a had long lived in the region as a minority group persecuted by the Sunni majority and, at the very least, sought to bring that practice to an end.[197] Their efforts were successful. As a result of their support of the Maronites, the Shi'ites soon materialized as a distinct and important faction in Lebanon; a position they had not been able to assume previously. Indeed, beginning in 1926, the French allowed the Shi'ites to create their own, autonomous, religious-based infrastructure and to practice their religion without outside interference.[198]

As expected, the Christian Maronites emerged as the dominant political actor in the mandate. Out of respect for the diverse factions however, political power was divided among the various religious entities. In addition, certain political arrangements were established in an attempt to maintain regime stability and legitimacy. For example, the presidency of Lebanon would always be in the hands of the Christian Maronites, the prime minister would always be a Sunni Muslim, and the speaker of the National Assembly would always be in the hands of the Shi'as. Additionally, the ratio of Christian members of the assembly to Muslim members was fixed at six to five, a relationship that reflected the demographic majority of the Christians in 1932. This arrangement guaranteed that the Sunnis and the Christians would control the leading political and military positions in the new state of Lebanon.[199]

Throughout the 1940s and 1950s, a significant gap was growing, economically, politically, and socially, between the Shi'ites and the rest of the country, largely because the government in Beirut tended to neglect them. Perhaps worse yet, semifeudal, landowning elites in the south were far more interested in their own personal gain than they were in the welfare of the Shi'a community as a whole. As a result, whereas the rest of Lebanon was modernizing, the Shi'ites lacked basic necessities: schools, hospitals, roads, and even running water in many instances. "In comparison with the prospering areas of the Sunnis and Christians, their standard of living was medieval."[200] As an example, in an analysis prepared in 1943, at the time of Lebanon's independence, it was noted that there was not one hospital in the entire south Lebanon area. The closest health clinic was in Sidon, Tyre, or Nabatiyya, all in the middle or northern sections of the country. Further, the availability of water for irrigation or human consumption was a persistent problem in the region. Nonetheless, there was very little that the new Lebanese state was willing or was able to do for the minority and increasingly marginalized Shi'a community.

In the 1950s, hundreds of thousands of Shi'ites relocated from the rural regions of Lebanon to metropolitan Beirut in the hope of a better way of life. Nonetheless, their experience was not what they had expected. Most were relegated to the slums of the city in a segregation process that limited their access to economic and political upward mobility. At the same time, their exposure to the affluent and Westernized lifestyle of the middle- and upper-class Christian and Sunni communities tended to exacerbate their sense of relative deprivation.[201]

Politically, the government of Lebanon did not support the recruitment and promotion of Shi'a civil servants in the state's bureaucratic framework. Indeed, throughout this period, the Shi'a community was considered by many observers as politically irrelevant in Lebanon.[202] They were underrepresented, when compared to their sizable portion of the population, in virtually all areas of public life.[203] This had the effect of de-legitimizing the government and its policies in the eyes of not only the Shi'ite community, but others as well. At another level, Shi'a religious leaders and many members of the lay public did not trust the government, which they perceived of as a secular, unworthy, activity. As a result, members of the Shi'ite community purposely held back from participating in public affairs, even within those fields that were within reach to them professionally.[204]

In 1958, a civil war erupted in Lebanon, largely as a result of the increased factionalism caused by the political arrangements established over 20 years earlier. Predictably, the Christian community had developed an increasingly pro-Western orientation, gaining the favor of not only France, but the United States. This orientation came into conflict with the growing pan-Arab ideology of the Sunni Muslims throughout the region. Ultimately, U.S. troops intervened in the fighting and order was established when the leader of Lebanon's army, Fouad Chehab, was elected president.[205]

Conclusion

Although such a process is universal, societies characterize religion—the organized search for transcendence—in different ways. They seek a personal God, on their own terms, in their own way. In turn, that which is sacred is represented and characterized through a similar methodology. In the process, every group attaches their ideals to society as whole. The most significant moments in these processes are shaped by crisis and tragedy: war, sickness, famine, and conquest, to name just a few. It is the tragedies of life that provoke people to pursue a search for the spiritual, to bring some meaning to what otherwise appears to be random, arbitrary, and disheartening events. And it is this convergence of tragedy and the need for transcendence that creates the potential for millenarian or apocalyptic forces to arise from dormancy.[206]

In addition, all societies come to deal with conflict in a way that is culturally unique. This is no less so in the cases under present study. Conflict resolution is pursued through the unique vernacular of the cognitive maps of these societies. In all three cases, a distinctive component of this cognitive map is a millenarian stream of faith: the belief that a Messiah or Savior figure will someday return and lead their society into a Golden Age.

The onset of Western imperialism beginning with the Spanish conquest of Peru in the sixteenth century, foreign intervention in Japan, and the Middle East in the nineteenth century engendered the most significant challenge and social disturbance that these three societies had faced. This was exacerbated in Japan in the aftermath of their defeat in World War II.

The effect can only be described as a complete and distressing disaster for traditional life in each case. The peoples of these communities came to see their old way of life and its traditional cultural system as no longer viable, outmoded, and seemingly useless in the presence of more powerful forces of modernization injected into these cultures by Western power.

The evidence is clear that a direct relationship exists between intercultural contact and the emergence of millenarian movements, either passive or violent. In all three cases, millenarian expectations frequently erupted in the presence of the conquering culture of the West.

The invasion of their way of life by a seemingly superior race, possessing new forms of material wealth, status, and military might, was seen as a significant, genuine, and dangerous threat to their way of life. It came to be associated with the roots of all evil and problems that pervaded their community: discrimination on the basis of race, relative deprivation, injustice, and oppression. All of these lead to a condition of righteous indignation.

Intercultural contact exacerbates a preexisting dichotomized perspective of all things in life falling into one of two categories: "light" versus "dark," "good" versus "evil," "god" and "anti-god." Millenarianism acts as an agent of countervailing force in such conditions. It sets in motion the idea that the community cannot be conquered or destroyed but, rather, must be renewed. Such renewal will come about through the intervention of cosmic forces. Nonetheless, the peoples of these communities did not believe that they were merely passive bystanders in such a process. Renewal was possible only through conformity to strict rules established by prophet founders. When the community obeyed these rules in an unquestioning way, the present vicious and evil circumstances could be defeated and a new era of extraordinary happiness, peace, and harmony could be allowed to begin.

Tracing its roots to antiquity, millenarianism survives to the present day in all three of these societies and continues to provide sacred reinforcement and legitimacy in the presence of profound socioeconomic and political change.

Millenarianism establishes the prospect that present difficulties can be transcended through the intervention of a cosmic and healing force. It provides the community with a clear ideology of progress, the end point of which is an idealized society, free from pain, alienation, oppression, injustice, racism, and want. The symbols that surround the rituals associated with millenarian beliefs are capable of inspiring powerful motivations for action, even if such action requires violence.

In each of these cases, the process of cultural renewal took the form of modifications to traditional devices in these societies. Characteristics of the conquering culture were gradually overlaid onto the traditional society, creating a unique syncretic mixture of new religio-political practices.

In the case of the Indians of Peru, for example, Christianity, brought by the Spanish, was heaped onto traditional Inca ritual. Indeed, in the twentieth century, as we shall see, the secular ideology of Marxism was effectively mixed with traditional Indian millenarianism. What emerged, in either case, were new religions and ideologies representing a desperate search for a divine truth that might allow their adherents to find a means to transcend present difficulties.

In Japan, Buddhism effectively converged with Shinto in the traditional era. And in the nineteenth and twentieth centuries, as Japan's intercultural contact with Western ways has expanded significantly, New Religions have literally exploded in numbers. An important consistent characteristic is their millenarian nature.

Among the Shi'a, the traditional rituals of their religion have remained largely unchanged. Nonetheless, the doctrine of the Imamate, a concept that began following the death of Muhammad as a primitive form of millenarian desire, has evolved into newer and far more intricate theological and political meanings regarding the role of the hidden Imam and his deputies on earth. Such an evolution has been significantly impacted by Western intervention into the life of the community. Nonetheless, once again, the millenarian paradigm remains intact.

In all three cases, traditional life is not perceived initially as something that is changing but, rather, as something being "disturbed." Rather quickly, modernity and secularity are seen as things to be feared, not embraced.

Eruptions of apocalyptic expectations in response to intercultural conflict in these three cases have been marked by a striking similarity in the use of violence. Such actions were seen to possess a sacred justification in defense of traditional life. Nonetheless, these traditional communities have always been resource poor in relation to the more material and powerful conquering cultures that have historically invaded their culture. As a result they are forced to rely on whatever means necessary to fight off perceived forces of evil and achieve a satisfactory form of cultural renewal on their own terms, not on the terms of the impinging culture. This means utilizing, at times, what is seen by many as egregious violence, lashing out at any target that symbolically represents the impinging cultural force. The destruction of these forces of evil and injustice is an imperative. It is conceptualized by members of the community as a requirement to hasten the idealized renewal of society that they so desperately seek.

CHAPTER 3

The Mediating Role of the Prophet

Leadership is a concept essential to a full understanding of the politics of terror. An important characteristic of leaders of social movements utilizing political violence and bent on transformative change, including millenarian movements, is a profound sensitivity to the present conditions of society and to the unique needs and desires of their potential followers.[1] The millenarian leader comes to define their role as that of the creator, communicator, and overseer of a radical, new political program, which is frequently inadequately defined and without bounds, but nevertheless grabs the attention of group members because it so effectively resonates with their expectations and aspirations.[2]

As a result, in order to understand the relationship between millenarianism and terrorist group leadership, we must carefully look, not only at the unique individuals involved but, more importantly, at the sources of hope, identity, and collectively held values within societies that engender such movements.

The study of leadership remains controversial. For example, empirical research that has focused attention on such factors as distinct personality traits of individuals as the active independent variable in effective leadership have had limited results. Such narrowly defined characteristics have been found to be much less important than first believed. More recent studies have tended to focus attention not on the characteristics of the leader but, rather, on the specific situation or set of events that appear to set the stage for effective leadership to occur. In other words, under what conditions do leaders gain their salience and effectiveness? Leadership, it is assumed, depends largely on the ability of the leader to react in such a manner that allows him or her to quickly alter their behavior to cope with emergent dynamic or complex situations.

Ultimately, the influence of any leader is most significantly dependent upon the particular cultural narrative that he or she communicates or actually personifies to the receiving audience. Rather than relating a litany of facts or boring, didactic recaps of the problems that exist within a group or society, in a communication process that merely confirms what virtually everyone is already aware, effective leaders present a vigorous, lifelike, and perceptual vision that resonates on the same wavelength (to use an electronic metaphor) as that of the audience. In this way, the effective leader speaks to the audience in a jargon and language that is easily understood, molds to their cultural imagery, and engages them in three important steps.

He or she must reconfirm the fundamental values of the society, by reminding the audience of who they are (identity) and why they have important meaning and value (transcendence).

Leaders must construct a workable solution to problems out of the cultural material available exclusively within that society. Indeed, this cultural material is far more important to their success than any unique or exceptional personal characteristics or qualities that they may possess. Such a workable solution requires linking the past with not only present conditions, but also, an idealized future, when problems will be effectively pushed aside.

Finally, the leader must mobilize society for action. However, this must be accomplished on terms dictated by the audience, not by the leader, and he or she must be fully cognizant of that fact from the beginning. Premature action can be incomplete and ineffective, whereas action that is too late can be fatal. Timing is of utmost importance to the leader.

The audience is not merely an impassive receptor in this process. They are not simply going to listen and follow the first would-be leader who shares his or her dynamic crusade for change. On the contrary, members of a group or society arrive fully equipped with a variety of optional and available cultural narratives. These have gained salience by being told and retold over an extended period of time within the family, community, village, and town. The message of the potential leader, whether it is conventional or radical, must be able to effectively contend with these other, preexisting tales. If the new message is to achieve any degree of success, it must somehow come to supplant, balance, supplement, harmonize, and, indeed, prevail over the earlier narratives.[3]

Leadership necessitates three essential components: one who will guide the way forward, a willing group of followers, and an end state that they wish to achieve. Indeed, it is the goal of the movement that establishes the basis for the other two.[4] As a result, it is out of the goal of imminent salvation that the leader of a millenarian group derives much of his or her power to mobilize, focus, direct, and provide a sense of urgency. Without this powerful target, the leader would have no followers to join in the struggle. The passionate appeal of the new dogma espoused by the leader to group members is, ironically, largely based on its quick satisfaction of the need to uncover an exceptional and compelling leader.

More recent scholars of leadership have concluded that its effectiveness is not determined by a single personality trait or even a set of specific traits but, rather, by the nature of the structure that surrounds the leader and the environment in which he or she must lead.[5]

The requirement for a divinely inspired leader, who champions solutions to circumstances of group alienation and stress by proclaiming the possibility of complete community transformation, begins with group members themselves. This relationship with the leader-prophet is primarily determined by the "displacement of transference dependency wishes" onto the leader as a symbol of unquestionable power sanctioned by mystical forces.[6]

In millenarian movements, the prophet-leader carries out three important tasks. First, he or she interprets history in an attempt to place the current circumstances into a form of relative, meaningful context. Such an interpretation is informed by and wholly consistent with the cognitive map of both the leader and the community.

Second, through such an interpretation he or she creates the ideology of the movement. It is carefully shaped to meet the exclusive needs of not only the movement but, also, to ensure that it meets the demands of the moment.

Finally, his or her actions and leadership mediate the condition of group stress. In this process, the relationship between the powerful notion of imminent salvation and the millenarian leader is critical. The immediate rescue of the group and, perhaps, the community as a whole, becomes the overarching and preeminent goal. In this way it becomes an important ingredient in the leadership process.[7]

Millenarian leaders arise as cultural idols, offering the community both spiritual stimulation and a plan of action to ameliorate the perceived stress.[8] Such leaders invariably arise from within the community itself, perhaps based largely on their detailed, firsthand knowledge of the uncertainty and difficulty of the times. Directed by what they interpret as divine inspiration, they present a message of hope and confidence to the community that the present conditions can and will be overcome.

They provide the impression that they uniquely understand the causes of the present sources of stress and can provide salvation from it. The prophet-leader's plan of action is both exalted and worldwide in scope. Such a plan offers his or her followers a sensation of meaning and aspiration for the future. The followers' transformed position in the world becomes cast in a focused, divinely endorsed context.[9]

As a result, millenarian movements are neither capricious nor impulsive. They do not emerge as the exclusive result of the needs and inspirations of the prophet-leader. Rather, they are contextual, relying largely on the psychological nature of their potential adherents who are drawn to a prophetic message and charismatic stimulation, forming a symbiotic relationship between leader and followers.

Millenarian leaders often show up in a community characterized by extreme stress or perceived crisis. In such conditions, if the incumbent political authority does not effectively respond or seems unwilling to take action to ameliorate present circumstances, then people will begin to feel a sense of alienation from the system. As a result, they will become particularly susceptible to the appeal of new leaders, who come to be seen as both the symbol and the device of rescue from distress.[10]

Nonetheless, the roots of millenarian leadership lie much deeper than simply the levels of anxiety and distress a leader can exploit or even the millenarian doctrines he or she can put forth.

In every potential sociopolitical movement there is intense competition for leadership. Why, then, does one individual out of this pool of potential leaders succeed in exploiting the situation and gain control?

As we have already seen, the sources of millenarian beliefs in a community can be found in the sacred myths that are transmitted from one generation to the next. The leader who comes to be seen as most relevant is the one who successfully keys into the significant myths of his culture and who is capable of extracting those specific myths that are linked to the sacred icons of society: its legendary heroes, sufferings, and achievements. Under such circumstances, the millenarian leader is the one who can successfully invoke and assimilate the traditions and folklore that provide the society with its unique identity.[11] As a result, millenarian leadership gains its legitimacy though the successful enforcement of the predominant traditional beliefs that are generally accepted within a community.

In this way the existence of durable millenarian beliefs creates the potential for prophetic and charismatic leadership that will drive sociopolitical action, not the unique qualities of the leaders themselves.[12]

Abimael Guzman and the Emergence of Sendero Luminoso

Abimael Guzman was born in the town of Tambo, not far from the southern Peruvian coastal city of Mollendo, on December 3, 1934. He was the illegitimate son of a wealthy, import wholesaler. His mother, Bernice Reynoso, lived not too far from his father's store. At the age of five, Guzman's mother died. Eventually, he went to live with his father in the city of Callao and it was here that he began school. Within a few years his father moved once again to the more upscale city of Arequipa, where he and his family lived in a large and stylish home in an expensive neighborhood. Today, this home is a school in Arequipa, and has been named the *College of the Divine Master*, in honor of Guzman.[13]

A very bright and studious young man, Guzman later matriculated at LaSalle College. He did quite well in his academic work and by his third year was the top scholar in his class. Early on, Guzman began to demonstrate certain skills at grasping abstract philosophies and also exhibited a keen aptitude for organization.[14]

At the age of nineteen, Guzman entered the National University of San Agustin in Arequipa to study both law and philosophy. Here, he began to cultivate a strong interest in Marxism and in the late 1950s decided to join the Peruvian Communist Party (PCP).

As a young ideologue, Guzman was particularly moved by the continuing, appalling poverty and injustice that he observed in Peru. The more of Marx that he read and studied, the more he seemed convinced that these ideas had relevance to the circumstances in his own country. He was in a rather unique position to understand the nature of modern Peruvian life. On the one hand, he had lived the comfortable life as the son of a wealthy family. On the other, he was taken aback by the inequity, poverty, and injustice that he saw in the daily life of Peru.[15]

In 1961, while completing his second of two doctoral theses,[16] Guzman began to interpret the economic and political history of the Andes in a revisionist Marxist perspective. He condemned the Spanish exploitation of the indigenous peoples of the region and asserted that, in fact, there was no difference between traditional colonialism, modern neocolonialism, and outright slavery in South America. He concluded that all oppressed societies possess an unqualified right to rebel against their oppressors.[17]

Following the completion of his graduate studies, Guzman was offered the opportunity to teach at the newly reopened University of

San Cristobal de Huamanga. Originally established in 1677, the university had been closed since the latter years of the nineteenth century but was reopened in 1959 by a reform-minded Peruvian government in an attempt to educate the indigenous youth of the region.[18] The education of the Indians was seen as the first step toward modernization and development.

Located in the remote southern highlands of Peru, Huamanga is the largest city in Ayacucho. The province is largely an indigenous region and one characterized by some of the poorest socioeconomic conditions in the country.[19]

At the time of Guzman's arrival, the total population of Ayacucho was approximately 450,000. About three-quarters of those living in the province were Indian peasants. Indeed, about 20 percent lived in what can only be described as a serf-like condition, owing virtually all of their sociopolitical and economic existence to the hacienda system. Here, in return for every acre and a quarter of land that he was provided by the landowner, the local peasant was required to work three days a week on the lands controlled by the master of the hacienda. He agreed to supply the master with labor to ensure the success of the entire operation, including servants for the elite families.

Nonetheless, it was the hacienda system that had perpetuated poverty in the region since the arrival of the Spanish. Indeed, the peasants possessed no social mobility, were singled out largely on the basis of their race and ethnicity, and, generally, much like the generations before them, lived a life of misery, despair, and isolation from the mainstream of Peruvian life.[20] It cannot be surprising that such conditions provided an effective base for recruitment to radical Marxist ideas that were quickly spreading into the area.[21]

Guzman proved to be a very effective teacher in his new academic post. His lectures were among the more popular on campus and very soon many students came to see him as a charismatic and captivating intellectual who stood apart from the other faculty members. Much of his influence was drawn from a philosophy that was both easy to understand and, equally so, genuinely relevant to the lives of those within the community. Guzman was quite successful at linking Marxist philosophy to the socioeconomic conditions of the Ayacucho region. And, he did so in a very forceful way. "He was a fanatic who had the power to fanaticize others," one of his fellow faculty members remarked. "Like a pastor talking with his flock about the Virgin Mary," said another.[22]

Guzman utilized both his time and position at the university shrewdly. He realized the importance of having a presence on a college campus as an agent that provided legitimacy to the cause. He also realized the impact that an influential professor can have on the life of young impressionable students.[23]

One year after his appointment to the faculty at the Universidad Nacional de San Cristobal de Huamanga, Guzman was elected to the university's Executive Council and served as the director of the Graduate Studies program. In these positions he was able to influence and shape curriculum. He combined his above average administrative skills with his dynamic ability in the classroom in order to sustain the growth in the number of students who were attracted to Marxist–Maoist doctrine. As a result, many of the student organizations on campus began to take on a definite Maoist tone. It was from these groups that Guzman was able to draw the most dedicated and reliable members and assign to them duties and tasks in his growing political movement.[24]

In addition, Guzman was appointed director of Personnel for the university, which allowed him to control the hiring and firing of faculty and staff, dismissing those that did not support his political agenda and ideology and replace them with those who did. Many of these individuals would eventually form the senior leadership of Sendero Luminoso.[25]

By 1970 he had recruited and organized a solid base of socialist cadres. Following their academic and ideological experience, many of these individuals returned to their local villages as teachers. As a result they were in a position to both influence and recruit new young people to the cause.[26]

For most of the next ten years, Sendero adherents worked in a clandestine way to build support for the movement and prepare for that day when they knew that armed political action would begin. In 1973, the party began to establish *organismos generados* or party-generated organisms. These organizations were designed to perform a series of services for the movement including the distribution of propaganda, recruiting and training new recruits, and, in general, to provide a conduit to broad-based mobilization within the region.[27]

The Communist party of Peru in the 1960s was in serious disorder and becoming increasingly out of date. Since the death of its founder, Jose Carlos Mariategui, the party had remained solidly loyal to Moscow at the expense of popular support within Peru. It was during this period that Guzman and other young intellectuals became harshly critical of the party and sought to transform it in order to meet the needs of the future, not those of the past.[28]

Guzman was convinced that the PCP was insufficiently activist, overly bureaucratic, and wholly lacking in any type of political drive.

His feelings were deeply influenced by the recent victory of Fidel Castro and his movement in Cuba; an event that bolstered Marxist-based political parties throughout Latin America and brought a renewed sense of urgency and meaning to their cause. To many, Castro's success indicated that the time was now to take action. Guzman argued, "if you are admirers of the Cuban revolution, you have to be like Fidel, because to do the same here it is necessary to work, work, work."[29]

In addition to pressures from within the region, in the early 1960s the PCP became caught up in the much larger international schism between orthodox party officials in the Soviet Union and the Maoists in China; a split that affected national communist parties around the world.

In 1964, at the Fourth National Party Conference of PCP, significant ideological differences led the party to finally split into two important factions. The first was a pro-Maoist minority that formed the Bandera Roja (red flag). Second, the pro-Soviet group chose to follow the political line that continued to be fostered by Moscow.[30] The pro-Chinese faction came to be convinced that the only path to liberation from Western imperialism was to follow the example of Mao and mobilize the peasantry throughout the rural regions and pursue violent struggle.[31] This pro-Mao faction of the PCP became the foundation of Sendero Luminoso.

It was within this context in the mid-1960s that Abimael Guzman began to develop a political philosophy that eventually became known to his followers as the "Fourth Sword." Guzman and those intellectuals loyal to him perceived of themselves as a part of a profoundly historical and deterministic path: as the lineal ideological successors of not only Marx and Lenin, but now Mao. These three icons had been committed to the violent overthrow of capitalism and foreign oppression and Guzman perceived of an intellectual progression that allowed him to firmly establish the Sendero movement as its descendent.

In 1965, Guzman actually visited China and observed firsthand the unfolding of events that led to the Great Proletarian Cultural Revolution the following year. The visit enhanced his position within the party in Peru and soon after his return he was made its secretary general. He made a follow-up visit to China in 1969.[32]

Guzman insisted that Sendero Luminoso be grounded ideologically in a thorough and fundamental approach to the study of the classic Communist writings of Marx, Lenin, and Mao. These were increasingly presented by the movement as possessing a kind of scripture-like quality. Sendero ideology was built on this firm and seemingly sacred foundation, utilizing basic principles derived from them and then modified to fit the unique needs of twentieth-century Peru. In the process, Guzman sought to satisfy the political needs of himself and that of his followers to achieve legitimacy, identity, and a sense of purpose.[33]

In addition to the philosophies of Marx, Lenin, and Mao, Guzman was deeply influenced by the ideas of Mariategui who had asserted that "the shining path of socialism" could lead Peru to an idealized future. Guzman began calling his new movement *Sendero Luminoso*, the Shining Path.[34]

The Sendero movement, operating from its base in Ayacucho, was initially considered rather inconsequential by the government of President Fernando Belaunde Terry in the 1970s and the movement was allowed to develop rather freely with little interference from the capital. Even after Sendero violence began to emerge in the Ayacucho province, the Belaunde government largely ignored the rebellion for nearly two years and only dispatched small special police units to the region in response.[35] As a result, during the first two years of armed conflict the Sendero movement was allowed to take almost unrestrained action. This allowed the movement to recruit new members, train its personnel, and expand its base of operation in a remarkably unfettered environment.

In 1974, in a bold move reflecting the rapid growth of the movement, Guzman relocated the headquarters of Sendero to Lima itself. The move was out of organizational necessity and a clear recognition of its growing influence. The total number of party cells had grown rapidly and Sendero Luminoso now had strong followings at most of the major universities in Peru.

By the early 1980s, Sendero Luminoso began to prosecute a persistent war of terror in Ayacucho and elsewhere. Their tactics not only included the bombing of local government buildings and physical attacks on property owned by the private sector but, eventually expanded to include the assassination of local politicians. In relatively short order their activities became so dangerous that the state police were forced to leave the area. This allowed Sendero leaders to declare a "liberation zone" throughout the province; political power in the area was now completely in their hands. Eventually, a more general violence ensued following a daring raid and jailbreak from the Ayacucho prison in March 1982.[36]

By December 1982, the escalation of violence, bombings, and power blackouts resulting from Sendero attacks on power stations forced the government to declare a state of emergency across five provinces; an expansive area encompassing roughly 60 percent of the population of Peru. This government action was the clearest indication yet that the power of Sendero Luminoso was a direct challenge to the regime itself.[37]

In early 1983, as support for Sendero intensified, the state launched a counterinsurgency campaign that was both abusive and brutal. Sendero responded in 1984 with a new offensive that was even more violent than past operations. The government declared a state of emergency and suspended constitutional rights in the area encompassed by the "emergency zone." As a result, Sendero Luminoso really came into its own in the early 1980s within a background of rapid sociopolitical and economic change and profound crisis in Peru in which rural society, particularly the Andean region of Ayacucho, was hit hard. Sendero's growth was rather dramatic—in 1980 it possessed perhaps only about 100 freedom fighters. By 1990 it numbered well over 10,000.

The Millenarian Ideology of Sendero Luminoso

The ideology of Sendero Luminoso drew upon a durable tradition of indigenous socialism among the Peruvian Indian peasantry. Its fundamental principles included the historical model of Incan agrarian communalism as much as it embraced the modern classless aspirations of Marxism.[38] In this way, it closely resembled traditional Indian millenarian movements as well as the teachings of a pure indigenous communism that had been articulated by Mariategui in the 1920s.[39]

Guzman worked with other party leaders to carefully create and circulate the political ideology of Sendero. A significant component of this process was the establishment of the *Jose Carlos Mariategui Center of Intellectual Work* (CTIM) in Ayacucho. It was here that Guzman and other Sendero intellectuals were able to build upon and preach their ideology in its most complete and untainted form. What emerged was a unique Peruvian historicism that seemingly explained the inevitable destiny of the Sendero Luminoso through its program of a people's war for social and political justice. For many of the students who attended CTIM classes, the combination of Guzman's articulate explanation of the relationship between the history of oppression in Peru and the idealized, inexorable goals of Sendero led to a growing belligerency within the movement.[40]

In contrast to other models of revolution in Latin America, particularly in the aftermath of Castro's success in Cuba, the Sendero ideology focused its attention on theory over pragmatism. Sendero's mission was more ideological and pedagogical than other contemporary Marxist movements in the region. It emphasized "guiding thought" rather than simply practical military and political guerilla tactics.[41]

Sendero prospered on its leadership's ability to successfully overlay its political ideology onto traditional Indian myths and rituals, largely because, early on, they became aware of the fact that it was not easy to gain, or to keep the support and adherence of the majority of the regional population simply on the basis of a European-inspired, secular ideology like Marxism.[42]

Guzman and his colleagues worked diligently to craft an ideology that successfully merged the millenarian stream of the Inca past with the dialectic of Marxism. Traditional Andean themes were often referenced in Guzman's speeches and even in the methods of Sendero. He successfully merged Maoism with Inca culture into an effective, violent, millenarian ideology that sought to destroy, in the minds of his young followers, centuries of disgust, oppression, and injustice.[43] What emerged was a unique syncretic mixture of apocalyptic Indian mythology, Marxism, Leninism, and Maoism, all brought together into a durable web of seemingly unquestionable historical destiny for Peru. As Guzman explained:

> For us, Marxism is a process of development, and this process has given us a new, third and higher stage. Why do we say that we are in a new, third, and higher stage, Maoism? We say this because in examining the three component parts of Marxism, it is clearly evident that Chairman Mao Tse-tung has developed each one of these three parts . . . I am referring to Mao Tse-tung's development of Lenin's great thesis on imperialism. This is of great importance today, and in the historical stage that is presently unfolding . . . [Lenin] discovered a law of imperialism when he said that imperialism makes trouble and fails, makes trouble again and fails again, until its final doom. He also specified a period in the process of development of imperialism, which he called "the next 50 to 100 years," years, as he said, unparalleled on earth, during which, as we understand it, we will sweep imperialism and reaction from the face of the earth.[44]

Nonetheless, Guzman's conscientious and meticulous manipulation of Indian traditions was subtle. At the same time, his supporters were quite aware of the syncretic mixture that he had created and were comfortable with it. One poetic interpretation of the "people's war" declared:

> Thousands of Indians and Mestizos
> Descend to the town

Like a red avalanche
With muscles of steel
And voices of thunder, shouting "freedom!"
Because they know that the days of Pachacutec
And the Inkarri have arrived[45]

The ideology of Sendero Luminoso placed its highest priority on the achievement of social justice and the promise of an idealized life to its Peruvian peasant adherents, in the context of a durable cultural tradition that they fully understood and held sacred. It promoted a complex and significant relationship between the ideology and the peasantry that transcended the mere use of violence to achieve their sociopolitical objectives. As a result, Sendero adherents became convinced that their movement would usher in a new utopian age in Peru.

> Communism is the only and unsubstitutable new society, without exploited and exploiters, without oppressed or oppressors, without classes, without the state, without parties, without democracy, without arms, without wars. [It is] the society of great harmony, the radical and definitively new society towards which fifteen billion years of matter in movement, of that part we know as eternal matter, is directed necessarily and irrepressibly, [and] to which humanity must arrive only passing through the highest expression of the class struggle . . . and through the rifles of the invincible people's war.[46]

Sendero forces, when carrying out acts of violence against the state, purposely utilized the widely known Inkarri myth of Indian resurrection. In addition, in 1980, they chose to openly celebrate the one hundred and ninety-ninth anniversary of the execution of José Gabriel Condorcanqui, Tupac Amaru II. This was a highly symbolic action and afterward, one can clearly discern that consistent and meaningful elements of Quechua Indian culture and ritual pervaded the Shining Path and significantly influenced their activities.[47]

Guzman viewed Sendero at the forefront of the international Communist revolution, which, he believed, would accompany "humanity's third millennium." In a speech entitled "For the New Flag" delivered at a Sendero conference in 1979, Guzman divided Peruvian history into three important epochs. First, he referred to "how darkness prevailed," a clear reference to the colonial period. Second, he asserted, was an age that explained "how light emerged and steel was forged." Finally, he concluded with "how the walls were destroyed and the dawn spread."

These three epochs were designed to purposely coincide with the transformation in the colonial period of the initial five ages of the Andean world. According to traditional Indian myth, each of these five ages lasted 1,000 years and was made up of two distinct halves, each proclaimed by a *pachacuti*—the end of one age and the beginning of another. In many areas that had fallen under Christian influence during the colonial area, the *pachacuti* had already arrived by the seventeenth century, and was, by then, clearly associated with the Christian Last Judgment. By the time of Juan Santos Atahualpa, the five ages had been cut to three—the age of the Father, the age of the Son, and the age of the Holy Ghost. It was in this third age that the separation between the Indian and European worlds would be reestablished.[48]

Guzman theorized that the age of darkness in Peru was enlightened by industrialization and the appearance of a modern working class. With the assistance of Marxism, he argued, this "light becomes steel," and "there began to appear a purer light, a shining light; that is the light that we have, in our breasts and in our soul."[49]

In the aftermath of both Marx and Lenin, Guzman declared, it was Mao Tse-tung who shone a "dazzling" light on the people. Only the party, gradually, "as its retinas adjusted" and "lowered its eyes," began to understand its power. As a consequence, the Communist Party of Peru reestablished itself in order to "illuminate" the path of the people.[50]

Sendero Luminoso effectively utilized symbolism to enhance Abimael Guzman's image as a savior of the people.[51] For example, many of Guzman's closest advisors were known as the "holy family."[52] This appeared to indicate the stature possessed by Guzman and how simply being linked to him could somehow raise the status of mortal men to that of the near sacred.

As the perceived "father of a new age in Peru" Guzman was portrayed as a "bright, soaring flame, burning with ideological passion and power."[53] Among the Quechua-speaking Indians, who held a traditional reverence for the sun, Guzman was known as Doctor *Puka Inti*—the Red Sun.[54] By most, he was lovingly referred to as Father or President Gonzalo and was considered by many to be nothing less than the savior of Peru.

> To the greatest man of the present era, leader of our party and the revolution, President Gonzalo: Glorious years of struggle and victory as we march towards the takeover of power. Today we open our popular open committees, part of our war of movements. We are guided by the shining light of the greatest man of the era, President Gonzalo. Who is President Gonzalo? He is the new leader of the heroic struggle, teacher

> amongst teachers, great among the greatest, and the eagle of our party. Look at the years of the triumphant revolution. Look at how he forms legions of iron willing to overcome any storm. Look how he builds new power, brick by brick. Revolution is justified. What do we have? Nothing. What do we want? Everything. We want a new society without rich or poor; a society in total harmony, guaranteed by President Gonzalo. By defending and applying Marxist, Leninist, Maoist and Gonzalo Thought, we will light the shining path. Follow President Gonzalo![55]

Further enhancing this image was the common technique of Guzman to invoke Biblical phrases into his speeches. He regularly portrayed the revolution as not only the realization of the laws of history but, also, the fulfillment of traditional Christian prophecy. Such phrases as "you will know them by their works," "many are called, few are chosen," "It is written," "The future is assured" lent further enhancement to the religious image of Guzman.[56]

At the Sendero Luminoso Party Conference II held in 1982, the position of Guzman was elevated to that of near sacred status, as the leader, guide, and ultimate ideologue of Sendero doctrine and thought. In a way that was modeled on the notion of "Mao Tse-tung thought" as the guiding light of the Chinese Revolution, Conference II approved the need to "enthrone the guiding thought of [Chairman] Gonzalo" and also authorized the new party slogan to be "Learn from [Chairman] Gonzalo . . . because he is support, is leadership . . . because he has firm principles, maintains the course, and brings it into being."[57] In addition, Guzman was clearly linked in an effective way to the great icons of the Sendero movement: Marx, Lenin, Mariategui, and Mao.[58]

From that point forward, a necessary part of each Sendero member's commitment to the revolution would be an "absolute submission to [Chairman] Gonzalo and to guiding thought" without question or disapproval. Guzman's word became final and absolute. His position was messianic. And this exaltation was not ephemeral, it had been prophesied.[59]

The literature of the Sendero Luminoso was dotted with messianic references designed to strengthen the belief that they were leading the people to a new age. According to one document, "the people's war in Peru is unstoppable and is sweeping away the order of exploitation and oppression, and building the new society on the debris."[60] Sprinkled throughout is a significant sense of determinism and inevitability—that they were destined to ultimately prevail. "Our people know consciously and completely that the wheel of history cannot be detained, that's why they continue to struggle heroically alongside the PCP striving for a new dawn to come."[61] Biblical references often appeared in party pamphlets circulated around Ayacucho. In particular, these glorified the image and symbol of Guzman, asserting, "we are communists as your image and as your simile . . . fortunate the eyes that see you, fortunate the eyes that hear you." In this way, Guzman's role as a god-like figure was embellished and "the principles of Marxism–Leninism–Maoism were internalized as dogmas."[62]

In an interview with El Diario, Guzman asserted,

> We believe that bureaucratic capitalism has entered into a general crisis. Moreover, we believe that this bureaucratic capitalism was born sick, because it derived from semi feudalism (or is tied to it) and from imperialism. What kind of child could come from these two parents condemned to death by incurable disease? A sick, stunted monster that has entered its phase of destruction. We believe that the crises will become sharper and sharper, that, even as some economists say, there have been more or less thirty years of crisis from which we have not emerged except for some small ripples of recovery. We can see that each new crisis is worse than the previous one. And if we add to this the two critical decades of the 80s and 90s, back-to-back, the situation becomes clear.[63]

Thus, according to Guzman, the only hope of salvation for the Peruvian masses is to completely destroy liberal democratic capitalism and build a socialist state and a reframed Indian identity on top of the ashes. Indeed, they assert, such a scenario is inevitable.

Asahara Shoko and the New Religion of Aum Shinrikyo

Asahara Shoko was born Chizuo Matsumoto[64] in 1955 on one of Japan's main islands, Kyushu. From birth he was blind in one eye and possessed little vision in the other. As a result, at the age of six, Asahara's father sent him away to the Kumamoto Prefectural School for the Blind from which he graduated in 1977.[65]

From a young age, Asahara exhibited what might be considered leadership qualities. Reports of his experience at the Kumamoto School describe a young Asahara, who possessed a rather distinctive personality that rather early on set him apart from his classmates. For example, he routinely boasted to his classmates that he possessed supernatural powers such as clairvoyance, the ability to meditate underwater for long periods of time, and even to levitate his body.[66]

Later, while in high school, Asahara continued to hold a rather audacious and lofty image of himself and the personal goals that he sought. For example, he would often boldly assert to those around him that he was going to pursue a career in politics and that one day he would rise to the position of prime minister of Japan.[67] Indeed, he began to detail an ambitious step-by-step plan that would allow him to achieve his goal. First, he would attend Tokyo University, an important requisite for anyone who sought an elite position within the Japanese hierarchy.

His vision of greatness began to crumble, when, upon his graduation from the Kumamoto school, he failed to meet the rigid academic admission standards of the university. At around the same time, he failed to meet the requirements to enter the medical college at Kumamoto University.[68] Disappointed by what he perceived as personal failure, Asahara returned to his family's home both disillusioned and cynical about his life and future prospects.[69]

In 1978, Asahara set up a professional practice as an acupuncturist, which was a traditional line of employment for the blind in Japan. His concern was soon thriving, delivering a variety of services, including both acupuncture and yoga training, and various medicinal products to his clients.[70] Some of these services, particularly the cures that he sold to his customers, were of dubious quality. Yet, he charged up to $7,000 for a three-month program of treatment. In addition, he promoted his services and products in Tokyo's finest hotels. Dressing himself in a white lab coat and a stethoscope, he portrayed himself as a true therapeutic professional who examined elderly people in their hotel rooms and convinced them he could cure rheumatism, among other infirmities.[71] Very early then, Asahara was demonstrating a clear ability to persuade and self promote. His skills were made all the more noteworthy when one considers the fact that he was handicapped.

That same year, he married a young college student, Tomoko Ishii. Over the next few years they had a total of six children. Matsumoto Tomoko, the name Asahara's wife assumed after marriage, eventually became a prominent member of the Aum organizational hierarchy.[72]

Though his small business was doing well, Asahara began to seriously question where his life was going. In his later books, he described himself at this time as overwhelmed by a deep-seated anxiety and experiencing a "raging conflict of self confidence and personal complexes," which made him feel that he "could not go on like this." "For the first time," he later wrote, "I stopped to ask myself, why am I alive? What do I need to overcome this emptiness? I wanted to find something absolute."[73] He also seems to have had some deep frustrations regarding his ability to help his acupuncture patients more effectively. Through a study of religion he hoped to gain new spiritual knowledge that might enhance his power to heal.[74]

It was in this context that Asahara's first experience with an organized religion began in 1978. He joined *Agon Shu*, which he found profoundly compelling and seemed to be a defining moment in his quest for spiritual meaning in his life.[75]

The doctrine of *Agon Shu* consists of three distinct elements. The first is a firm grounding in early Buddhism, which stressed the purging of karmic obstacles—the unhealthy emotional, psychological, and bodily habits that prevent the achievement of personal enlightenment. Such a purging takes place through a series of spiritual steps.[76] The elimination of the "bad karma" in one's life is considered central to the salvation and redemption of the individual from evil and pain. Freedom from its effects, it is believed, provides immediate improvement.[77]

Asahara was personally inspired by what he found in the early Buddhist writings, particularly in a group of texts called the *Agon Kyo*, which are believed to document the original sermons of the Buddha in the ancient Pali language. "I read Buddhists texts and I meditated" he would later recall. "I realized that everything in the world is sin. When I realized that I myself was a polluted person, I could not stop weeping. I also learned the spirit of self-sacrifice."[78]

Stirred by his experience with *Agon Shu*, Asahara began to study traditional Chinese medicinal practices and astrology. Both of these are closely linked to one another as well as to the practice of acupuncture. In addition, he read the writings of Shinji Takahashi, founder of the new religion *God Light Association*. Takahashi claimed that he was a modern incarnation of the Buddha and effectively mixed his teachings with those of Christianity. In addition, Asahara studied the writings of such eminent Buddhist scholars as Hajime Nakamura and Fumio Masutani. In particular, he became deeply interested in their work on early or "primitive" Buddhism.[79]

The second major component of the doctrine of *Agon Shu* is Vajrayana or Tantric Buddhism. A much more recent movement than that based on writings in *Agon Kyo*, the Tantric form of Buddhism makes use of spells, symbols, complex rituals, and the attainment of magical powers that lead one to higher and higher stages of enlightenment. Tantric Buddhism requires a completed set of extensive and complex meditation devices that are learned through a series of initiation rituals delivered by the master and passed along to the disciple through a variety of obscure and mysterious methods. This accounts for why the Tantric form is sometimes referred to as Esoteric

Buddhism. It assumes that the individual is capable, through the mastery of wisdom, to achieve superhuman powers particularly in the area of sexual practice.[80]

Third, *Agon Shu* taught the use of the ancient Hindu system of Kundalini Yoga and Taoist Yoga—concepts that had been imported from China. Followers of the religion were taught that if they ardently practiced the fundamental precepts of the religion and successfully applied its practices that they would literally never age and achieve everlasting mortality.[81] This linkage between the practice of a particular brand of Yoga, release from "bad karma," through the use of esoteric and highly disciplined ritual practice, culminating in an everlasting life for the adherent seems to have been particularly appealing to Asahara. These are consistent themes that appear frequently in his later writings.[82] Many argue that it was here that Asahara began to develop the foundation of what would later become his apocalyptic vision of the future.[83]

In 1982, Asahara was arrested and charged with selling fake Chinese cures to his clients. He was convicted and sentenced to 20 days in jail and forced to pay a fine equivalent to US$2,000. Following a highly critical local newspaper article detailing his arrest and conviction, his business went bankrupt. Asahara was devastated by his conviction and the failure of his business. This dramatic reversal pushed him ever more aggressively in the direction of religion and the comfort and relief that it provided him.[84]

In the spring of 1985, Asahara claimed that he was visited by Shiva, a Hindu god, while meditating on the beach at Miura in Kanagawa Prefecture just south of Tokyo. He declared that Shiva had appointed him to be "the god of light who leads the armies of the gods"[85] and charged him with building an ideal society made up of those who had attained psychic powers: the Kingdom of Shambala.

The Kingdom of Shambala is an ancient concept appearing in Zoroastrianism, Hinduism, and Buddhism, but Asahara's knowledge of it derived from Tantric Buddhist texts in which Shambala is portrayed as a hidden valley located somewhere in northeast Asia; a sort of paradise for those who have achieved very high levels of spiritual enlightenment. According to Buddhist tradition, at some unspecified future date a messiah-king will appear in Shambala, defeat the infidels and nonbelievers in a final, apocalyptic war, and establish a universal reign of Buddhism.[86]

Asahara claimed that Shiva had charged him with preparing for the coming of an ideal society, which would be made up of those who had personally achieved high levels of spiritual development and psychic powers. He interpreted this encounter as a sign that he was the chosen one—a messiah who would destroy the sin and corruption in modern Japanese life and set the stage for a new age.[87]

In 1987, Asahara officially founded Aum Shinrikyo and began conferring on himself such titles as "Today's Christ" and "the Savior of this Century." Increasing numbers of young people, in particular, were drawn to its teachings and vision of world renunciation and the denial of worldly pleasures. They were compelled by its exclusive focus on the improvement and personal salvation of the inner self at the expense of the empty material possessions of modern affluence and the alienation it engenders.[88]

Increasingly, Asahara began to experiment with deeper religious rituals and apocalyptic notions. In 1985, he visited Mount Goyo in Iwate Prefecture in northern Japan to see a shrine that possessed a text supposedly given by the gods to the prewar historian and rabid anti-Semite Sakai Katsutoki. In the content of this text was a vision that "Armageddon will occur at the end of this century. Only a race of compassionate sages will survive. Their leader will come from Japan."[89]

Aum Shinrikyo went to great lengths to portray Asahara in overtly messianic imagery. Photographs and cartoons that appeared in Aum publications depicted the leader in the garb of an Indian ascetic meditating alone in the mountains or holding small children in a loving and patriarchal pose. He was always presented as larger than life, with his beard, hair, and body assuming huge proportions, almost dwarfing those around him. Perhaps the most famous and explicit example of this millenarian imagery was his appearance on the cover of his work *Declaring Myself the Christ.* Here he was represented as Jesus Christ, hanging on the cross, possessing a crown of thorns—an image of enormous self-sacrifice offering redemption to a world craving deeper and deeper spirituality.[90]

Slowly, Asahara was formulating a true plan of salvation and more frequently spoke of his vision of establishing an ideal society on earth.

> The legendary utopia of Shambala . . . ruled by the god Shiva, is a world that only those souls who have penetrated the full truth of the universe may enter. There the world's saviors, whose goal it is to save all souls and lead them to *gedatsu*, progress in their own training. Master Asahara has been reborn from that realm into the human world so that he might take up his messianic mission. Thus the Master's efforts to embody truth throughout the human world are in accordance with the great will of the god Shiva . . . This is why Aum Shinrikyo has developed a plan to transform Japan into Shambala. This plan, unequalled in scope, will extend Aum's sacred sphere throughout the nation and

> foster the development of multitudes of holy people, making Japan the base for saving the entire world. This plan cannot be realized without the help of our believers. Please come and join us![91]

Asahara presented his interpretation of the New Testament Book of Revelation in *The Day of Destruction* in 1989. He predicted that the Soviet Union would collapse in the year 2004, China would be destroyed at the end of 2004 or the beginning of 2005, and that "the American president elected in 1995 [sic] and the Soviet Party Secretary at that time might lead the world to Armageddon." In addition, he prophesied that Europe would survive this Armageddon and that a "super-human race" would come to rule the world.[92]

By the late 1980s, Aum was selling what they portrayed as "powerful spiritual tonics" formulated from the hair, bath water, and the blood of Asahara. For the equivalent of US$10,000, Aum offered its new members a "special cult initiation rite" that consisted of drinking Asahara's blood. Such a tonic would place them on the correct path to *saishu gedatsu*, or "final liberation." Other special medications included a tea that was brewed from Asahara's hair clippings and a small container of his personal bath water, which was described as a "miracle pond."[93]

Following a visit to a Himalayan retreat, Asahara declared that he had achieved *satori*, or enlightenment. In addition, while he traveled in Tibet, he met with the Dalai Lama who, he said, received him with courtesy and great warmth. Asahara had his picture taken with the Dalai Lama and often used it in Aum promotional material. He quoted the Dalai Lama as saying, "what I've done for Buddhism in Tibet, you will do for Buddhism in Japan." Later, reporters asked the Dalai Lama if these statements were true. He denied ever making such claims and asserted that he had simply greeted Asahara in a hospitable way. Asahara also claimed that he met with religious leaders in Sri Lanka and declared that they had also accepted him as a great spiritual master. Whether any of these stories are true is irrelevant. They were quite convincing to Asahara's followers and that's all that mattered.[94]

Aum Shinrikyo spread quickly in Japan and soon established branches in foreign countries including the United States, Germany, and most significantly Russia. Indeed, Asahara once preached before a crowd of 15,000 in a Moscow sports stadium.[95] He appeared to be a masterful storyteller who was quite adept at assessing the emotional needs of his audience and, in turn, delivering to them exactly what they sought.[96]

Aum, much like Agon Shu, connected individual salvation to the salvation of society, and Japan as a whole. In 1988, Asahara broadened this vision by calling for not only the salvation of Japan, but of the world. In an Aum recruiting pamphlet published that year the sect laid out its scheme for bringing happiness to all mankind:

> Let us take a look, however, at the situation of Japan and the world. Clearly we face a very dangerous situation, due to the rapid growth of egoism. Master Asahara's prophecies, such as a worsening of the trade friction between the United States and Japan, an increase in defense spending, and abnormalities in the Fuji volcanic region and the Pacific Plate have already proved true. If we allow the demonic energy to increase, it will be extremely difficult to prevent the slide towards a nuclear war at the end of the century.[97]

By 1994, the movement's character took on an increasingly militant nature. Asahara claimed that the Aum commune was being threatened by individuals possessing both poison gas and biological weapons. Growing paranoia led them to focus their attention on simple physical survival. Nonetheless, in the process they were slowly isolating themselves from a temporal world that they perceived could not be trusted.[98] Asahara's preaching's increasingly focused on a supposed threat from the United States, which he believed was a creature of both Freemasons and Jews who were bent on destroying Japan. He went so far as to predict that the world would end at some point between 1997 and 2000.[99]

Aum's militant nature centered on widespread suffering. This was a natural theoretical outgrowth of the notion that removing bad karma from the group's adherents justified strict, severe religious training techniques that effectively sought to purge and remake the individual. In turn, what was good for the soul of one was equally beneficial for society as a whole. If torturing or even murdering one individual could "transform" his or her life, then mass killing could "transform" the life of an entire society. Such a concept eventually came to be known as *poa*. Asahara, on several occasions, went to great lengths to clarify what was meant by the term.

> Suppose there was someone who would accumulate bad karma and go to hell if allowed to live. And suppose an enlightened individual thought that it was better to terminate the person's life and gave the person *poa* . . . Objectively speaking, it is a destruction of life . . . However, based on the notion of Vajrayana, it is no other than respectable poa . . . when your guru orders you to take someone's life . . . you are killing that person exactly at the right time and therefore letting that person have his poa. [Under such circumstances] any

> enlightened person will see at once that both the killer and the person to be killed are going to benefit from the act.[100]

In this way, *poa* was perceived to be, not a device of destruction, but, rather, a "form of life-power to both killer and victim. Above all the immortality of both was to be enhanced." It became a powerful, convincing, and convenient rationalization for acts of violence that was perceived as necessary if, first, the cult and later society as a whole were to survive.[101]

The idea of killing in order to heal is not a new one. The Thugs sect of Indian Hinduism perceived of the victims that they plundered and murdered as little more than sacrifices to the goddess Kali. Kali was linked to disease, death, and destruction. By killing their victims, the Thugs believed that they were actually ensuring that they would reach paradise.[102]

Nonetheless, the concept of *poa* was greatly expanded within the context of Aum theology and exemplified a fundamental characteristic that distinguishes the group from other political movements. To Aum, *poa* came to mean a "vision of altruistic omnicide" that could successfully justify and engender mass violence and murder.[103]

On the morning of March 20, 1995, Aum Shinrikyo placed containers of a crudely manufactured sarin poison gas (of the sect's own construction) onto five trains of the Tokyo subway. The attack was centered on Kasumigaseki Station, which is near many Japanese government offices. The attack claimed 12 dead and over 5,000 injured and, of course, initiated massive chaos and panic.

Following a long investigation by the Japanese authorities, nine former members of Aum Shinrikyo, including Shoko Asahara, were tried and sentenced to between 22 months to 17 years in prison. Asahara, himself, was sentenced to death in 2004. One member was acquitted of all charges. Nonetheless, Aum Shinrikyo, despite its imprisoned prophet, continues to proselytize its message and attract new converts.

Musa Al-Sadr and the Revitalization of the Lebanese Shi'a

In the late 1960s, in response to their growing alienation from the greater Lebanese state, the Shi'ite community began what can only be described as a sociopolitical awakening. Ironically, this movement was not led by either an Arab or a native-born Lebanese but, rather, an Iranian Shi'ite immigrant, Musa al-Sadr.

Born in the Iranian religious center of Qom, and educated in Najaf, Iraq, al-Sadr was invited to become the religious leader of the Shi'ites of Lebanon in 1959. A charismatic figure, who possessed ties to both Ayatollah Khomeini and President Hafez al-Assad of Syria, Sadr began to work to transform the Shi'a community by developing a plan to firmly establish a strong sense of communal identity. He took on a role that had long gone wanting, that of the champion of the Shi'a cause. He worked hard to organize and educate the community. In the process he was able to slowly contribute to a true sense of identity among the Shi'a and foster a growing awareness that they were a part of something beyond just south Lebanon. He instilled in them the idea that they were connected to the much broader tradition in the Islamic world; something that they could take great pride in.[104]

In addition, al-Sadr harnessed a profound and meaningful sense of righteous anger within the community regarding their deprived condition and lower socioeconomic and political status in Lebanon. He inspired the notion that through action and organization they could, in fact, do something to correct their position through a reform-minded political cause.[105]

Al-Sadr clearly understood the power of religion and cultural symbols to promote these ideas. And, he understood that his capacity to resonate with the community rested in part in his responsibility as the perceived guardian of those images. [106]

Musa al-Sadr had arrived at an opportune time in the late 1950s. To no small extent the Shi'a were beginning to feel a sense of relative deprivation as some elites within the community began to accumulate modest wealth. Just as important, al-Sadr arrived at an early moment in the evolution of Shi'a urbanization, when those from the rural regions would be exposed to a wealthy, cosmopolitan lifestyle. As a result, al-Sadr was entering a society that was just beginning to see the inequalities that they had dealt with all of their lives in a quite different light. For decades they had passively tolerated the inequities. Al-Sadr convinced them that something could and should be done about it.[107]

The chaos in Lebanon—a civil war with seemingly no end in sight and an Israeli invasion—seemed to create the appropriate time for a great millenarian legend to unfold. Musa al-Sadr's powerful message of identity slowly began to merge with the millenarian tradition among the Shi'a. Their messianic expectation of an extraordinary man who brings history to its appointed consummation and who appears when it is God's will for him to do so "was there for Musa al-Sadr in a natural way" from almost the very beginning of his campaign.[108] To the historically passive and restrained Shi'a community, a unique and special new leader who would provide them with courage and resilience in such difficult times was necessary. In the minds of many in the community, al-Sadr became that special figure who would be the one to take vengeance on the unjust and immoral and finally save the community in its time of dire need. Perhaps more importantly, he would become the model, much like Imam Husayn, many centuries before, for young Shi'a fighters who would give their lives in a great cause.[109]

In 1967, Musa al-Sadr founded the *Lebanese Shi'ite Islamic Higher Council* or Majlis al-shii-al-Aala, and was appointed its first president. In 1974, he established the *Movement of the Deprived* or Harakat al-Mahroumeen. Through these organizations, Musa al-Sadr sought to reform the system and make it more equitable for the Shi'a. In addition, he sought vocational schools, medical clinics, as well as civil service reform within the government. Finally, he wanted a much larger and fairer distribution of the national budget to repair the towns and villages of south Lebanon that had gone ignored for too long.[110]

These new organizations provided the community with important new tools. They supplied the Shi'as full recognition as a distinct and viable political movement and religious force in Lebanese affairs. They offered al-Sadr a much-needed public forum to mobilize the community for action. Finally, they established a solid base from which the Shi'a community could pressure the government for reform.[111]

Nonetheless, it must be noted that all of this political activity aside, Musa al-Sadr was seen first in a religious and cultural sense, as a man of God, the son of a cleric. More than reform and politics, his basic message was a religious one. For this reason, it was very important that the traditions and rituals of Shi'ism underlay both his words and his actions, because that was the basis of his and the community's legitimacy. Very quickly, the spiritual imagery of al-Sadr became intertwined with the identity of the community as a whole.

For example, it was well known that al-Sadr was directly descended from the Seventh Imam, which, of course, contributed significantly to his aura and legitimacy.

> The men who were to follow him—the patricians and upwardly mobile professionals in the first decade, the Shi'a masses in the second—read into his life themes of Shi'a history, and projected onto him long dormant attitudes about legitimate authority and who was entitled to it. The career of an "Imam" . . . had to be anchored in a religious base . . . The exemplary leader had been the Prophet Muhammad himself; the Imams who in the Shi'a doctrine inherited his religious and worldly power worked out of the same progression—from the religious

> toward the political. And, in Musa al-Sadr's case, it was an inheritor of tradition who was insinuating—really bringing back—into the world of politics an old notion of the primacy of the religious over what was worldly and political.[112]

Musa al-Sadr's most influential sermons and speeches dealt with the issue of modernization. More specifically, he sought to tackle the old question of how does the Muslim world contend with the modern world. This topic had been broached many times by Shi'a scholars and preachers who had sought an Islamic response to the power of the West and the requirements of a secular, scientific culture.

Al-Sadr asserted that in the presence of modernization, Islam has been converted into nothing more than ritual. In the process it had lost much of its true spiritual essence and thus its power. Indeed, he argued that many modern clerics, those that he referred to as the "deviant" men of the religion, had actually gone along with this conversion and thus exacerbated the problem, because they wanted to live in a modern world in which religion would become largely ritual and doctrinally nonsubstantive.

At one time, he asserted, Islam had been a religion of strength, purpose, and vibrancy. It was the religion of those who were achievers and doers. Now, he argued, its outlook was grounded in weariness, laziness, and resignation. Nonetheless, Islam and the process of modernization were not incompatible processes. They could effectively converge in a satisfactory manner. But such a process, he preached, must be guided by the Qur'an and not the secular.[113]

Al-Sadr's public confrontation with the question of Shi'a tradition and the sustainability of its doctrines in a modern world were part of a much greater debate taking shape throughout the Muslim world. For example, beginning in the 1960s at the Shi'ite religious schools in southern Iraq, particularly in the cities of Najaf and Karbala, young Shi'ite seminary students from Iran, Iraq, Lebanon, and many other Arab states were becoming increasingly influenced by growing intellectual radicalism stimulated by recent events, particularly in Iran.[114] Many of these students and faculty members became closely associated with the emerging and secretive Iraqi revolutionary movement *al Da'wa al-Islamiyya* (the Islamic Call or Da'wa), which had formed in 1968.

A number of these Najaf-educated Shi'a clerics, who would eventually become an important component of Hezbollah leadership, returned to Lebanon, where they formed Shi'ite schools based on the Najaf model, which would offer the ideas of emerging radical Islam to a new generation of students. In addition, they formed a Lebanese counterpart of the Iraqi al-Da'wa al-Islamyya, the Lebanese al-Da'wa party. Under the spiritual guidance of Sheikh Muhammad Hussein Fadlallah, this organization would become a core component of the Hezbollah movement in the 1980s.[115] According to Subhi Tufeili, who characterized himself as the "Godfather" of Hezbollah and played a significant role in its early years:

> The Dawa party was a clandestine presence which incorporated the main religious cadres of Amal and those outside Amal. Hezbollah is in essence the Dawa party from which we removed the title of Dawa and entered it into military rounds in order for it to start the resistance.[116]

In 1978, Musa al-Sadr mysteriously disappeared during an official visit to Libya to meet with President Mommar Qadaffi. Libya claimed that al-Sadr had actually left the country, boarding a plane headed for Rome. Nonetheless, he was never heard from again.

To many Shi'ites, Sadr's unexplained disappearance seemed to reflect the fate of the hidden Imam. As we have seen, even prior to his sudden disappearance, al-Sadr had been considered a savior to the Shi'ite community. Now his status was elevated to that of a martyr.[117]

No leader of the Shi'a in Lebanon, before or since, had achieved the unique and powerful status as that of al-Sadr. Now, such status was enhanced by the way he left the community. He was gone, but not dead, in the eyes of the community. He was now above the battle. In his absence, people came to wrap him as a critical component into the sacred history of the community. He could now be seen as a part of their destiny and belonged to them in that way. Salient features of Shi'a tradition were now embodied in his image—the martyrdom of Husayn and the occultation of the hidden Imam.[118]

As with Khomeini in the late 1970s, the title of Imam, which had been bestowed on al-Sadr, was offered by followers and "accepted" by al-Sadr. In both cases the label, loaded with messianic expectation, emerged in the political arena. In Lebanon in the late 1960s, as in Iran ten years later, a cleric was set apart from the other clerics and accorded a title with great evocative power and prestige. Both cases represented a break with Shi'a orthodoxy and both cases represented the triumph of political activism over religious restraint.[119]

Indeed, during the summer of 1982, only four years after al-Sadr's disappearance, during the Israeli invasion, a story circulated through the Shi'a community that al-Sadr had been discovered by the Israeli Army. The story declared that al-Sadr had been quietly biding his time in Lebanon waiting for the right moment to reemerge.[120]

The Emergence of Hezbollah

In 1968, the Palestine Liberation Organization (PLO) began utilizing bases in south Lebanon as staging areas for raids across the border into Israel. The region had become the only PLO base that could be used for such purposes following the organization's forced removal from Jordan by King Hussein. As one might suspect, Israel began a series of reprisals into Lebanon in order to secure their northern frontier from further attacks. As these reprisals continued, al-Sadr demanded of Israeli authorities that the Shi'ites of the region be protected from these military incursions. Nonetheless, no guarantees came forward. Eventually, al-Sadr was involved in establishing training camps in which Shi'a men could be armed and trained to protect the community.[121]

In 1978, Israel launched "Operation Litani." Their goal was the establishment of a "security zone" between the PLO and the Israeli border communities.[122] In the end, the operation had costly consequences. It has been estimated that over 2,000 died and approximately 250,000 were made homeless. The violence unleashed by the campaign swept over 100 villages and about 25,000 homes were completely destroyed; approximately 47,000 were damaged. Of course, the large majority who endured the attack was Shi'a.[123]

Four years later and in the presence of a continuing frustration with PLO activities in the region, the Israelis actually invaded south Lebanon.[124] This proved to be even more destructive than previous campaigns.

The Israeli invasion was a violent event that engendered catastrophic damage on the Shi'ite communities. This invasion became the most significant catalyst in the formation of Hezbollah because it was the final phase in a process that truly radicalized the community and made it clear that the Shi'ites must take action to protect not only themselves but their way of life. Over 80 percent of villages in the area were damaged. Indeed, seven were completely destroyed. In the process, 19,000 Shi'ites died and 32,000 more were injured.[125]

The invasion increased the flow of Shi'ites out of the south and into the urban areas of Beirut. This exacerbated the mounting problem of poverty among these refugees and increased the size of the Shi'ite "Belt of Misery," which was rapidly becoming a hotbed of militant Shi'ite groups.[126]

A second factor contributing to the emergence of Hezbollah was the Iranian Revolution of 1979. This upheaval was a watershed event in the history of modern Shi'ism because it engendered a wholly new form of Islamic Radicalism on the political map of the entire Middle East. As a result, it inspired a chain of political violence and actions that still challenge both the incumbent regimes and Western powers in ways never before seen.[127]

The revolution in Iran reshaped the relationship between the Shi'a community and the greater Arab world. Prior to the revolution, the perception of the "Persian connection" of the Lebanese Shi'a community was that of a sociopolitical burden "to be carried like a yoke around their necks."[128] In the aftermath of the revolution, perceptions of Shi'ism took on a much different character. For the first time in the modern age a significant revolt had succeeded in the name of Islam. This was perceived to have added enormous cultural authenticity to the Shi'a community. Finally, the old tradition of social and political fatalism and submission had come to an end, for good. What replaced it was a powerful messianic political, social, and cultural movement led not by the military, nationalists, or even radical secularists but Shi'a clerics. "Now the same individuals who had called men to worship were now calling them to armed revolution."[129] And, this model was having a profound influence on the young Shi'a radical clerics of Lebanon. They quickly offered their allegiance to Khomeini and his religio-political ideology and began to envision a similar revolt in Lebanon.[130]

As early as 1982, pictures of Ayatollah Khomeini began to appear in Shi'ite communities in southern Lebanon. This was a clear indication that the Hezbollah movement now unfolding would be dominated by two characteristics. First, it would be a religious-based movement, not a secular one. Second, assistance and ideological influence would come from Iran.

Following the Israeli invasion, Iran sent 1,500 Revolutionary Guard troops to Baalbeck in the Bekaa Valley of Lebanon, which had become the base of the movement, to aid the emerging Islamic Resistance.[131] Almost immediately, these troops took charge of Hezbollah's security operations.[132]

Accompanying the Iranian Revolutionary Guards were religious instructors, who immediately went to work recruiting a number of young, radical Lebanese clerics affiliated with the Lebanese branch of Al-Dawa and Islamic AMAL, a splinter faction from the larger Amal movement, which had become more secularized under the leadership of Nabih Berri.[133]

In 1984, as Hezbollah moved in to take effective control of west Beirut, the presence of its militia became more visible on city streets. Hezbollah fighters wore green bands around their heads that carried inscriptions such as *Allahu Akbar*, or "God is Greater," and *Qaaidouna Khomeini*, or "our leader is Khomeini." Posters that bore the image of the Iranian leader were everywhere in sight.[134]

Hezbollah Political Leadership and the Concept of the Velayat-E Faqih

The notion of the leadership of Hezbollah can be a bit confusing. In contrast to Western models of structured organizational management and clear lines of authority, no such arrangements exist within the Party of God. As a result, authority within Hezbollah is not easily understood in the context of conventional Western-style models of power, structure, and compliance. Rather, it is grounded in the capacity to simply influence and convince members and followers to pursue organizational goals. And, in the Shi'a worldview, the capacity to influence and sway the public at large rests in one's ability to construct and articulate your message in the jargon of Islam. So, religio-political authority is not endowed; it is conveyed through eloquence and perceptions of a divinely ordained communication. As a result, a more successful way to pursue the question of political leadership and authority within Hezbollah is to inquire as to who is in the best position to influence and convince the community, "whether that means convincing hostage-holders to release their hostages, or persuading young men to offer their lives in suicidal assaults."[135]

It is important to acknowledge the public bond between Khomeini and Musa al-Sadr. To Khomeini, al-Sadr was both a "son and a disciple." At one juncture, Khomeini declared: "I can say that I nearly raised him." On another occasion Khomeini speculated that al-Sadr's mysterious disappearance in Libya, which he referred to as his "detention," represented a form of "suffering in the cause of Islam," and suggested that, similar to Imams of the past, al-Sadr "would return to his followers."[136] In addition, in many of the predominately Shi'a communities of Lebanon one can frequently observe posters of the image of Khomeini and al-Sadr side by side.[137]

From the very beginning of Hezbollah, the concept of the velayat-e faqih has remained a central component of party ideology and doctrine. Just like Khomeini, the party accepts the notion that the Faqih is the chosen representative of the Twelfth Imam that rules over the community during his occultation.[138]

Hezbollah makes it quite clear that their uncompromising support of the velayat-e faqih is not a "political" requirement as much as it is an "intellectual commitment to a sacred individual and to those who follow in such an exalted position, the commands of whom are considered to be 'fixed truths.' "[139]

In the "open letter" of February 1985, Hezbollah clearly accepted the theory of velayat-e faqih, which symbolized a statement of loyalty to Khomeini as a divinely guided authority in the Shi'a community in Lebanon.

> We are sons of the nation of Hezbollah, whose vanguard God made victorious in Iran, and who reestablished the nucleus of a central Islamic state in the world. We abide by the orders of the sole wise and just command represented by the supreme jurisconsult who meets the necessary qualifications, and who is presently incarnate in the imam and guide, the great Ayatollah Ruhollah al-Musawi al-Khomeini, may his authority be perpetuated—enabler of the revolution of the Muslims and harbinger of their glorious renaissance.[140]

Hezbollah adherents envision themselves as "fighters for God." This image is informed by those members of the community who are perceived to be entitled to speak in the name of God. As a result, the rhetoric of Hezbollah is, at its foundation, theocratic—government and leadership of God. Among its most faithful, the movement is perceived to be endowed with the presence of the sacred.[141]

As explained by Sayyid Hasan Nasrallah:

> The faqih is the guardian during the absence [of the Twelfth Imam], and the extent of his authority is wider than that of any other person . . . we must obey al-wali al-faqih; disagreement with him is not permitted. The guardianship of the faqih is like the guardianship of the Prophet Mohammed and of the infallible Imam . . . His wisdom derives from God and the family of the prophet, and he approaches the divine . . . When [velayat-e faqih] orders that someone be obeyed, such obedience is obligatory.[142]

Hezbollah Organization

Hezbollah's organizational structure ensures that even if the current operational leader is removed, incapacitated, or killed, the group can successfully continue its mission. Day-to-day decision-making policy is never in the hands of one single individual. This is so, out of functional necessity—it guarantees the long-term survival of the movement.[143]

In early 1983, Hezbollah made the effort to establish its first centralized leadership, known as the *shoura* or council, which incorporated three members; although, over time, this number has averaged around seven members. It is the responsibility of the *shoura* to make final decisions about all political, military, and social policies.[144] As a result, Hezbollah's structure is, in some respects, rather loosely organized. In other respects, it is quite clearly defined. This results in two distinct components of the movement. The first component includes the key party officials. The second component includes the mass of the party adherents.[145]

The *shoura* is led by the secretary general of Hezbollah, although he is not permitted to make any decisions unilaterally. The role of the secretary general is a functional one. He acts more as a coordinator and facilitator of the council, than as a powerful leader.[146]

Consistent with the teachings of Khomeini, power within Hezbollah centers on clerics who provide the community with both spiritual and political guidance, as they have always done. It is through these individuals and their teachings that the community hears of Hezbollah's position on major political issues and even their justification for violence. This takes place in a very decentralized environment in which every cleric has his own particular mosque, much like that of a parish priest, in which he ministers to the people at the grass roots level.[147]

By the mid-1980s, a new spiritual leader of Hezbollah—Ayatollah Sayyid Muhammad Husayn Fadlallah—had emerged. Born in Najaf in 1935, Fadlallah was also educated there during the religio-political ferment that pervaded the great center of Shi'a theology in the 1950s.[148]

In 1962, Fadlallah visited Lebanon and assisted Musa al-Sadr in preparing a written letter of protest against the policies of the shah of Iran. During this trip, he was impressed with what al-Sadr had been able to accomplish in Lebanon in such a short period of time. In addition, he may have been influenced to move there because of ancestral ties on his mother's side. His mother's father had been a notable figure among the powerful Bazzi family that lived in Bint Jubayl and his uncle had been a minister of the Lebanese government.[149]

Fadlallah arrived for good in Beirut in 1966. He was able to immediately recognize the confusion and dissatisfaction on the faces of young Shi'ites in the community and committed himself to opening a *husayniyya*, a space within the community where the faithful could come and mourn the martyrdom of Husayn. He also established a small collective organization called the Family of Fraternity or *Usrat al-Ta'akhi*, which oversaw the successful operation of clinics, youth centers, and a middle school for the study of Islam known as the Islamic Law Institute or *Al-Ma'had al-Shar'i al-Islami*.

During the 1970s, while Musa al-Sadr took on the mantle of Imam, Fadlallah remained in the background. He used this time to develop his own backing at the grass roots level within the community and to strengthen his scholarly credentials.[150]

The disappearance of al-Sadr in 1978 "opened a gate of opportunity for Fadlallah and his message."[151] He was now in a position to gradually assume the mantle of mystical guidance within the community. Because he knew, in particular, the Shi'ite youth of Beirut so well he could fully appreciate their anger and disappointment, and could harness its force for the achievement of a political purpose. His capacity to mold his message in such a way as to respond to the messianic expectations of the community made the endeavor complete. Nonetheless, despite his growing power, he preferred to remain outside of any formal connection to Hezbollah, asserting:

> The claim that I am the leader of Hizbullah is baseless and untrue. I am not the leader of any organization or party. It seems that when they could not find any prominent figure to pin this label on, and when they observed that I was active in the Islamic field, they decided to settle on me. It could be that many of those who are considered to be part of Hizbullah live with us in the Mosque and they might have confidence in me. Who is the leader of Hizbullah? Obviously he is the one who has influence. So, when they cannot see anybody on the scene, no spokesman, no prominent political figure speaking out for Hizbullah, they try to nail it on a specific person, whose name is linked to every incident.[152]

At the time that Fadlallah made this statement, his mosque had become one of the principal meeting locations for Hezbollah operatives.[153]

So, to no small extent, Fadlallah had succeeded to the "radical religious mantle of Musa al-Sadr." Yet, his reliance on force and power to achieve the goals of the Shi'a community were even greater than those of his predecessor. In his book *Islam and the Logic of Force*, Fadlallah formalizes his argument that only through militancy can the Shi'ites achieve their political goals. And, it is here that we can discern the further evolution of traditional Shi'a quietism in Lebanon toward an ideology of violence and confrontation.[154]

Only through the use of violence, Fadlallah asserts, can a man be himself and not someone else. It enables him to take control of his own life.

> Force means that the world gives you its resources and its wealth; conversely, in conditions of weaknesses, a man's life degenerates, his

> energies are wasted; he becomes subject to something that resembles suffocation and paralysis. History, the history of war and peace, of science and wealth, is the history of the strong.[155]

Here we see a clear break with the Shi'a ideological past to the extent that the acquisition of power was now a requirement of the good and moral life.

But, what about the notion of the hidden Imam? Fadlallah hypothesized that the notion of the Imam Mahdi does not require the Shi'a community to wait passively for his return, while accepting an unjust state in his absence. The concept does not demand that Shi'ites forsake the political realm. "Society needs a state," he asserted, it "needs to be organized . . . the issue is not the existence of an infallible Imam but society's innate need for a ruling order, to rescue men from confusion and chaos." It also does not require that men remain disengaged and passively accept the oppression and injustice imposed on them by others. Armed confrontation, he argued, did not come to an end with the death of Husayn. It is an incorrect interpretation of history to assume that after the tragedy at Karbala that Shi'ism entered a long-term period of silence in which the community quietly accepts the rule and accepts him without question. The evasion of struggle does not have to be an enduring condition of the community and an undeviating response to injustice and oppression.[156] So, Fadlallah was articulating the concept of an Islamic state well before that of even Khomeini.[157]

In addition, he argued that Shi'ism can be and is an ideology of revolution and a response to the injustice of the world. His writings and speeches came to be a call to arms for the community by injecting the necessary justification for political violence in response to immorality and unworthy leadership in the state. What this allowed was the convergence of two Shi'ite movements in Lebanon into one: Hezbollah. At one level, it represented an "extremist millenarian revolt" that did not hesitate to utilize political violence to achieve its political and social goals. At another level, it was a "reformist mainstream" movement that could equally utilize humanitarianism and provide social services to the community to assist them at a time of dire need. And, both of these "were grafted onto the legacy of Musa al-Sadr by their respective adherents."[158]

Conclusion

Millenarian leaders don't require charisma to achieve success. Rather, their power rests in their capacity to restructure preexisting and durable cultural strains into agents of mobilization, organization, and collective action. The evidence of the cases under analysis indicates that millenarian leaders possess a unique sensitivity for understanding present conditions within a society. They have the capacity to interpret sociopolitical disturbance in the context of the cognitive map of their society and come to understand how present conditions impact the needs of the community at large.

Millenarian prophet figures shape and formulate a radical prescription for sociopolitical renewal in response to these conditions. They articulate that prescription in a unique, culturally defined jargon that appears to the community to be exclusively for them and resonates with their cultural expectations/aspirations and their cognitive maps.

In each of these three cases, millenarian leaders possessed no personal inventory of skills that may be described as extraordinary. Rather, the active variable here was the condition of their audience. In this context, we may begin to develop a model of millenarian leadership within the three groups under investigation:

> Intercultural Contact → Social Disturbance → Indignation and a Sense of Injustice → Cosmic Expectations → Millenarian Leader

Such a model is fully congruent with a durable and pervasive millenarian component of the cultural worldview of these societies. In that context, many members of society yearned for the time when a seemingly divinely guided figure would emerge. This was not simply a longing, it was genuinely expected to occur.

The ability of the prophet figure to communicate with the community in a cultural narrative that is fully congruent with these apocalyptic expectations is what distinguishes him from other potential leaders. Indeed, under less disturbing social circumstances, such a narrative would have little impact on society. Existing on the margins, it would be perceived as well outside the mainstream of conventional and legitimate sociopolitical activity. Nonetheless, as conditions worsen, charismatic prophets and the hope that they offer become drawn much closer to the center of political activity and their message becomes increasingly resonant and salient. They are able to offer a vital, convincing vision of hope, action, and change.

The ability of the prophet figure to achieve success in this endeavor is determined by his ability to confirm fundamental values that exist within society and link those fundamental values to present conditions. In the process, he is called upon to interpret current events through a historical lens. Second, he must construct a workable ideology;

one that offers a purposeful solution constructed from culturally available material. Finally, he must organize and mobilize the group experience to pursue the idealized outcome: a paradise, free from oppression, pain, and alienation. In this way, it is the goal of the movement, cast in apocalyptic terms that drive group action. Both the action and message of the prophet figure mediate the conditions of group stress and anxiety. He becomes an agent of salvation by effectively linking the past with the present.

In all three cases, movement leadership took the form of a millenarian-inspired prophet who came to define his role as that of the shaper, articulator, and director of a new political program. Such a program was poorly defined and boundless; nonetheless, it appealed to the expectations and aspirations of movement followers.

The origins of all three leaders varied. Guzman, a Criollo, was nonetheless capable of leading a primarily indigenous political movement. Al-Sadr, a Persian by birth, and thus non-Arab, was capable of leading the Arab Shi'a community of south Lebanon. Asahara was the only one of the three whose ethnic background was fully consistent with group membership at large.

The socioeconomic and educational backgrounds of the leaders also varied dramatically. On the one hand, Guzman and al-Sadr grew up in upper-middle-class surroundings and provided the opportunity to gain a formal education that prepared them well for their work to come. On the other hand, Asahara was raised in poverty. In addition, because of his disabilities, he was prevented from pursuing education beyond the secondary level.

The forum or platform utilized by each of these leaders to launch, promote, and fully develop the movements also varied. Guzman shrewdly utilized his position as a university professor to his advantage politically. Asahara utilized the venue of yoga, enhanced spiritual enlightenment, and the power of seemingly curative medicines to foster his messianic appeal and nurture a new religion. Al-Sadr was able to effectively utilize an explicitly Shi'a religious forum to promote his call for action and renewal.

In all three cases, the prophet leader was able to shape a syncretic mixture from both old and new ideologies that effectively linked the past with the present. Guzman linked a traditional indigenous apocalyptic cognitive map to the modern ideas of scientific socialism. Asahara concocted a strange, yet effective brew of Tantric Buddhism, Agon Shu, Christianity, the occult, and new age ideas to serve the needs of his adherents. Finally, al-Sadr modified ancient interpretations of the martyrdom of Husayn to create a far more activist form of

Shi'ism in a bold and powerful confrontation between the passivity of the past and the enormous challenges of a contemporary modern world. In each case, the ideology that they offered was explicitly millenarian.

The messianic aura that came to surround each of these leaders was a critical component of the movement. Guzman was perceived as the "Father of a New Age in Peru," the savior of the people, "Doctor Puka inti—the Red Sun." Asahara was seen as a modern guru of healing, "today's Christ," and "Savior of the Century." And, al-Sadr, particularly following his strange and unexplained disappearance, led to him being perceived in the context of the occultation of the hidden Imam, the central character in the Shi'ite messianic cognitive map. In addition, he was effectively connected to the sacrifice and martyrdom of Imam Husayn.

In all three cases, these movements performed a religious-like function for their adherents. The inevitability of change was widely accepted and critical to action by the movement. The outcome, arising out of the catastrophic imposition of a foreign cultural paradigm disguised as modernization, was considered to be certain. And, the change that the movement would engender was expected to be total and complete social salvation.

CHAPTER 4

Alienation and the Quest for Renewal

The faith in an imminent, divine intervention that will rescue society from conditions of oppression and injustice holds a powerful healing capability. As a result, millenarianism possesses the power to move a community away from a sense of despair and return it to a feeling of renewal, integration, and a spiritual wholeness. It is curative and can provide a solid foundation for a restoration process to take place. Such a process is not only beneficial to the mental and emotional health of the individual but, equally important, it is necessary if the overall society is to carry on in the future.

Millenarian reactions to perceived stress may be seen as a collective desire to return to conditions that have provided stability and comfort in the past, often in the form of traditional sacred customs and rituals. Psychologists assert that the potential for "suggestibility," under such circumstances, is quite high.[1] That is, under conditions of anxiety and strains on a society, it is more likely that absurd rumors and fanatical arguments can emerge in an attempt to explain such difficult conditions. Absent such stress, when conditions are quite normal, such arguments would be considered excessive, outlandish, and marginal thought, outside of the mainstream of society. But, in the presence of challenging circumstances, such notions may be grasped at out of sheer desperation by a populace hungry for simple, seemingly plausible solutions to otherwise complex and confusing troubles. Thus, we may reconfirm what was asserted in chapter 3: the most important variable at work here is the condition of the group. As victims of anxiety and social strain, they are acutely vulnerable to those remedies that seem most actionable, pleasing, appropriate, and culturally relevant.

It is under such conditions that millenarianism is not only possible, but flourishes. As an ideology of hope, it offers simple explanations for confusing conditions. As an ideology of action, it offers a seemingly appropriate response to perceptibly stressful conditions by putting forward the appealing promise of a total and immediate way out of otherwise intractable problems.

An important factor that contributes to such social healing is the boundless, utopian-seeking quality of millenarian beliefs. This allows the potential for ideological foundations to be shaped into a call for complete, unqualified, and, if necessary, violent, total, societal change that will, first, cleanse the community of iniquity and, second, restore its fundamental purity and goodness, ushering in a new age of justice and freedom.

Alienation, Millenarianism, and Political Violence

Alienation has been one of the more durable notions in the social sciences. Despite the fact that it's often difficult to define and even to identify, there are some characterizations of alienation that have achieved a degree of consensus among scholars.

First is the idea that alienation is rooted in human society; it is considered to be an inherent part of the human experience and one that distinguishes us from other members of the animal world.

Second it is sourced by a variety of human activities and circumstances. In other words, it is derived from social, political, and/or economic interactions. As such, it is inherently a group phenomenon.

Finally, alienation is most readily expressed through cultural devices. These can range from elements of popular culture, such as music, literature, or art, to more sacred forms, for example, ritual, sacred conceptualizations, and, as we discuss in this analysis, religious beliefs, to include millenarianism.

We can trace alienation as a major philosophical perspective to antiquity. The Apostle Paul, in the New Testament of the Bible, taught that humankind, by its innately sinful nature, alienated itself from a forgiving and loving father (God). Indeed, a centerpiece of modern Christian doctrine is that such alienation should and can be reconciled.

At the beginning of the modern era, alienation increasingly came to be seen as a secular idea. For example, the Romantic Movement viewed alienation as a manifestation of the increasing structural features associated with modern life and that such features estranged humankind from nature itself. Later, the concept came to occupy a central role in German Enlightenment thought, beginning in the late eighteenth century. For example, in *Phenomenology of Spirit*, Georg W. F. Hegel asserts that humankind strives to attain actually what he is potentially, but that this realization is mediated by conscience, defined as conformity to one's own sense of ethical conduct, and manifested in social institutions and moral customs. According to Hegel, these impede Man's full realization. That is, they are an alienation from self.[2]

One of Hegel's disciples, Bruno Bauer, popularized the term self-alienation when he proposed that religious beliefs cause a separation in the human conscience between perceived ideas of the world and the world as it is actually experienced.[3]

Ludwig Feuerbach, a contemporary of Bauer and another disciple of Hegel, argued that religion and religious rituals were a projection of human inner nature and desire and are agents of alienation because they force humans to situate their humanity in an "external idea" and subject themselves to the irrationalities of religious dogma.[4]

The work of Hegel, Bauer, and Feuerbach came to have enormous influence on the studies of Karl Marx in the mid-nineteenth century. Marx perceived of alienation as a manifestation of economic exploitation. He used the term to refer to the ways in which human powers of perception, orientation, reason, and creation became stunted and crippled by the very nature of modern industrial organization and by the capitalist economic system.[5] Yet, it should be noted that he also perceived of religious as well as political forms of alienation.[6]

Later in the nineteenth century, Emile Durkheim drew slightly different conclusions than Marx about the sources and consequences of alienation. Durkheim used the term *anomie* to describe the rootlessness that resulted in various forms of violent behavior—from suicide at the individual level to political violence at the group level. Durkheim argued that such rootlessness resulted from the breakdown of traditional community and religious values, engendering mass alienation. Anomie, he argued, means a condition of normlessness, a moral vacuum, the suspension of rules—a state sometimes referred to as deregulation. Anomie presupposes a prior condition in which behavior is normatively determined. A powerful and terrible social crisis or intervention disrupts the traditional equilibrium, disturbs a large group of people within society, significantly eases the normalized force of traditional values, and engenders broad-based anomie.

Such a crisis is characterized by economic distress and social dislocation. As Durkheim saw it, civil violence was simply the ultimate symptom of widespread anomie engendered by the weakening of the regulative powers traditionally held by social morality, mores, and norms of behavior. In this sense, Durkheim perceived of the concept of alienation as a meaningful facet of sociological analysis.[7]

Beginning in the 1950s, research on alienation tended to focus more on the psychological base of the phenomenon. It was conceived of as an intensely personal feeling of separation of oneself from others, manifest as feelings of discontent and a sense of powerlessness linked to a concurrent belief in the individual's inability to communicate with others.

Melvin Seeman attempted to differentiate a variety of psychological states characteristic of the alienated individual. He conceived of alienation as "the expectancy or probability held by the individual that his own behavior cannot determine the occurrence of the outcomes, or reinforcements he seeks." In this social-psychological view of alienation, Seeman hypothesized that it possessed five distinguishing characteristics: meaninglessness, normlessness, powerlessness, isolation, and estrangement.[8] He sought to restrict the application of the concept to those expectations that are actually under the influence of the individual with respect to sociopolitical events.[9]

Further development of Seeman's typologies allows us to draw some important conclusions about the nature of individual and group alienation. First, alienation contributes to devaluation of the self, in the form of lower self-esteem and sense of self-value. In turn, this contributes to a concurrent devaluation of other groups and those who compose them.

Alienated individuals share a deep distrust of others. This leads to a clear rejection of socially approved norms of behavior, which tends to enhance the probability of conflicts over demands for conformity. In such an environment, individuals begin to collectively search for new forms of normative behavior. They seek to reconstruct a new value system to replace the traditional one that has disintegrated or is disintegrating.

Robert Merton observed that such societies, disrupted by widespread alienation, were frequently characterized by a broad-based "craving for reassurance, an acute need to believe, a flight into faith."[10] Indeed, it is through religion, and more specifically apocalyptic belief systems, that groups of alienated individuals can seek reintegration into a transformed society disrupted by economic stress, social dislocation, or significant intervention by external forces.[11]

Millenarianism provides a normative framework that sets the stage for the righting of injustices. It provides a call for action connected to the concept of the future idealized. This call to action has many different components, all of which are related to millenarian expectations.

First is the possibility that the idealized can be achieved and a perfect state of affairs is doable.

In addition, the use of egregious violence provides the millenarian-inspired terrorist the opportunity to fulfill sacred duties associated with persistent theological commands. As a result, such violence elevates the terrorist to a lofty, transcendental position that frees him or her from obstacles that confront others who choose violence as their tool of political action.[12]

Messianic foundations of political violence trace their roots to sacred struggles of the past. Prior to the nineteenth century, religion was a recognized, virtually exclusive substantiation for terrorist activities. Rapoport refers to this tradition as "holy terrorism." "The holy terrorist," he argues, "believes that only a transcendent purpose, which fulfills the meaning of the universe can justify terror, and that the deity reveals at some early moment in time both the end and means and may even participate in the process as well."[13] This is a significant and durable form of justification for violence. It is perceived of, by the faithful, as a necessary and unremitting vigilance against what they see as evil forces, which are often equally committed to the destruction of what is sacred. Only when such forces are finally annihilated, it is believed, can a perfect peace be achieved.[14]

It is appropriate at this juncture to reemphasize the fact that not all messianic movements utilize violence. The turn to violence by a millenarian-inspired movement depends on the presence of two conditions. The adherents must have complete faith that deliverance is at hand. In addition, they must also believe that the actions that they take can hasten the end time.[15] When these two prerequisites are met, the apocalyptic group considers the use of terror as not only justified, but as a requisite step to fight the evil among them.[16]

The millenarian terrorist assumes that society is corrupt. Nonetheless, as a member of that society, he or she is also corrupt to the degree that they remain committed to the status quo. Thus, the choice of violence allows the millenarian terrorist to confront the corrupt reality of the community and his or her role in it. The true believer is the one that is capable of breaking through conventional social norms and pursuing a new world free from corruption, injustice, and oppression. The act of violence becomes a significant moment of transcendence for both the individual and the movement.[17] In this way, the millenarian terrorist is able to overcome a deep sense of alienation from the corrupt world in which he or she exists.

Sendero Luminoso

The early 1960s was a period characterized by broad-based poverty exacerbated by double-digit inflation in Peru.[18] By the end of the decade, the military government of General Juan Velasco announced a sweeping new national land reform policy in response to the continued economic difficulty. Under this plan, much of the lands in the rural regions of the country would be seized and redistributed to the peasants in the form of communal ownership.[19] The goal of the policy was to transfer land control from the predominately White, rural economic elites—the owners of the haciendas—into the hands of the predominately indigenous peasants.[20]

Nonetheless, the plan was ill-conceived and encountered serious problems from the very beginning. The reforms were slow to take shape and were not as comprehensive as the problems of the nation required. At the time of the termination of the program in 1976, only about seven million hectares of the total nineteen million subject to expropriation by the government had been placed into the hands of peasant families.[21] And, by 1979, only 13 percent of the rural lands of Peru were actually under the control of the peasants. Most of the land remained under the control of the state itself. This created disillusionment and in some instances indignation in many of the rural peasant communities. It led many to believe that even a government seemingly sympathetic to their economic plight could not be trusted. Rather than rely on a top–down approach to reform, many believed that it was time to take action at the grass roots level.[22]

In addition to the problems in the rural regions, the national government's fiscal condition grew worse in the 1970s. By 1978, the Peruvian national treasury was almost bankrupt and the nation was unable to pay the service on its foreign debt obligations.[23] As a result, inflation of Peru's currency became a persistent, frightening problem throughout the 1980s. From the difficult level of 60 percent in 1980, inflation accelerated. In 1984, the rate was 100 percent. In 1988 it had soared to a rate of 1,722 percent, 2,600 percent in 1989, and 7,650 percent in 1990.[24] As a result, the nation's financial markets were in chaos; the Gross National Product declined and real wages nose-dived.[25]

In addition to economic catastrophe, the people were forced to cope with the government's reduced ability to care for the needs of its citizens. Health care and other social services declined significantly. The availability of clean drinking water and adequate waste facilities deteriorated to the point that "an estimated forty percent of Lima's mushrooming population and approximately seventy-five percent of Peru's rural population did not enjoy access to clean water or sewage."[26]

Many people during this period, particularly in the rural regions such as Ayacucho, came to believe that they completely lacked sociopolitical mobility, as well as the basic necessities of life and that no remedy was in sight. Indeed, conditions continued to worsen. For the peasantry, even relying on the legitimate political and legal system, as they had for so many years, no longer appeared to be a viable option.

For those that had done so, attending the university and receiving a formal education had provided them with very little—jobs were not forthcoming and their status had not changed. In most cases they returned to their own villages after graduation in order to become relatively low-paid teachers.[27] Nonetheless, their education had opened their eyes to their relative deprivation and acted as an agent of mobilization for action.

Life in urban areas was no better. Unemployment and underemployment rates remained high. Those that had migrated to the cities often found themselves in a worse situation than they had left. Many people lived in growing urban shantytowns and, in contrast to life in the country, had no way to grow their own crops for food.[28]

These conditions set the stage for the rise of an indigenous movement that could offer the people hope, while at the same time taking care of pressing human service needs as much as possible.

Sendero Luminoso first began to organize grass roots support for the movement in 1973. Their initial step was the creation of the *organizmos generados* or party-generated organisms. These were characterized as "natural movements generated by the proletariat in the different organizational fronts."[29]

A variety of organizmos generados came into being including the Popular Women's Movement (MFP), the Poor Peasants' Movement (MCP), the Class Workers' and Laborers Movement (MOTC), the Popular Intellectual Movement (MIIP), and the Neighborhood Class Movement (MCB).[30]

Beginning in the 1970s, in the region surrounding Ayacucho, Sendero workers began the process of establishing and maintaining the notion of the "popular school." These grass roots institutions, directed at the poorest strata of the Peruvian population, sought to overcome the inadequacies of the state schools and bring education to all of the people. By the 1980s, the popular school concept had expanded to a national campaign.[31]

In 1979, Sendero also established a military school in order to "train cadres to lead the armed struggle."[32] The purpose of the school was to continue the training process and prepare guerilla fighters in military tactics.

In addition to functions that promoted overt party goals, these organizations also provided services for Sendero members. For example, *Popular Aid of Peru*, founded in 1982, consisted of several smaller aid groups that offered medical, legal, transportation, food, and housing assistance to Sendero adherents.[33]

Rather than a rigid structure, the organization of Sendero Luminoso was quite fluid, allowing its adherents to rise to higher and more responsible levels as they proved themselves to be worthy. As they gained positions of higher authority they received additional party indoctrination. As a result, by the time an individual reached the top echelons of party hierarchy they were fully committed to its cause and methods.[34]

In addition to its primary hierarchy, the party structure contained intermediate and ancillary support organizations that helped the movement run smoothly. These were designed to assist the party leadership in coordinating and supporting regional committees. These included the Department for Organizational Support, the Group of Popular Support, the Department of Finance, and the Department of International Relations.[35]

Many Sendero members claimed that socioeconomic misery drove them to join the movement. Others claimed that government duplicity and incompetence were important reasons. In short, they saw society as corrupt.

Nonetheless, these were not the only variables at work in the movement's membership and mobilization.[36] For many, the problems of Peru stemmed from a society dominated by people who were perceived by the Indians as foreigners in their own land. They were convinced that if this dominant and seemingly "foreign" class of elites could be removed from the positions of power in Peruvian society, the country's problems would be much closer to being solved.[37]

The movement perceived of violence and terror as agents of rebirth and renewal. As Guzman asserted:

> Mariategui said, "power is seized through violence and is defended with dictatorship," "today revolution is the bloody process through which things are born," and throughout the years of his glorious life he persistently upheld the role of revolutionary violence and class dictatorship . . . Revolutionary violence is what allows us to resolve fundamental contradictions by means of an army, through people's war . . . What Marx held, that violence is the midwife of history, continues to be totally valid and monumental contribution . . . without revolutionary violence one class cannot replace another, an old order cannot be overthrown to create a new one.[38]

He argued that violence and terror were keys to achieving the inevitable destiny of Peru.

> I believe that the heroic destiny of destroying the old state and the glorious destiny of beginning to build a new society will be a monumental effort. These will be times of sacrifice and difficulties, but the people will emerge victorious . . . the only solution, therefore, is people's war, which conceived of in waves, will lead to a worldwide people's war and the coming together of the legions of steel of the international proletariat, of the people, who in the end will carry out our historic mission.[39]

In perhaps his most famous speech titled "We Are the Initiators," given in April 1980, Guzman eloquently portrayed the cause of Sendero Luminoso in apocalyptic terms:

> Revolution will find its nest in our homeland; we will make sure of it . . . the people's war will grow everyday until the old order is pulled down, the world is entering a new era; the strategic offensive of world revolution. This is of transcendental importance . . . The people rear up, arm themselves, and rise in revolution to put the noose around the neck of imperialism and the reactionaries, seizing them by the throat and garroting them.
>
> The trumpets begin to sound, the roar of the masses grows, and will continue to grow, it will deafen us, it will take us into a powerful vortex . . . there will be a great rupture and we will be the makers of a definitive dawn. We will convert the black fire into red and the red into light. This we shall do, this is the rebirth. Comrades we are reborn![40]

The symbolism here is clear: conflict, dark, light, death, sacred intervention, destiny, rebirth, paradise. The war that Sendero Luminoso found itself engaged in was to be the most significant in the history of Peru. It was of transcendental importance, and would result in the solution of all problems that now faced society.

Sendero military operations were well organized and purposeful. In their methods, for example, they followed a well-disciplined plan of five steps that came to constitute an effective tactical policy. Step one required a decision by party leadership on a specific plan of action before its execution. The second involved an assessment of the physical and manpower assets that were needed to complete the operations and guarantee its success. The third and fourth steps involved thorough preparation and the actual carrying out of the plan.[41]

Operations could take one of many different forms: street protests, recruitment, disruption of daily life in the country—such as destruction of power plants or a physical attack on individuals or other groups—confiscating agricultural harvests in the rural regions to meet the needs of the party, and armed confrontation with agents of the state structure, for example, the Civil Guard or the Republican Guard.[42]

The fifth step called for an after-action report that involved a detailed analysis of the action. This report was forwarded to party leadership where it was utilized in the formulations and preparation of new party action.[43]

Sendero literature glorified war and violence. War was not characterized as an historical necessity, but as a way of life, a cleansing process, a way of reinforcing the power of both the individual and society, and a method of separating the wheat from the chaff: those who are prepared for the promised utopia and those who will be left behind. Between 1980 and 1993, it is estimated, the terrorist war carried out by Sendero resulted in the deaths of about 30,000.[44]

Aum Shinrikyo

To understand the rise of Aum Shinrikyo and the tragic events of the attack of March 20, 1995, it is necessary to evaluate much more broad-based social conditions that existed in modern Japanese society. Although the attack itself was planned and carried out by Asahara Shoko and a close group that surrounded him, these individuals were a product of their times and the group that they fostered can only be explained in the larger light of their surrounding circumstances and the culture that nourished them.[45]

To begin with, the rise of New Religions in Japan is widely recognized to be in response to "acute anomie" in which the Japanese people found themselves cast into, through their rapid process of modernization and by their humiliating defeat in World War II.[46] Although the physical damage left by the war has been repaired, many, less obvious wounds remain.

To understand this problem, we must look briefly at public sentiment in the period leading up to and including the war. The commitment of the Japanese to the cause of nationalism and the needs of the state were enormous in the 1930s and 1940s. The people pledged everything they had emotionally and materially to a cause based on the notion that a divine emperor was directing a chosen people, who lived in a sacred land, toward achievement of their god-given right and responsibility as leaders of the world. In light of their profound commitment, Japanese defeat and surrender was not only failure in war, but the failure of their way of life and a massive invalidation of their cultural heritage and legacy.[47]

Although the passing of time soothed some of the pain, many Japanese, even in the 1980s, were still affected by these scars. There had been a discernable weakening of Japanese respect for authority, in particular, political authority. In addition, there had been a notable increase in individual freedoms in Japan, in a way that the people were not altogether comfortable.

From a Western perspective, the unleashing of such forces as democracy and individual freedom would be viewed as a great change for the better. Cognitively, it resonates with our dominant worldview. Nonetheless, the opening up of unprecedented new individual freedoms, combined with a declining respect for traditional sources of authority and stability, opened the door to moral confusion, anxiety, anomie, and alienation for the Japanese. Cultural options were now abundant, yet no clear direction was forthcoming.

In particular, the young people of Japan have had a difficult time coping with the available yet contradictory options available in modern Japan. Personal freedom requires the making of choices and many young people, primarily because of their frequently ambiguous system of values, discovered the selections available to them, on the one hand, to be wide-ranging, yet, on the other hand, to be virtually immobilizing. There was little in the way of authoritative perspective and no genuine system of personal values to guide their path in an environment of independence of choice and action.[48]

The message of Aum Shinrikyo was particularly compelling to an alienated generation of Japanese young people: a demographic segment that some sociologists have estimated to be in excess of ten percent of the total population of Japan in the late 1980s.[49] Membership in the organization was skewed younger. Documentation contained in membership lists uncovered by police confirmed that a little more than 47 percent of the 1,114 members living in the Aum commune at the time of the attack were in their twenties. And, over 75 percent were in either their twenties or thirties.[50]

An important factor in attracting these young people to Aum was their intense alienation. As many of the members of this generation completed their education and entered the workforce, they began to question the very societal norms and conformist requirements that they had ostensibly fully committed themselves to participate in. Many of them felt lost and wondered whether job security and social conformity were all there was to life. Indeed, they became alienated from themselves and their environment.

The Japanese economy was booming in the 1980s. Rapid economic growth and rising per capita income contributed to a high quality of material life. Nonetheless, this continued rise in national prosperity also broadened the gap in a series of lingering generational differences. The young generation coming along in the 1980s did not automatically accept the traditional values of their parents. They did not share their parents' goals of status and material success and therefore rejected their drive to find a respectable educational and professional niche that offered status and financial reward.[51] They saw their parents as workaholics who were employed by companies that dominated their lives as well as that of their families.[52]

Many were driven to pursue careers decided on by their parents, not because they were satisfying or gratifying but because they portrayed an image of acceptability and compliance with the expectations and aspirations of the culture as a whole.[53]

The young people of Japan in the 1980s have been portrayed as the "fun" generation largely because they were far freer in their spending and more leisure-oriented than previous ones. At the same time, they seemed to reject the values of hard work and loyalty to one's employer.[54] Some have argued that they were neither emotionally nor intellectually prepared for the stiff pressures of the stringent Japanese public education system or corporate life after graduation. This accounts for why many of this generation decided to avoid the "rat race" to search for a more "humane" life. Many of this generation found such humanity in the tranquility of esoteric mysticism and the religious practices of the new age religions.[55] In a quest for understanding and explanations, many of this generation would frequently seek out, usually in a very naive fashion, anyone or any group that presented a solution or offered the assurance of engaging them in a social power that fulfill two requirements: (1) satisfied their affiliative need to be a part of something bigger than themselves and (2) free them from the seemingly ubiquitous forms of alienation that now surrounded them.

Probably the most common theme among late-twentieth-century New Religions in Japan focused on the idea that the current age of materialism was coming to an end. In turn, because society as a whole was so firmly entrenched in this material lifestyle, it was, itself, teetering on the brink of chaos and failure. Japanese society, many asserted, had entered a condition of decline, largely as a result of a gradual, inexorable decomposition of community spirituality. Many preached that Japanese society was now much too concentrated on the acquisition of material wealth. Many young people were disillusioned by the promise of scientific rationalism that placed such enormous emphasis on economic development and seemingly worshipped technological innovation.[56] Material satisfaction appeared to be the chief aim of the people and many could perceive of the dark side of that social phenomenon.

A consistent theme in the popular youth culture of Japan in the 1980s was the notion that some form of apocalyptic event was imminent. This became a frequent device within the popular culture. "For example, this generation was bombarded with television programs and cartoons depicting a final war between the forces of justice and invaders from outer space."[57]

In addition, there was a persistent undercurrent of alienation, not only at the substantive level but equally so at the spiritual level. Under such circumstances, many people rejected a value system that they found to be foreign. Others had a great deal of trouble finding their way in a system that did not clearly work for them personally.[58]

Many came to believe that a comprehensive spiritual transformation was required. A transformation that would complete the destruction of materialism and all of its accompanying evils and usher in a new age of authenticity and a higher level of human consciousness.[59]

Haruki Murakami, who interviewed numerous victims of the Aum attack as well as Aum members, asserts that it is impossible to simply write off the tragic incident as merely the work of crazed fanatics. It must be understood, he argues, in the context of late-twentieth-century Japanese society as a whole.

> We will get nowhere as long as the Japanese continue to disown the Aum "phenomenon" as something completely other, an alien presence viewed through binoculars on the far shore. Unpleasant though the prospect might seem, it is important that we incorporate "them," to some extent, within that construct called "us," or at least within Japanese society . . . by failing to look for the key buried under our own feet, where it might be visible to the naked eye, by holding the phenomenon at such a distance we are in danger of reducing its significance to a microscopic level . . . The Aum "phenomenon" disturbs [us] precisely because it is not someone else's affair. It shows us a distorted image of ourselves in a manner none of us could have foreseen.[60]

Obviously, Aum's doctrine of world rejection, getting away from one's family, and establishing an individual identity on one's own terms, was appealing to a small group of younger generation. It provided them with the crucial tools of denying their parents and the society whose values they represented.[61]

Many adherents perceived of Aum as an ideal place. They found its ascetic lifestyle more appealing than living in everyday Japanese society, where they found little of spiritual value. For many, "Aum was a kind of paradise."[62]

Aum Shinrikyo's ideology was akin to many other New Religions in Japan in the later years of the twentieth century. Aum asserted that the people seemed oblivious to the inevitability of total socioeconomic collapse that would be brought about as a result of a global war involving the Japanese state. The solution was simple. Once Japanese society agreed to accept Asahara as their leader then they would escape destruction—Japan would become a land of peace, harmony, and spirituality. Just as important, it would spearhead these values to the remainder of the world, engendering an epoch of global peace.[63]

Inherent in this ideology was the notion of pervasive sinfulness in the world and that life itself is principally a process of struggle toward perfection. The only available escape from such sin and struggle was through an act of withdrawal from mainstream life, and devoting one's energies to spiritual practice and meditation, which would manifest themselves in personal enlightenment and increased spirituality. Indeed, Asahara Shoko asserted that his own personal enlightenment had presented him with extraordinary powers such as levitation, clairvoyance, and the capacity to free him from the natural cycle of birth and death and achieve Nirvana. He promised similar powers to those who would follow his preaching. In addition, their lives would be spared in the approaching world Armageddon.[64]

Many Aum members seemed to have major doubts about the genuineness of Japanese life. Authentic Love, friendship, or social relations—these seemed to be lacking in a Japanese society almost exclusively focused on the material self. This lack of authenticity led many to conclude that life was no longer sustainable and was headed down a treacherous road of destruction and that there was no turning back. The only way out was the "afterlife." As one former member put it, "that's the sole remaining hope."[65]

So, many in Japan, especially the younger generation, had an expectation of change. This led large groups of them to search out new spiritual possibilities that were deeply intertwined in apocalyptic expectations. Upheaval and destruction of the old way of life was, for many, a prerequisite for the coming of the new age. For others, it was not so much an expectation, as it was a hope for a better future—that the overly material world of the present would be brushed away and in its place a new, much simpler, divine world would emerge. This imagery became central within Aum. Yet, it contained two opposing perceptions. On the one hand, the future was bright, offering great optimism about what was to come. On the other hand, there was a darker side. Increasingly "doom and destruction were not merely seen as inevitable, but were openly welcomed."[66]

A number of factors had converged to strengthen the appeal of new age religions in Japan in the 1980s and set the stage for Aum Shinrikyo's rise to notoriety. Economic uncertainty, a clear breakdown in the traditional Japanese sense of family and community, alienation, rootlessness led many Japanese on a search for less conventional forms of spirituality. Asahara and Aum Shinrikyo, before 1995, appealed to some as one of the more interesting of the counterculture movements because their syncretic religious ideas seemed like a useful and appropriate convergence of the past traditions and new realities.[67]

The need for the New Religions, such as Aum, was made all the more significant because of the lack of any type of effective support system for a growing population living on the margins of Japanese society. Although they functioned outside of the mainstream and, as a result were avoided by most Japanese, they were perceived of as legitimate sanctuary for those alienated by conventional life.[68]

Aum offered its adherents a vehicle to satisfy their thirst for spirituality through an apocalyptic imagery unsurpassed in their previous attempts. This imagery often included massive death and destruction engendered by a nuclear holocaust. Training within Aum was intense, yet remarkably rewarding to those who pursued it with high energy. Many of these training sessions were augmented further through the use of hallucinatory drugs such as LSD. Indeed, following the collapse of the movement, many former members interviewed by Lifton yearned for a return of the sense of energy and inner peace that they had known during their Aum experience.[69]

The story of Aum member Akio Namimura was not atypical: in high school, he felt deeply alienated by an educational system that he perceived only met the needs of society as a whole, while ignoring his own. After graduation, he drifted from one job to the next. Throughout the experience, he perceived that he was just "out of sync" with the world in which he lived. "Any way you cut it, the concrete jungle had burned me out and I longed to see the ocean in my hometown." At first he joined Soka Gakkai, but saw that it did not meet his needs. Eventually, he found Aum to be what he seemed to be looking for.[70]

What Aum did, in the minds of its members, was to reduce the psychological stress of modern life in Japan. In return they all perceived that they had increased their own personal power. The vast majority of those who were attracted to the movement saw it in this "problem–solution" context.[71] As one member put it, "when you reach liberation you are freed from the sufferings of the impermanent world."[72]

The ideology of Aum Shinrikyo was grounded in the belief that the whole world was awash in sin and that life was primarily a process of suffering. It stressed the importance of breaking away from the suffering through spiritual practice. Life's meaning must be detached from the materialism of the world and understood in the reality of religious discipline and meditation.

Aum emphasized the important step of withdrawing from the Japanese world of consumption and the greater accumulation of wealth in favor of "spiritual progress through asceticism, yoga, and meditation." Its rejection of worldly values was directly tied to its millenarian character because such a rejection allowed the triumph over temporal corruption that would set the stage for a new civilization.[73] In the process, Aum believed that in order to cleanse the world of iniquity, corruption, and sin it had to be destroyed. It was then that a new, pure, and ideal spirituality could be achieved.[74]

Asahara preached to his adherents that they were both special and unique, that they did not fit well into the present transient world.[75] As a result, members tended to view those in the outside "secular" world with some degree of disdain. They saw them as suffering, whereas they were working to solve their problems and move to a level above the psychological stresses of temporal life.[76]

In this way, the destruction of temporal life became an act of compassion. Death and murder would be an act of liberation in which God's chosen few would free the common man in Japan from "bad karma" and "enhance their immortality, or their subsequent reincarnation, or their journey to the pure land." Although not everyone in Aum believed in this notion in the ruthless and cold way that it was presented, it was the message that Asahara stressed over and over.[77]

Life inside of Aum was far more difficult than life on the outside. Nonetheless, most accepted this as part of the sacrifice required to achieve the satisfaction that the group offered them. Everyone was aiming at the same goal, the achievement of a far higher degree of spiritual satisfaction. In the process, they assumed all of their problems would be resolved. It provided a sense of direction and certainty that they had not achieved elsewhere in their lives.[78]

Alienation, Shi'ism, and the Message of Musa Al-Sadr

Since the era of the Ottoman Empire, the Shi'ite community has been on the margins of Lebanese society—economically, socially, and politically. The major activities of the state, including its primary economic interests tended to center around Beirut and not in the Shi'a south.

Following World War II, Lebanon began to modernize. This process had a significant impact on all members of the state both socially and politically. And, this was particularly true of the Shi'ites. The infrastructure of the entire country began to both expand and improve. Transportation was made easier, which contributed to an influx of Shi'ites into Beirut, searching for a better life. Nonetheless, an almost immediate result was the rapid expansion of the "Belt of Misery."

Modernization impacted the media and the availability of information among the entire population. Radio and television contributed to a growing awareness among the Shi'a that their position within Lebanon was not what it could be, in a way that they had not been impacted before. This exacerbated their sense of relative deprivation and "made their unfavourable situation, and the lack of social mobility, all the more painfully obvious."[79] It was quite clear, especially to Shi'ite elites, that the system in Lebanon, at least for their community, was blocked.[80] Most Shi'a saw an almost continuous sequence of what they perceived of as unjust government and a society that simply did not seem to work for them. And, Sunni hegemony within the Islamic community, placing the Shi'a in a sort of permanent minority status among the faithful, tended to exacerbate these problems.[81]

As a result, Lebanese Shi'ites have long felt a sense of social discrimination and political disenfranchisement, with constant reminders of their distinctive, minority position. Alienation within the community is widespread.

Historically, the Shi'ite community had dealt with this alienation in a passive manner. This passivity was directly related to religious interpretations of long-established Shi'a status within the umma. For example, Shi'ite clerics traditionally interpreted the tragedy at Karbala as a statement of submission. As a result, they taught that there was nothing to gain in fighting evil in life and that one must simply accept their position in day-to-day life. In their interpretation, the clerics relied on the Doctrine of Religious Dissimulation or *taqiyya*, which traced its roots to the eighth century AD. It put forth the idea that deviations from living the religious model of Islam are only permissible and lawful in Shi'ism in those situations "where there is overwhelming danger of loss of life or property and where no danger to religion would occur thereby." Thus, while living as a minority and dominated politically by other laws, Shi'ites were still protected through their faith in God.[82]

Because of *taqiyya*, the Shi'ite community was able to live in peace, untroubled in their messianic belief that the Twelfth Imam would one day return and reestablish God's rule on earth.

Each year, Husayn's death is commemorated in the month of Muharram on the day of Ashura. The events of the tragedy at Karbala are played out in a public ritual that often attracts thousands of Shi'ites. Long parades are held during which narrations from religious texts are read to the crowd. The scene is dramatized by a sense of mourning for Husayn. Both men and women cry and, in many cases, eventually work themselves into a passionate, frenzied state. In some pageants, men cut themselves with razors in a style of self-flagellation and then proceed to beat their bloodied wounds in sync with the rhythm of the narrations being read to the crowd.[83]

Through such rituals, Husayn's own self-sacrifice in the face of perceived oppression has become a deeply moving and durable icon for the Shi'a. This is particularly so in Iran and Lebanon, where he is referred to as the "Prince of Martyrs."[84]

Musa al-Sadr challenged these traditional interpretations of both the ritual and meaning of Karbala and the martyrdom of Husayn. Rather than simply accepting their alienation and sense of injustice resulting from a secondary position in society, al-Sadr developed a far different perspective that brought a much deeper analysis to the significance of Karbala.

He sought to remove the message of mourning and grief and replace it with a sense of self-worth and righteous indignation. He preached that, in fact, the Karbala tragedy must be interpreted as an extreme expression of political choice and heroism by Imam Husayn and those who fought with him. As a result, rather than largely a reminder of their vanquished past, the annual ritual celebrating Karbala should not be a demonstration of submission, but rather an expression of defiance and a refusal to no longer accept what they perceived to be injustice at the hands of others.[85]

Such a transformation of traditional Shi'ite doctrine was evident in a speech given by al-Sadr as early as 1974. He began by recounting the difficult period that surrounded the life of Husayn, and the challenges that were faced within the community:

> The umma was silent, free men were fugitives; fear reduced men to silence. Islam was threatened . . . A great sacrifice was needed to . . . stir feelings. The event of Kerbala was that sacrifice. Imam Hussein put his family, his forces, and even his life, in the balance

> against tyranny and corruption. Then the Islamic world burst forth with this revolution.
>
> This revolution did not die in the sands of Kerbala; it flowed into the life stream of the Islamic world, and passed from generation to generation, even to our day. It is a deposit placed in our hands so that we may profit from it, that we draw out of it a new source of reform, a new position, a new movement, a new revolution, to repel the darkness, to stop tyranny and to pulverize evil.[86]

Through this reinterpretation of a significant Shi'a ritual, al-Sadr was provoking the community to take action. He sought to use the ritual more effectively as a modern political tool by attaching it to new ideas of involvement and activism.[87] For far too long, al-Sadr declared, the Shi'ite community had kept quiet. The result of this passiveness was quite clear: continued injustice. By prodding the Shi'ite community to fully grasp their own sacred history, traditions, and conviction, he now provided them with the spark that they required for assuming a posture of innovative protest.

In 1975, al-Sadr created AMAL, an acronym for *Afwaj al-Muqawamah al-Lubnaniyah* or Battalions of the Lebanese Resistance. The organization quickly became known as simply AMAL, or "hope." Al-Sadr conceived of AMAL as an agent that could bring both social justice and an increase in government services to the community as a whole. What he built was the first modern mass political movement within the Shi'ite community.[88]

Al-Sadr himself held no official, functioning leadership role in AMAL. Rather, he was identified as simply the group's spiritual guide or *murshid ruhi*. In this role, he was moving along a political path that the community could increasingly understand and support. Through his utilization of a new type of political rhetoric that he believed would bring together all of the classes within the community and which appealed to the "wretched of the earth" and the "disinherited," al-Sadr was able to shrewdly go around both the political Left and Right. He was able to tackle both the poor class, which was susceptible to the ideology of the Left, and at the same time, he gained the support of economic elites within the community who tended to lean to the political Right. As a consequence, religious activities and events in south Lebanon began to appear more like armed political rallies rather than assemblies of worship and sacred praise. At the same time, it was becoming increasingly clear that a new spiritual bond had been created between an uplifted community sense of self-worth and the charismatic image of al-Sadr. One was now an unmistakable function of the other.[89]

The Ideology of Hezbollah

At the foundation of Hezbollah's ideological organization is an idealized Islamic state: a profoundly messianic construction, which has, as yet, not been fulfilled. This pan-Islamic republic will be headed by religious clerics. Only when the Mahdi or hidden Imam reappears can the utopian state of the Shi'ites truly achieve fulfillment. As a result, Hezbollah must focus its attention on the pre-Mahdist construction of the state, which they perceive, in one form, is represented by the Islamic Republic of Iran. In turn, much of their theory of the state is directly taken from the theories of Khomeini.[90]

The solution to Lebanon's problems, Hezbollah proclaims, is the establishment of an Islamic republic. Only this type of regime can secure justice and equality for all of Lebanon's citizens. Concurrently, Hezbollah refuses to accept the idea of an independent Lebanon. Instead, it appeals for the assimilation of Lebanon into a greater Islamic state.[91]

According to official party statements, Hezbollah follows a doctrinal path firmly grounded in Islam. Its message is one that seeks to establish universal peace and justice. "The kind of Islam that Hezbollah seeks is a civilized one that refuses any kind of oppression, degradation, subjugation, and colonization. Hezbollah also stretches its arm of friendship to all on the basis of mutual self-respect."[92]

Hezbollah seeks to restore Islam to a position of supremacy in the political, social, and economic life of the Muslim world. It is this goal that has attracted the material, financial, political, and social support of the Islamic Republic of Iran. Indeed, there is a great deal of cooperation between Hezbollah and the Iranian government. Throughout the 1980s and early 1990s there were several hundred Iranian Revolutionary Guards in the Bekaa valley training and assisting Hezbollah soldiers. In the political realm, Iran administers the affairs of Hezbollah through the guise of the Lebanon Council or *Majlis Lubnan*.[93]

Hezbollah leaders routinely invoke the names and deeds of Shi'a martyrs as a tool of mobilization and action within the movement, linking the cause of Hezbollah to the historical Shi'a search for justice and freedom from oppression.

> 1360 years ago today, Imam Hussein stood on the battlefield of Kerbala, surrounded by a large force of thousands of enemy soldiers.

> With just a small band of followers, Imam Hussein's stand was aimed at reminding the soldier's who faced him of God, His messenger Mohammad, and of how they would be held accountable for their own deeds on the Day of Judgment. In fact, Imam Hussein's rallying cry didn't just address those enemy soldiers. It has addressed the generations of all coming ages since then . . . Though heavily outnumbered, Imam Hussein decided to fight, recognizing that Islam has no place for humiliation . . . Kerbala is the one, which inspired our souls and spirits and gave us struggle and steadfastness. The blood of Imam Hussein has breathed life into the souls and minds of all who have since followed him. 1360 years after Imam Hussein's blood was spilt, that same blood runs in our veins and helped us to defeat the Israelis in South Lebanon. This holy blood will always keep us on the side of the oppressed and motivate us to defend the just causes of the nation and reject humiliation and oppression.[94]

Hezbollah perceives of the West in a religious and political context shaped by two important notions. First is a traditional confrontation and antagonism between Islam and Christianity going back to the Crusades. Second, is their perception of modern European and American imperialism in the Middle East beginning in the aftermath of World War I.[95] They assert that Western objectives in the region are grounded exclusively in their self-interested pursuit of power, in particular, the control of oil in the region. Hezbollah openly condemns many leaders in the Arab world, especially Saudi Arabia, for kowtowing to American interests.[96]

The principal weapon of Hezbollah has been suicide bombing: young Shi'ite combatants who have volunteered to maneuver vehicles loaded with explosives into Israeli targets and, in the process, kill themselves. Such a powerful weapon was new to the region—prior to Hezbollah no one had utilized such a tactic before.[97]

At the foundation of such a tactic is not secular authority, strong discipline and training, or even personal anger—it is a religious faith growing out of a pervasive sense of alienation. As one young resistance fighter asserted:

> We have a firm belief in our land. It is rightfully ours and we have the right to defend and liberate it from the occupiers. The Resistance is not led by commanders, it is directed by the tenets of Islam . . . it is faith [that drives us]. No one might believe us, but it emanates from our faith—that wondrous weapon, which no armaments in the world can destroy, united our town's residents, despite the fact that they had belonged to different political parties and affiliations before the invasion.[98]

Between 1982 and 1985, 30 or more suicide bombings were carried out in Lebanon by young Hezbollah fighters. Bombs were placed in automobiles, suitcases, and even, in one instance, on the back of a donkey.[99] These suicide bombings had a significant effect on events in the region. Perhaps the two most powerful examples occurred in 1983. First, on April 18, the U.S. Embassy in Beirut was destroyed in a massive explosion carried out by a young suicide bomber, killing a total of 63. Six months later, a U.S. Marine compound located near the Beirut airport and a French military compound four miles away were bombed within seconds of one another killing 299.[100]

Hezbollah is very much an indigenous organization. Its fighters are mostly local men.[101] They have significant local family ties, jobs, professions, homes, networks of local support, and hopes and aspirations for Lebanon. These members do not choose to join the organization because they have no alternative, but, rather, it is because the organization more closely fits their ideology and beliefs.[102]

Their principal motive is to defend the ideals of their social, religious, and economic way of life. Embellishing this motivation are the signs and symbols of the movement proclaiming Israel as a terrorist state and accusing the Israeli Defense Forces (IDF) of carrying out acts of genocide and making reference to the traditional sayings of the chief characters in Shi'ism. Numerous banners stress the pain and violence that have marked the region since the invasion and call for acts of retaliation against Israel. For example, one sign reads: "Qana is the Karbala of the twentieth century; it is a land made holy by the Lord Jesus and contaminated by the Zionist Satan."[103]

Members of Hezbollah are convinced that they will ultimately triumph in their war with Israel. At the same time, they are quite capable of putting this conflict into a historical perspective that assists them in characterizing the struggle in a way that provides meaning and determination. As a senior Hezbollah spokesperson has stated: "The Crusaders stayed in Palestine for 200 years and have gone. Israelis have only been in Palestine since 1948."[104]

Hezbollah represents a collective and violent response to the alienation that pervades the region. It seeks to remove the Western presence from Lebanon. This has been perhaps most clearly articulated by Naiim Qassem, Hezbollah's deputy secretary general:

> In our region we have a problem with the West, which at one time placed us under the French mandate, at other times under the British mandate and over certain periods we were politically governed by the whims of the United States . . . When the West moves into a region, it

> does so with the intention of marketing its principles. It establishes schools, its own educational curriculum, Western cultural institutions, its own media, practically its own way of life and thinking. All of this, in a bid to impose its own ideologies in our region . . . they seek to impose their own Western principles, not taking ours into consideration, in an attempt to suck us into their own agenda. From here we consider that there is a cultural conflict between us and the West and it is our job to invalidate their concepts here, to prove their evil and to spread our vision instead. If we succeed we will have obstructed their political agenda and this is our first kind of confrontation.[105]

The leaders of Hezbollah claim they possess a large number of young Shi'ites who are ready to give their lives in martyr attacks in order to play their part in ultimate success of the movement. Although many scholars of Islam have condemned the practice, the leadership of Hezbollah defends it. They assert that these young martyrs follow in one of the more powerful and durable traditions of Shi'ism, inspired originally by Husayn.[106]

Perhaps one of the more potent expressions of this is the action of Salah Ghandour. In 1995, Ghandour drove his car, laden with bombs, into an Israeli military compound. Before his death, he recorded one final message.

> I shall, insha'allah [God willing], shortly after saying these words, be meeting my God with pride, dignity, and having avenged my religion and all the martyrs who preceded me on this route. In a short while I shall avenge all the martyrs and oppressed of Jabal Amel, South Lebanon, as well as the children and sons of the Intifada in Palestine. I shall avenge all those suffering in the tortured security zone. Oh sons of Ali and Hussein and sons of the great Imam Khomeini, God bless his soul. Yea sons of the leaders Khameini and sons of the martyr Abbas Musawi and Sheikh Ragheb Harb, your jihad, insha'allah, is the preparatory jihad for the anticipated Imam, so let us continue until we achieve our desired target and the Godly gratification and thus arrive at our Godly promise. We belong to God and to God we shall return.[107]

From an early age Shi'a Children are taught the value of self-sacrifice. The notion is presented in a sacred context through Islamic religious studies, which all students are required to take in Hezbollah schools.[108]

Hezbollah takes enormous credit for forcing Israel's withdrawal from south Lebanon and, as a result, has gained vast prestige, not simply among its core of Shi'ite supporters, but, also, throughout Lebanon and the Middle East region.[109]

As the campaign for the liberation of south Lebanon from the throes of the Israeli invasion continued, the Shi'ite community continued to suffer. Thousands of refugees fled to the north, into metropolitan Beirut. Conditions in the "Belt of Misery" continued to worsen. Shi'ites began to build makeshift homes in areas of the city where no one else would live: near garbage dumps and next to the common sewer system. Few of these improvised communities had electricity or running water and, by any standards, were unhealthy. Yet, they continued to expand. Although the government of Lebanon felt threatened by this massive flood of refugees from the conflict, it did little to help the situation. Nonetheless, as time went by, the privation and inequity provoked the indignation of the Shi'ites, turning the region into a hotbed of Hezbollah activity and an important recruiting ground for new fighters.[110]

The Shi'ite leadership came to understand that something must be done to improve the conditions of their people. With the help of resources from Iran, Hezbollah began to pursue a large-scale project to construct a social welfare infrastructure for the Shi'ite community of Lebanon.[111]

Ironically, the project meshed quite effectively with Iran's goal of exporting its revolution. As a result, millions of dollars of assistance and credit was passed to Hezbollah to assist the community. The end result was twofold. First, it provided help for the community, which needed it desperately. Second, it guaranteed the loyalty of the Shi'ite population of the region to both Hezbollah and its Iranian benefactors.[112]

In 1984, the first two of many organizations were established: the Construction Jihad or *Jihad al-Binaa* (JAB) and the Islamic Health Committee (IHC). In 1987, the Relief Committee of Imam Khomeini (RCIK), which is based in Tehran, created a branch, at the personal insistence of the Ayatollah, in the Hrat Hreik neighborhood in south Beirut. Khomeini thought that the new branch would help ease conditions in the area. It was his personal attention and sanction of the project that raised the organization's status in the minds of Hezbollah and the Shi'ite community as a whole.[113]

Another very important organization established by Hezbollah was the Martyr's Widow or Armalat al-Shaheed. This aid group takes full responsibility for the financial needs of the widows and families of young Shi'ite martyrs. They provide them with housing, social amenities, and even see to their children's education.[114]

All of these relief associations have performed a vital service in assisting the Shi'ite community in dealing with the effects of the conflict in the south. For example, early on, each time that a village was bombed the JAB would show up on the scene ready to fix the damage. Later, JAB expanded and included the building of houses and repairing sewer systems. Other organizations collect garbage and deliver water.[115] The agencies have expanded dramatically to locations throughout Lebanon. Indeed, they are not limited to aiding only the Shi'ite communities but have broadened their reach into some Sunni and Christian regions as well.[116]

Some scholars have dismissed the relief efforts of these agencies sponsored by Hezbollah and funded by Iran as merely a step in the political evolution of the movement. They argue that Hezbollah only seeks to utilize these social welfare projects as a base for furthering their political strength in Lebanon.[117]

Nonetheless, such efforts are wholly consistent with the faith and must be seen, first, in that context. The suffering, alienation, dislocation, and social stress engendered by the conflict in the south created conditions that required a collective form of therapy, a mass cure for the problems encountered by the community. Such a cure went far beyond the material aspects of building homes, collecting garbage, or delivering water. It was also forced to confront the spiritual damage that had been inflicted on the community. It seems obvious that only an organization of the nature of the "Party of God" could assist in such revitalization.[118]

Conclusion

Faith in an impending, divinely guided intervention—one that will rescue the community from conditions of oppression, injustice, despair, and hopelessness—holds a powerful healing capability.

In the presence of a potent, conquering culture, societies become alienated. Traditional ways begin to be seen as both useless and outmoded. One's sense of self within the community is challenged and things simply don't work like they used to. Worse than that, life seems increasingly "foreign," "corrupt," and no longer of "genuine" meaning.

In response, this alienation breeds discontent and a profound sense of powerlessness. This is expressed through a variety of cultural devices—music, literature, art, and religion, among others.

It is important to understand that a divergence of forces is at work under such conditions. On the one hand, there is a collective desire to return to theological and mystical roots: to a time when things were "real," "meaningful," and life was "on track." On the other hand, concurrently, there is a search for new forms of normative behavior and new interpretations of sociopolitical structures and processes.

Millenarianism provides groups with the opportunity to reintegrate themselves in a society impinged upon by disturbing and corrupting forces. The ideas of reintegration, reinterpretation, and renewal are powerful. First, they establish the possibility of an idealized state of affairs. Second, they provide a call for action. Finally, such ideas promote the mobilization of resources to achieve their goals through whatever means necessary. Not only does millenarianism provide sacred justification for political violence but, also, it elevates those who carry out such acts to an exalted, transcendental position.

In this way, millenarianism allows the community to "break through" conventional sociopolitical norms in pursuit of a pristine world liberated from corruption, indignation, and alienation.

Failed efforts at reforms by the Peruvian government helped set the stage for the rise of Sendero Luminoso in the 1980s. Such a failure exacerbated a sense of alienation and relative deprivation among many, especially peasants and the indigenous community, leaving them drained by hopelessness, despair, powerlessness, and disillusionment.

Sendero offered these groups hope, a renewed sense of power, self-esteem, and social services; it organized the community and mobilized it for action, in a purposeful and satisfying way.

Aum Shinrikyo, a rather small movement when compared to Sendero or Hezbollah, arose in the presence of severe economic turbulence. It offered a seeming haven away from the alienating world of modern Japan: a historically traditional society that had seemingly gone wild with materialism in the second half of the twentieth century. Having been conquered by the West at mid-century, a foreign culture now pervaded Japanese life. Despite modern conveniences, life in the community was uneasy.

New religions have thrived in postwar Japan in response to the alienation engendered by a contest between, on the one hand, traditional values, customs, and time-honored forms of identity and, on the other hand, secular materialism and the unique life that it engenders.

Aum declared that the current age of materialism was coming to an end. It called for a rejection of modern values and the move to a new age of enlightened spirituality and global peace. Nonetheless, to hasten this new age, all that has come before must and will be destroyed. This was a compelling message to many.

Among the Shi'a, the injection of modern Western culture into Lebanon brought disruption and significant alienation to their community. This was brought to a head when Israeli Defense Forces invaded south Lebanon in 1982. Under such circumstances, Hezbollah was born. It provided the community with physical defense against foreign invasion but, just as important, hope for a future ideal world, a sense of purpose, power, and self-esteem.

In all three cases, outbreaks of powerful millenarian expectations arose as an unambiguous resolution to the miseries associated with social, cultural, and economic disruption. Through the use of traditional images of sacred redemption a remedy was forthcoming that temporal devices seemed powerless to repair. The savior appears as an immediate and unequivocal reaction to the cravings of the people for a restoration of their traditional ways, which have now been reformed into an image of paradise on earth.

Millenarianism functioned as a mitigating factor in the capacity of the peoples of these societies to (1) cope with the disastrous consequences of an impingement upon their traditional way of life by projecting their problems onto a broader screen that helped them to clarify and objectify their social issues; (2) reduce the resultant dislocation and alienation; and (3) thoroughly purge and cleanse themselves in an effective act of mass catharsis.

Violence is perceived to be a requirement of destroying the old and hastening the new. Nonetheless, each of these groups was resource poor. In the process of making the most efficient use of available resources, justified by their sacred millenarian goals and a dichotomized worldview, they turned to the warfare of the poor: terrorism.

CHAPTER 5

Identity and Millenarian Violence

All millenarians require a god and a satan, a christ and an anti-christ, the lamb and the serpent, the holy and the unholy, lightness and darkness, heaven and hell, and in-groups and out-groups. All of these concepts exemplify the dichotomized world inhabited by adherents to an apocalyptic faith. Such conceptualizations define, sustain, and legitimate their identities.

The worldview of the millenarian tends to be dominated by an anxious, paranoid commitment to in-group survival. Frequently they perceive that they are threatened by a conspiracy of out-group members, whom they are convinced are out to destroy their way of life. And, the anxiety that accompanies this commitment cannot be sustained.

Under stress, many millenarians come to believe that the only solution is the destruction of the present untenable conditions: termination of the now and hastening the utopian hereafter. Frequently, such destruction includes members of the in-group itself. But that's an acceptable proposition: passing from the pain, stress, anxiety, and alienation of the past to the blissful paradise of forever.

Experiences of severe social stress, alienation, oppression, and injustice tend to give rise to certain psychological needs among the members of a community. The nature and intensity of the needs and, more specifically, the mechanism that the community chooses to reduce the intensity of such stress are strongly influenced by cultural and social factors.

Under severe, difficult conditions, for example, the need for physical safety and confidence in one's ability to satisfy necessities, including food and shelter, are greatly heightened. The inability to take care of oneself and one's family and to control the circumstances of one's life greatly threatens the psychological self: the self-concept, values, beliefs, and ways of life of the individual and the group. When "their" group (family, clan, village, or other) is in chaos, or at least functioning poorly and unable to provide its members with protection and a feeling of security, then their self-concept will become threatened, because all people have strong needs to protect both their individual and collective identities.[1]

In a complementary way, a breakdown in the traditions and customary ways of life in a society profoundly challenges and threatens people's assumptions—not only assumptions about their self-concept, but also their interpretation and assumptions about their world. Under such circumstances, lacking clear beliefs that help make sense and guide one's relation to it, life becomes filled with uncertainty and anxiety. As a result, peoples' traditional worldview and comprehension of reality become untenable and they will seek a "renewed comprehension of reality," that is, a revitalization of their society.[2]

Acute social crisis, in the form of perceived catastrophe, oppression, injustice, and sociopolitical alienation can challenge identities. Groups come to feel that their collective self-concept is no longer viable. This, in turn, can precipitate a revitalization movement as a device for achieving a new identification—one that is feasible and capable of dealing with society's problems. This new cultural identification may be characterized by a resurrection and reinstitutionalization of ancient socioeconomic ways, the institutionalization of imported or newly invented ways, or, more likely, the fusion of the old and the new.[3] Nonetheless, the crisis is ultimately resolved through a reassertion of their own identity in the context of the overarching cultural scheme.[4]

Human nature strives for identity based on two important components. First, one can achieve identity on the basis of a competent ability to maintain productive social and personal relations with others. Second, identity rests on a sense of structure that is created by our cognitive map. In other words, who we are becomes a function of a greater world of meaning, authority, and spirituality. As a result, when each of us is asked to characterize our identity we tend to assert our own unique position within a context of a sociopolitical and cultural structure: for example, as adherents to a religious faith, believers in a particular brand of ideology, and living in a certain geographic location. These affiliations delineate the borders of the world in which we live.[5]

Until just a few years ago, those who studied politics paid little attention to the concept of identity. They assumed that it had very little relevance to the subject. Nonetheless, in the post–Cold War environment, the politics of identity have been thrust onto the front page of global events. Scholars have come to realize that political action inherently and fundamentally involves human identity.[6] But, what is the nature of human identity? How can we relate the individual experience to that of the group, and, thus, the political?

The strength and stability of one's personality rests on the effective formation of a satisfying and functioning identity. Identity is a fundamental component of the individual's character and basic to the framework and stability of the personality.

It is a phenomenon that is not developed in a vacuum but, rather, in the collective experience of one's ethnic, familial, communal, and national past. The foundation of a satisfying identity is a sense of trust that begins to form almost immediately following birth. Every individual possesses an innate need to internalize the behavior, mores, and attitudes of major individuals in his or her social milieu. It is this instinctual urge that sets the stage for identity formation. Further, once such identities have been established, there exists an equal human desire to both enhance and protect this identity, for the remainder of their life. What is critical here is the fact that given the same structural surroundings, there is an equivalent propensity for a group of individuals to create the same identity and to take on the same identity. In the same fashion, provided the same structural surroundings, there will be an equivalent propensity for members of the groups to enhance and protect their identities at the collective level. In this way, identity formation occurs simultaneously at the individual and group levels in very similar processes and very similar patterns.[7]

The outcome of this is a social pattern in which those people who share a common identity will tend to act as one and possess the capability to mobilize for group action if provoked to do so. Such a process provides the foundation for political action. To take this one step further, if forced to, such a movement of commonly identified individuals will, if called upon to do so, utilize political violence to defend their common identity.

Although one's sense of identity is a state of mind it demands that there be a world of meaning that the psyche can make sense of. In other words, an identity cannot be formed in a sociopolitical void. It is a function of the sociopolitical and economic structure in which the individual and the group exist. For example, systems of social affiliation, such as religions, political loyalties, and ethnic ties, exert a significant influence on identity. As a result, identity is determined not simply by ego, or some conceptual sense of self, but by the necessary achievement of a sense of capability and reliability amid the dynamic demands of physical changes and the interchange of powerful social forces.[8]

At a minimum, then, a basic requirement for a psychologically satisfying sense of well-being is a secure sense of identity. In contrast, but equally of significance to the individual, is what happens when the individual's identity loses its integral structure. Under such circumstances, it becomes very difficult, if not impossible, for the ego to cope with the inevitable changes that social life brings. This lack of adaptive capacity to deal with the stress and difficulties associated with social change can lead to a significant personal disruption of one's worldview. In response, there is a psychological necessity for the individual to craft an adaptive identification consistent with the context of his structural circumstance. This is always pursued within a group context. Eventually, the individual and the group must both enhance and defend such a crafted identity.[9]

As the human infant evolves to adolescence, from the family to the wider society as a whole, it is faced with further crafting and defending his or her fragile identity in the context of an expanding and increasingly complex world. Erikson recognized that "man, in order to be able to interact efficiently, must at intervals, make a total orientation out of a given state of partial knowledge." This led humans to a completely psychological concept of "ideology." He characterized "ideology" within a total worldview growing out of the synthesis of readymade, historical identifications and a culture that prescribes a specific mode of behavior.

> We are speaking here, not merely of high privileges and lofty ideals but of psychological necessities. For the social institution, which is the guardian of identity, is what we have called identity . . . Whatever else ideology is and whatever transitory or lasting social form it takes . . . we will view it here as a necessity for the growing ego which is involved in the succession of generations and in adolescence is committed to some new synthesis of past and future: a synthesis which must include but transcend the past, even as identity does.[10]

Ideology, then, becomes a psychological mechanism for the individual to integrate in a satisfying way with society. It represent an almost "off the shelf" generalized identification that is made to order for the individual to use to his or her satisfaction and requirements. In this sense, an ideology satisfies an inherent psychological requirement. As a result, Erikson theorized that there is a continuum among identity, ideology, and culture. Any threat to ideology or culture becomes a threat to identity. And, a change in historical circumstances or the structural arrangements of life, for example, cultural impingement, rebellion, revolution, economic depression, threatens the individual's and the group's sense of identity by eliminating the "external social coordinates by which people recognize their identity continuity." This will trigger anxiety that, in turn, engenders a "dynamic adaptive reaction" with two possible outcomes: (1) attempts are made to protect the identity, ideology, and culture at all costs, or (2) a new synthesis of identifications is crafted to meet new circumstances.[11]

We may observe this psychological process being played out in the nature of ethnic nationalism and ethnic conflict. The psychological foundation of the powerful ideology of ethnic nationalism is group identification: that is, an emotional attachment and affiliation with a group of like individuals. The process begins as a socio-psychological attachment. Nonetheless, almost out of a necessity, in order to defend the bond, it evolves to a political attachment, which manifests itself in the form of an articulated ideology. Individuals become willing to sacrifice for the group, community, or even a nation.[12] Our challenge in this study is to understand the nature of that group feeling and how it comes to manifest itself as political violence.

Humans hold both the desire and capability to form groups basically around any observed or imagined differences between themselves and other humans.[13] These differences may include proximity to one another, language, age, the color of their skin, a shared sense of history, and religious beliefs. Those who come to consider themselves alike in some way tend to gather together to form a tribe, village, community, or nation. In doing so they immediately set themselves apart from those who identify with other groups.

In the process of establishing such identities, group interests, beliefs, and expectations can both converge and diverge. On the one hand, interests tend to converge around in-group members. On the other hand, at the same time, group interests diverge from those of out-group members.[14] Tribes, villages, communities, and nations are in-groups, whose interests, beliefs, and expectations have converged on various levels, contrasting their convergent interests with members of corresponding but different groups. In this way, group identity performs a significant role in in-group–out-group relations. Indeed, it has been argued that movements utilizing terror as a primary tactic are aided by identities that emphasize the cultural diversity of peoples, primarily in the form of language and religious practices that actually overlap national boundaries.[15] In-group identities become the primary source of a group's values and beliefs, sustaining them in reference to other groups.

In periods of stress, anxiety, oppression, injustice, and perceived disaster, which may threaten the dissolution of the in-group's structure and thus its existence, in-groups come to rely on millenarian expectations as an agent of salvation. "Millenarian movements almost always occur in times of upheaval, in the wake of culture contact, economic dislocation, revolution, war, and natural disaster."[16]

To understand how it is that otherwise normal individuals can come to utilize violence as a political tool, it is necessary to recognize that their radical behavior is acquired slowly in an inexorable progression that moves from the conventional to the extreme.[17] Generally, this progression involves moving in a series of steps sometimes through a series of groups and causes, toward increasingly more violent-oriented activities.[18] In this progression, identity becomes a significant variable in the formation of millenarian terrorism. This is so for a number of reasons.

Millenarian terrorists do not view themselves as ordinary folk. They are special, at least in their own perception of the world. They see their cause and their role in its achievement as something significantly apart from life within "mainstream" society.

In addition, as we have already discussed, millenarianism is an ideology: it involves the projection of moral order onto society and subsequently translating such ideas into a practical reality through their attachment onto particular places and moments in time. The particular places chosen have a significant meaning or are "central" for the specific group involved. In this way, "any group that wishes to make some change to society and seeks to bring about that change will engage in some form of spatially located action."[19] Actions invested with the meaning of a particular site become ones that convey an option to those presented by the conventional, existing society. For those who come to reject the norms and beliefs of conventional society, it is those places of meaning that facilitate the organization of new identities. In this way, millenarianism offers a doctrine around which one can reassert one's identity and self-esteem: it provides a common rallying point for those who sense that their place in society had been lost.

Finally, millenarianism and terrorism are group activities. Indeed, individuals may be more attracted to the group experience than to the acts of violence per se. This is because those motivated by a strong desire to change their social and political environment can rarely hope to accomplish their goals alone and become dependent on the group to achieve their otherwise personal ideological objectives. Social networks, such as those seen in similar ethnic, cultural, or racial relationships existing before the recruitment to the movement takes place, are important variables. This tends to create a discernable homogeneity in terms of social affiliations within millenarian terrorist groups.

Identity and Sendero Luminoso

Adherents to Sendero Luminoso are primarily young, Quechua-speaking Indians who live in a country where their language is perceived of by many as an indicator of their racial and ethnic inferiority. For them, Sendero offers the opportunity to break away from disillusionment, racism, and cultural alienation. It offers them hope, identity, and the possibility of self-development as well as the opportunity to let loose traditional and durable ethnic and cultural revenge for past injustices.[20] Many believe that the problem with Peru is that it is being governed by individuals of foreign descent, possessing a uniquely different vision of the future. And, that if they could be removed from power the country would be much better off.[21]

The average age of Sendero members is relatively young. However, this average does vary by region. A study of convicted Sendero members indicated that 57 percent were under the age of twenty-five. A study of members in the Upper Huallaga valley, however, found that members were much younger. Of two groups studied, the age ranged from as young as ten up to twenty-five years of age.[22]

Women also play an active role in the Sendero movement. The movement itself claims that approximately 40 percent of its membership is female.[23] Other sources have estimated the number to be closer to 20 percent.[24]

Training forms the core component of preparing young Sendero recruits for the mission that lies ahead of them. The process is slow, deliberate, and comprehensive. It may take as long as three years and is designed to ensure the full commitment of the individual. Indeed, it is so complete that, once committed to the movement, the "people's war" takes on a form of personal calling for most members. They perceive of it as a private struggle to bring an end to the oppression of their ethnic group or social class. Not only do they feel that what they are fighting for is sacred, but that Sendero Luminoso is the only hope for Peru. In this way, for many, the movement becomes more important than their own lives.[25]

Guzman and the party leadership stressed thorough tactical military training for all party volunteers. In addition, a comprehensive ideological indoctrination was mandatory. A rigid and firm discipline was stressed from the time a fighter entered the party. In many ways this discipline was based on the Maoist paradigm including the "Three rules" and "Eight Warnings" of revolutionary China. In addition, fighters were taught to assist Peruvian farmers in their fields and in the day-to-day work in the villages.[26]

Central to this indoctrination was the Sendero concept of the "quota." The quota constituted a sacred covenant: a warrior expected to die in the people's war. Commitment to the quota was a highly ritualized process. It took on a mythical and powerfully symbolical aura. Nonetheless, it was central to the tactical objectives of the party—a dramatic increase in violence, the need to kill in a methodical and depersonalized way. The concept of the quota in the early years of the people's war lent an impression that Sendero Luminoso was much more of a "death cult" than a Marxist party bent on revolution. According to many observers in Peru at the time, Sendero's model was "not found in Marx or Lenin or even Mao, but in Reverend Jones and the Guyana cyanide pail."[27]

Nonetheless, such sacrifices were necessary according to Guzman and the party's leadership. Their objective was utopia—a society grounded in a new social justice. And without the massive spilling of blood, it was argued, their doctrines lacked content and their objectives could never be achieved. Without a disciplined, almost ascetic commitment to the destruction of evil and the old society, the energy that was necessary to achieve the new society could not be harnessed. According to Guzman, the only path to the Promised Land was the one that led over the "river of blood."[28]

All Sendero militants became preoccupied with the preparation of their own death in battle for the cause. The way they saw it, once they had committed to the quota they were no longer in direct control of their own life. Their personal identity was now under the control of the party. They were prepared for death by renouncing life. The quota became a death vow, which, once made, there was no turning back.

> This vision of death as an ardent surrender to the cause, a kind of sublimated sensual possession, opened unknown horizons in each militant's self-love. Combined with a millenarian vision and the personality cult of Guzman, this created ephemeral, fevered, and mythic forms.[29]

Sendero's identity is considered by its adherents as indistinguishable from its mission of "armed struggle" and the imagery of Guzman. Its adherents perceive of the party as the much anticipated redeemer and "guiding light" of the people, which will "spread the dawn" of deliverance, ending oppression and injustice that "kills the masses, consumes them by hunger, shackles them, and cuts their throats."[30]

Guzman perceived of the struggle being conducted by Sendero as a democratic struggle in which all of the people, not just a select few, would be allowed to enter the "promised land of Maoist utopia."[31]

Identity and Aum Shinrikyo

An important function of millenarianism in the ideology of Aum was its capacity to engender transcendence and a new form of personal identity. Adherents were committed to cleansing their world of its impurities by destroying it. It was only then, they believed, that an unadulterated new people could achieve a new plateau of spiritual evolution.[32] In the process, they believed it was an act of compassion to destroy an impure world and its inhabitants because it improves their own sense of immortality or the likelihood that they will reach a promised utopia. Not all Aum members believed in this in such a bleak context. Nonetheless, Asahara aggressively pursued this point of view. Over time, it gained increasing coherence and plausibility within the movement.[33] Indeed, such optimism was widespread among Aum members.

The ideology of Aum stressed the importance of breaking away from the suffering of life through spiritual practice. Life's meaning must be detached from the materialism of the world and understood in the reality of religious discipline and meditation. As a result, Aum, from the beginning, stood in contrast to other New Religions in Japan by asserting a profoundly critical view and rejection of society and, in particular, Japanese materialism. Aum emphasized the important step of withdrawing from the Japanese world of consumption and the greater accumulation of wealth in favor of "spiritual progress through asceticism, yoga, and meditation." "Aum's world rejectionism was closely linked to its millennialism, which promised the conquest of the corrupt material world and the triumph of a new, spiritually aware, civilization."[34]

Aum Shinrikyo carefully sought out new adherents by recruiting at top Japanese universities, because they knew this was fertile ground. Specifically, they aggressively pursued bright young scientists from chemistry, physics, and engineering departments.[35] For example, Masato Yokoyama, one of those responsible for carrying out the sarin gas attack, was a graduate in Applied Physics from the Tokai University Department of Engineering. Following graduation he had been employed in the electronics industry for three years before leaving to join Aum.[36]

As a result, the movement's leadership came to be dominated by a large number of men and women who, in many respects, were among the cream of Japanese youth. Many of them were graduates from Japan's top educational institutions and many came from sound, middle-class backgrounds.[37]

Aum Shinrikyo tempted the mystical, occult mentality that occupied the minds of increasing numbers of Japanese youth in the 1980s and 1990s. These younger Japanese rejected the pragmatic, utilitarian, and overwhelmingly material values of mainstream Japanese society, largely because they did not find it to be spiritually satisfying. Instead they sought a more favorable, humanistic worldview that sought to better explain and understand the true meaning of life. "When a religious movement such as Aum promised them special powers, an accepting community, and hope for happiness, a number of these youth responded positively."[38]

Members of the movement were persuaded to give up their temporal, this worldly status and become *shukkesha* or renunciates. The significance of this act cannot be overstated. It represented an enormous departure from the conventions of traditional Japan, which allowed the adherent to break away from the shackles of alienating social norms and firmly establish a new identity. In particular, Aum aggressively promoted the notion of breaking the traditionally powerful bond of family solidarity and the social convention of strict obedience to one's parents and grandparents. They achieved this by requiring all renunciates to leave their traditional home, to cut off all contact with their conventional family, and to turn over all of their material possessions to the movement. To the *shukkesha*, their commitment was now fully and exclusively to the principles and commands of Asahara, who would lead them to a new identity and a new personal enlightenment.[39]

A central ingredient in the doctrine of Aum Shinrikyo was the establishment of a "liberation-commitment" paradigm between the adherent and the movement. Asahara was able to relieve the pain and arduous responsibility of this world through the effective renunciation of one's identity in it. In its place, the member was required to firmly establish a new identity in a new spirituality: a world that fully transcended difficulty and alienation and offered honest authenticity to those who truly believed.

By the spring of 1995, Aum Shinrikyo declared that they had over 10,000 members, which included approximately 1,100 *shukke*. Of these, the vast majority was young, under the age of thirty.[40] Nonetheless, Aum was not in its entirety a youth movement. It possessed a proportionate share of middle-aged and elderly members, particularly in its early years.[41]

The organizational structure of Aum was distinctly hierarchical. It was based on a system of rank that fully encompassed the notion that humans exist at different levels of spirituality. What evolved was sort of an incentive system. As one achieved success at higher and higher stages of ascetic rituals, they gained the capacity to enter new and different spheres of being. Members were allowed to "challenge" these new levels in their daily worship. Success was confirmed by Asahara himself. In this way, adherents were prepared for not only higher spiritual practice, but increasing responsibility and power in the organization.[42]

As time passed and the group became more committed to the apocalyptic prophecies of Asahara, Aum prepared itself for global warfare and for that time following Armageddon, when its members alone would remain to rule Japan. As a result, by 1994, the group had taken on a dual organizational structure. One was based on the spiritual needs of the membership, the other on political goals. As one might suspect, Asahara held the top position in both structures.

On the spiritual level, members were classed according to seven ranks of "enlightenment" and all pledged complete allegiance to Asahara, the *Sonshi*. Below him were five "Seitaishi" or True Great Masters, the next rank down was called "Seigoshi," or True Enlightened Master, then Lesser Masters, then *Swami*, the Monastics or *shamana*. At the bottom of the pyramid were the lay members of Aum.[43]

At the political level, Aum organized itself in a way clearly modeled on the structure of the Japanese government. This included various ministries, administrative departments, and functional agencies. Such a structure was based on the belief that following the coming Armageddon, it would be the leadership and organization of Aum that would survive and become the functioning government of Japan.[44]

Shi'ite Identity and the Power of Hezbollah

To be a Shi'ite and live in the Levant region has always been problematic. As we have already noted, from the ancient period, the Shi'a community had represented a numerical minority within Lebanon. And, by the eleventh century, the Shi'a–Sunni split was clearly evident in the region when various religio-political leaders vied for power.[45]

During the era of the Ottoman Empire, the Shi'a played virtually no role in the politics of the region, because the Ottomans ruled in the name of Sunni Muslim orthodoxy.[46] The Ottomans were willing to recognize the Christian Maronites and other minorities in the region. Nonetheless, they were reluctant to extend any form of independent status to the Shi'a and treated them as a natural component of the overall Muslim population. As late as the end of the nineteenth century, the Shi'ites represented only about five percent of the population of what is now Lebanon.[47]

As Lebanese nationalism began to grow following independence in 1945, the Shi'a were in no position to participate. This was to be a sovereign state dominated by the Maronite community, which conceived of itself as a separate and distinct Lebanese Christian stronghold: independent and autonomous from other states in the region. Even the Sunni community could identify with the history and ethnicity of the region. For them, Lebanon was a natural extension of the Middle East and the tradition of Arab Sunni Islam.

Nonetheless, the Shi'a of Lebanon were in an untenable position with respect to the community's identity. They possessed no sense of independence and autonomy, even within their own state. And, despite the fact that they were Muslims, they were a minority sect who had traditionally been looked down on by the majority Sunnis.[48]

There remains a widespread sense in the modern Arab world that Arab culture is inherently the domain of the Sunnis. Many Arab Muslims believe that "Sunnism is the natural state of the Arabs." From this point of view, Shi'ism is perceived of as nothing more than an unnecessary and painful split in the faith. It is perceived by many to be purposely created by Shi'ites to reform their identity outside that of simply being Arab. Such reform efforts are significantly assisted by Iranian influence and aid.[49] As a result, Shi'ites throughout the Arab world, including Lebanon, are "left out in the cold" and suffer a sense of alienation from their own political state.[50]

For the vast majority of Shi'as, their religious faith is a conglomerate of theological, cultural, historical, and social characteristics, primarily acquired by the individual at birth. For the strictest of adherents, there is no distinguishing of the faith from their way of life. "Shi'ism as an identity is inseparable from adherence to the religious faith, and it is the active practice of Shi'ism that expresses identity."[51]

Hezbollah's conceptualization of its responsibility in the world is grounded in the way it conceives of itself in both historical and modern-day Islam. It does not see itself as just another confessional party in the fragmented Lebanese political structure. Rather, its role is far more significant and a component of a more universal movement. To its adherents it has come to be the continuation of a religio-political association formed by a sacred resolve first possessed by the Prophet Muhammad and pushed ahead through time in pursuit of one universal Islamic world. In the eyes of Hezbollah, the most recent agent of this sacred resolve has been the Imam Khomeini, whose victory in bringing about a true Islamic Revolution was merely the first stage in the much greater task of reestablishing Islam as the primary truth in the world. The mission of Hezbollah, it is believed, is to continue what Khomeini began by extending the revolution well past the geographic limits of the Iranian state.[52]

The foundation of Hezbollah identity rests in the single notion of struggle. Such struggle is aimed at a well-defined enemy: Zionism and, more specifically, the Israeli state, which Hezbollah members view as an illegitimate entity. Indeed, the more decisive moments in the evolution of Hezbollah tend to center on its identity as a movement of struggle committed to the destruction of Israel. The party does not officially recognize Israel and would simply like to see it disappear.[53]

The most important of these moments was the Israeli invasion of Lebanon in 1982. This led to the occupation of Beirut, which was perceived by Hezbollah as the second Arab capital to be occupied by Israel during the Arab–Israeli conflict. The first is considered to be Jerusalem.[54] Indeed, the linking of the liberation of both of these cities from the control of the Israelis became a source of inspiration and sloganeering with Hezbollah.[55]

From the beginning of the Israeli invasion in 1982 there was widespread concern that the identity of Lebanon as a state would be destroyed. From the Shi'a perspective there was a sense that the southern region of the country was "being amputated from Lebanon's body." Rather than entering Lebanon to protect its security, Israel was in fact entering Lebanon, it was widely believed, to erase its national identity.[56]

The significance of the millenarian nature of Shi'ite identity and its power to mobilize for action was clearly exhibited in events in the city of Nabatiyyeh in the fall of 1983. What transpired was a critical stage in driving the community toward their ultimate campaign of violence. Shi'ites were celebrating Ashura, the sacred ritual commemorating the tragedy of Husayn at Karbala.[57] In the course of activities, the celebration was interrupted by the IDF. What resulted, in the minds of the Shi'ite community, was intentional blasphemy and sacrilege; a deliberate impingement on the sacred identity of the faithful.

Whereas the Ashura ceremony has been interpreted throughout Shi'ite history as an act of penitence and redemption on the part of Husayn, it is important to remember that modern-day Shi'ites have reinterpreted these actions as a model of bravery and sacrifice that should be followed by all Muslims in their struggle against oppression. It is within this context that the violation of the ceremony of the Ashura procession by the IDF became a profound political event.[58]

The ceremony, which was attended by over 50,000 Shi'ites, was at its peak when on October 16, 1983, an Israeli convoy pushed through the town, driving directly through the crowds, angering the Muslim participants, who saw this as an offensive desecration of their holy day. Yelling insults at the Israelis, Shi'ite men, women, and children threw rocks at the soldiers, tried to set fire to the tires of their vehicles, and placed obstructions in front to slow their passage. In the confusion that followed, an Israeli truck was overturned and set afire. The Israeli soldiers who were caught in the middle of the angry crowd asked for support. Shots were fired and two Shi'ites were killed. Fifteen others were injured.[59]

Following news of the event, Shaykh Muhammad Mahdi Shams al Din, leader of the Higher Shi'a Council of Beirut, an otherwise moderate political figure within the community, immediately issued a fatwa, which called for "civil resistance" and "resistance to occupation in the south" against the Israelis. Negotiating with Israel or co-operating with them, he asserted, was "absolutely impermissible." "Every generation" he argued, has its own Karbala. And this was theirs. "Under these circumstances we make our own choice." We can "soar and sacrifice" or we can "submit and betray."[60]

Soon after, many other Shi'ite leaders issued similar calls for action. What ensued over the next few months was a series of escalating steps between the IDF and the Shi'ite community.

On November 4, just three weeks after the events at Nabatiyyeh, a twenty-year-old suicide bomber drove a vehicle into Israeli military headquarters in Tyre, killing 60 people, including 29 Israeli soldiers.[61] Subsequent reprisals against the Israelis rallied even more supporters to enlist in the cause. Before long, what had begun as simply a small core of activists expanded into large numbers and an official resistance organization, known as the Lebanese National Resistance, was created.[62]

Young Shi'ite fighters, prepared to give their life for the movement and asserting their loyalty to Musa al-Sadr, joined the ranks in large numbers. In many of their final testimonies, the closing words exalted al-Sadr, and proclaimed the "absent Imam's return."[63]

The Shi'a waged war with the Israelis with enormous fervor. In the process they were able to purge themselves of their minority status in Lebanon and their historical feeling of second-class citizenship within the Arab world. For many of these young people, the experience of retaliation against the IDF brought a sense of catharsis, relief, and a clear identity of themselves in the context of centuries of Shi'a tradition and ritual.[64]

On February 16, 1985, Hezbollah introduced its first public declaration to the citizens of Lebanon and to the rest of the world. The organization presented its Manifesto through its spokesman, Sheikh Ibrahim al-Amin. The contents of the Manifesto explained in great detail the purpose of the organization, its universal Islamic orientation, its support of Khomeini's radical ideology, and its messianic faith in the ultimate achievement of the ideal Islamic state.

> We are often asked: Who are we, the Hizballah, and what is our identity? We are the sons of the *umma*—the party of God (*Hizb Allah*) the vanguard of which was made victorious by God in Iran. We obey the orders of one leader, wise and just, that of our tutor and faqih who fulfills all the necessary conditions: Ruhollah Musawi Khomeini. God save him!
>
> We are an *umma* linked to the Muslims of the whole world by the solid doctrinal and religious connection of Islam, whose message God wanted to be fulfilled by the Seal of the Prophets, i.e., Muhammad . . . No one can imagine the importance of our military potential as our military apparatus is not separate from our overall social fabric. Each of us is a fighting soldier. And when it becomes necessary to carry out the Holy War, each of us takes up his assignments in the fight in accordance with the injunctions of the Law, and that in the framework of the mission carried out under the tutelage of the Commanding Jurist.[65]

At the core of Hezbollah's ideology is a division of the world into "oppressors" or *mustakbirin* and the "oppressed" or *mustad'afin*. Such a dichotomy was originally articulated by Ayatollah Khomeini in the years leading up to the Iranian Revolution. The concept is steeped in a powerful sense of moral dualism combined with traditional millenarianism. The forces of good and evil will battle with one another in one final, apocalyptic battle. And, in the end, the oppressed will emerge as the victors. This notion is so significant that it appears in virtually every official statement, speech, or letter prepared by Hezbollah officials.[66]

Who is identified as the "oppressed" and the "oppressor" in this dichotomy? The most significant variable in such an identity, according to Hezbollah, turns on one's attitude regarding "Zionism" and its American ally. Anyone who "resists Zionism" and is subject to danger because of this resistance is considered by Hezbollah to be "free" and qualifies as a member of the oppressed class. On the other hand, all of those who support the "Zionist enemy" and America are considered the oppressors.[67]

Hezbollah believes that it is capable of eventually establishing a working relationship with the Western world at some point in the future. Nonetheless, it cannot accept or imagine that such a possibility exists with the state of Israel.[68]

> We declare openly and loudly that we are an *umma* which fears God only and is by no means ready to tolerate injustice, aggression, and humiliation . . . the Zionist entity in the holy land of Palestine, attacked us and continue to do so without respite. Their aim is to make us eat dust continually. This is why we are, more and more, in a state of permanent alert in order to repel aggression and defend our religion, our existence, our dignity. . . . [Israel] is the hated enemy that must be fought until the hated ones get what they deserve. This enemy is the greatest danger to our future generations and to the destiny of our lands.[69]

Hezbollah rejects both nationalism and ethnicity as a basis for the identity of either the organization or its adherents. Loyalty to Lebanon is irreconcilable with the prophecy of Hezbollah. Indeed, the unrest that exists within the country is perceived of as the unavoidable result of synthetic and illegitimate formation. Hezbollah leaders assert that the country possesses no justifiable or lawful basis for its existence, and that its manmade borders were created by the great powers in order to facilitate a political deal in the 1920s.[70]

In the same way, there is no room in Hezbollah's vision of the future of the community for expressions of either Arab or Persian ethnicity, which, it is argued, splits Shi'ites along unnecessary lines.[71]

As a result, Hezbollah argues that the "ties of Islamic belief are the only ties which truly bind, and they bind without distinction of origin, nationality, race, language, or sect." The party does not acknowledge any of the state boundaries that exist among the Islamic states. This is particularly true of those that divide the Islamic *umma* and hinder the formation of a true Islamic identity.[72] According to their ideology: "all believing Muslims must work together to implement what Sayyid Ibrahim al-Amin calls the 'one Islamic world plan,' the aim of which is the creation of a 'Great Islamic State' which will unite the entire region."[73] In this way, identity within the movement is not grounded in ethnicity, nationalism, place of birth, or language. Rather, it is firmly grounded in the millenarian faith of Shi'ism that stands at its ideological foundation.

The plan of achieving the Great Islamic State, they perceive, will proceed in four phases. First is confrontation with Israel. Second is the toppling of the Lebanese regime. Third will be the liberation of Lebanon from interference by the Great Powers. Finally, these will be followed by the establishment of Islam as the exclusive basis of rule in

Lebanon "until the Muslims of Lebanon join with the Muslims throughout the world in this age, to implement the single Islamic plan, and so become the centralized, single nation (umma) willed by God, who decreed that 'your nation will be one.' "[74]

Hezbollah not only seeks to establish a republic in Lebanon based on the rule of Islam, they seek to incorporate such a state into a far broader entity that brings together all Muslims. According to Ibrahim al-Amin, "Lebanon's agony will end only 'when the final Middle East map is drawn. We seek almighty God's help in drawing this map as soon as possible, with the blood of the martyrs and the strength of those who wage the jihad.' This messianic notion that a final map of the entire region is now being drawn in blood sets the struggle of Hezbollah in a larger pan-Islamic context for its adherents."[75]

Hezbollah seeks the establishment of an ideal and universal Islamic state, ordained by God, and governed by the deputy of the hidden Imam (velayat-e faqih). Here we see the convergence of Hezbollah national identity and the messianic imperative of the Faqih.

Hezbollah asserts that Iran and Lebanon are one nation. Indeed, the party itself is a function of the universal Islamic Republic, symbolized by Iran. The Islamic Revolution only began in Iran. Ultimately it will spread throughout the community.[76] The underlying hypothesis here is that the *umma* is not just a religious community of submissive believers who rigidly follow the Qur'an and conform to Islamic rituals, but, also, a political community of Islamic activists and, if necessary, militants who fight to achieve God's purposes.[77]

Conclusion: The Identity Role of Millenarianism in Political Terror

Ideology is crafted from the cultural fabric of a community. It must complement and be consistent with the cognitive maps of society. Ideology is a psychological mechanism that allows the individual and the group to integrate into a society that is both satisfying and enduring. If an event or set of circumstances emerge that in some way threaten one's ideology, it becomes an equal threat to one's identity. Political violence becomes a toll of ideology/identity defense.

Humans form groups at a variety of levels. As a result, they possess many different identities. Nonetheless, some identities are more significant than others and, in turn, some groups are more important than others.

Each of the movements that we have investigated—Sendero Luminoso, Aum Shinrikyo, and Hezbollah—came to life in a society with a durable and pervasive tradition of millenarian expectations. Such expectations were ever present, lying just below the surface of daily life. They defined the nature of hope and aspiration within these societies and, in turn, performed a significant function in the process of identity formation within the group as a whole, as well as the individuals who composed it. In all three cases there existed a virtually complete institutionalization of millenarian-derived identity.

Millenarian expectations within these societies could bubble forth with enormous energy in the presence of sociopolitical and/or economic stress in which large segments of the population, particularly its youth, perceived of themselves as alienated from the mainstream. This alienation was exacerbated by a perceptive sense of profound "foreign" influence/domination as a component of a much larger worldview. Such pockets of millenarian eruptions manifested as episodes of political violence that in a brief moment in time and space were both heinous and perceptibly irrational. As a result, millenarianism became a significant source of political ideology that could justify the use of violence in the public sector in the search for complete justice and a better world.

Millenarianism provided sacred reinforcement and legitimacy to a specific vision of profound socioeconomic and political change. In addition, it provided its adherents with the tools to achieve such a vision because the symbols that surrounded the rituals associated with such beliefs were capable of inspiring powerful motivations for action. It engendered a strategic authorization for sociopolitical reaction to a pervasive sense of alienation within these cultures. As a result a powerful ideology was crafted—one that successfully merged the traditional millenarian "stream" that dominated the worldview of these societies with the material conditions that now surrounded them.

Millenarianism serves to structure sociopolitical thought as well as to structure sociopolitical action. It serves to establish a stage upon which a collective human sociopolitical identity can be framed. Indeed, the holders of such a temporal identity place themselves and their very nature at the integral center of such an identity. In this way, millenarianism establishes the foundations of collective identity that forces reaction to competitive (and perceptually superior) sociopolitical power arrangements that negate such an identity. Let's be clear here. The sociopolitical identity preexists. It must. Nonetheless, the millennial myth provides it with strength, durability, and the capacity for reaction to alienating forces. It engenders a strategic authorization for sociopolitical reaction to a pervasive sense of alienation within a culture.

Millenarianism serves to significantly validate a culture in their own regional power and protect an important symbolic form of their unity as a psychologically meaningful and identifiable social group.

A durable and persistent historical stream of structurally pervasive millenarian expectations can evolve into a significant political ideology that, in turn, becomes an important device of cultural organization. Such an ideology plays a significant role in the process of group identity formation. It helps to establish a group's distinctiveness and special meaning through myths of both origins and the end times, and reinforces claims to superiority and moral exclusivity. As a result it acts as a mediating device among alienation, group identity, and political violence.

Conclusions

This study represents a cross-cultural analysis of three non-Western communities that experienced notable episodes of political violence in the late twentieth century. Within each community a defined movement emerged that challenged the status quo within the society. The ideology of each of these movements was profoundly millenarian in form and content.

Beginning as early as the sixteenth century, all three of these societies were affected in one way or another by forces of cultural, economic, and political imperialism. Such intervention was dramatically augmented beginning in the nineteenth century. Eventually, all three communities could no longer escape the process of Western-style modernization and the powerful ideas that accompany it. Such ideas were perceived of as explicitly foreign. Their intervention was significantly disruptive to traditional ways of life in each of these communities. Indeed, the modern state that now exists in each of these cases is styled on Western models. Such a process was not voluntary, but, rather, forced upon these peoples by a conquering culture that was perceived of as superior.

The consequences of this foreign intervention were catastrophic. Many people in these communities came to see their old way of life and its traditional cultural system as no longer workable, out-of-date, and apparently worthless in the presence of more powerful forces of modernization forced into these cultures by Western power. The assault on their community by a perceptibly better ethnic group, flaunting all manner of materialism, greater affluence, and more powerful military might, was seen as a considerable, authentic, dangerous, and corrupting threat to their long-held cultural traditions. They could not identify with what was now seemingly pervading their life. In particular, they could not accept new conceptualizations of what was sacred.

The conquering culture was quickly perceived as the source of all evil and problems that now existed within their community: discrimination on the basis of race, relative deprivation, injustice, and oppression.

In each of these cases, the resolution of conflicts arising out of the difficulties associated with intercultural contact was pursued through the unique vernacular of the cognitive maps of these societies. In all three cases, a distinctive component of this cognitive map is a millenarian stream of faith: the belief that a Messiah or Savior figure will someday return and lead their society into a Golden Age.

The experiences in these three cases demonstrate that a direct relationship exists between intercultural contact and the emergence of millenarian movements, either passive or violent. Intercultural contact exacerbates a preexisting dichotomized perspective of all things in life: "light" versus "dark," "good" versus "evil," "god" and "anti-god."

Millenarianism acts as an agent of countervailing force in such conditions. It sets in motion the idea that the community, in fact, cannot be conquered or destroyed but, rather, must be renewed. Such renewal will come about through the intervention of cosmic forces.

Renewal of the community was seen as possible only through a rigid conformity to clear rules that traced their roots to the origins of society. It was perceived that adherence to these rules represented a powerful defense of society against the difficulties, oppression, and injustice that it now faced. Eventually they would be overcome and a new era of extraordinary happiness, peace, and harmony could be allowed to begin.

Eruptions of apocalyptic expectations in response to intercultural conflict in these three cases were marked by a striking similarity in the use of violence. Such actions were seen to possess a sacred justification in defense of traditional life. In each case, millenarian terrorists demonstrated a powerful belief in a world that must be destroyed in order to achieve their ultimate goals. This belief defines the character of both the participants and the organization. They are carrying out God's will.

Intercultural contact—social disturbance—indignation and a sense of injustice—alienation—apocalyptic beliefs: this sequence of events created a community bubbling with cosmic expectations about their future, fully congruent with a durable and pervasive millenarian component of their cultural worldview. Many members of society yearned for the time when a seemingly divinely guided figure would emerge. This was not simply a longing; it was genuinely expected to occur.

Millenarianism establishes the prospect that present difficulties can be transcended through the intervention of a cosmic and healing force. It provides the community with a clear ideology of progress, the end point of which is a liberated society, free from pain, alienation, oppression, injustice, racism, and want. The symbols that surround the rituals associated with millenarian beliefs are capable of inspiring powerful motivations for action, even if such action requires violence.

Millenarian leaders possess an exceptional compassion for understanding current conditions within a society. They have the ability to unravel sociopolitical disturbance and quickly come to understand how present conditions impact the needs of the community as a whole.

Millenarian leaders mold a sweeping prescription for sociopolitical renewal in response to these conditions. They express that prescription in a culturally defined language that appears to the community to be exclusively for them and resonates with their cultural expectations and aspirations.

In each of these three cases, millenarian leaders possessed no extraordinary characteristics or special skills. Instead, the active variable in their appeal was the condition of their audience.

In all three cases, movement leadership took the form of a millenarian-inspired prophet who came to define his role as that of the shaper, articulator, and director of a new political program. Such a program was poorly defined and boundless; nonetheless, it appealed to the expectations and aspirations of movement followers.

The origins of all three leaders varied. Abimael Guzman, a Criollo, was nonetheless capable of leading a primarily indigenous political movement. Musa al-Sadr, a Persian by birth, and thus non-Arab, was capable of leading the Arab Shi'a community of south Lebanon. Asahara Shoko was the only one of the three whose ethnic background was fully consistent with group membership at large.

The socioeconomic and educational backgrounds of the leaders also varied dramatically. On the one hand, Guzman and al-Sadr grew up in upper-middle-class surroundings and provided the opportunity to gain a formal education that prepared them well for their work to come. On the other hand, Asahara was raised in poverty. In addition, because of his disabilities, he was prevented from pursuing education beyond the secondary level.

The forum or platform utilized by each of these leaders to launch, promote, and fully develop the movements also varied. Guzman shrewdly utilized his position as a university professor to his advantage politically. Asahara utilized the venue of yoga, enhanced spiritual enlightenment, and the power of seemingly curative medicines to foster his messianic appeal and nurture a new religion. Al-Sadr was able to effectively utilize an explicitly Shi'a religious forum to promote his call for action and renewal.

The messianic aura that came to surround each of these leaders was a critical component of the movement. Guzman was perceived as the "Father of a New Age in Peru," the savior of the people, "Doctor Puka inti- the Red Sun." Asahara was seen as a modern guru of healing, "today's Christ," and "Savior of the Century." And, al-Sadr, particularly following his strange and unexplained disappearance, led to a revised, modern version of the occultation of the hidden Imam, the central character in the Shi'ite messianic cognitive map. In addition, he was effectively connected to the sacrifice and martyrdom of Imam Husayn.

In all three cases, these movements performed a religious-like function for their adherents. The inevitability of change was widely accepted and critical to action by the movement. The outcome, arising out of the catastrophic imposition of a foreign cultural paradigm disguised as modernization, was considered to be certain. And, the change that the movement would engender was expected to be total and complete social salvation.

Faith in an impending, divinely guided intervention—one that will rescue the community from conditions of oppression, injustice, despair, and hopelessness—holds a powerful healing capability.

In the presence of a powerful, conquering culture, societies become alienated. Traditional ways begin to be seen as both useless and outmoded. One's sense of self within the community is challenged and things simply don't work like they used to. Worse than that, life seems increasingly "foreign," "corrupt," and no longer of "genuine" meaning.

In response, this alienation breeds discontent and a profound sense of powerlessness. Millenarianism provides groups with the opportunity to reintegrate themselves in a society impinged upon by disturbing and corrupting forces. The ideas of reintegration, reinterpretation, and renewal are powerful. First, they establish the possibility of an idealized state of affairs. Second, they provide a call for action. Finally, such ideas promote the mobilization of resources to achieve their goals through whatever means necessary. Not only does millenarianism provide sacred justification for political violence, but, also, it elevates those who carry out such acts to an exalted, transcendental position.

In this way, millenarianism allows the community to "break through" conventional sociopolitical norms in pursuit of a pristine world liberated from corruption, indignation, and alienation.

All humans require an identity and these are formed in many different ways. While each is important, some identities possess more salience than others.

In each of these cases, millenarianism established the foundations of collective identity that forced reaction to competitive (and perceptually superior) sociopolitical arrangements that had eroded and ultimately negated traditional identity. Millenarianism played a significant role in sustaining group identity and provided a device for cultural organization.

Millenarianism served to establish a stage upon which a collective human sociopolitical identity can be framed. Indeed, the holders of such a temporal identity place themselves and their very nature at the integral center of such an identity. In this way, millenarianism establishes the foundations of collective identity that forces reaction to competitive sociopolitical power arrangements that negate such an identity.

In all three cases, outbreaks of powerful millenarian expectations arose as an unambiguous resolution to the miseries associated with social, cultural, and economic disruption. Through the use of traditional images of sacred redemption a remedy was forthcoming that temporal devices seemed powerless to repair. The savior appears as an immediate and unequivocal reaction to the cravings of the people for a restoration of their traditional ways, which have now been reformed into an image of paradise on earth.

Millenarianism functioned as a mitigating factor in the capacity of the peoples of these societies (1) to cope with the disastrous consequences of an impingement upon their traditional way of life by projecting their problems onto a broader screen that helped them to clarify and objectify their social issues; (2) reduce the resultant dislocation and alienation; and (3) to thoroughly purge and cleanse themselves in an effective act of mass catharsis.

Millenarian terrorists utilize violence in a perceived sacred cause. The cause is personally created from a worldview that allows the adherent to make sense of life and death by linking him or her to some form of immortality. This is required if one is to make sense of life and achieve some degree of transcendental satisfaction—an innate human need.

Millenarian terrorists are fanatics, which is not to imply that they are mentally disturbed or psychopathological. Rather, they are extraordinarily and exclusively focused on and committed to their political cause and are willing to exert enormous energy in its achievement. Although they possess a firm loyalty to the conventions of stable and orderly daily life within their society and are obliged to ensure their longevity, under certain conditions of disorientation, disharmony, and/or foreign impingement that threatens the institutions and norms of their way of life, they are driven to invoke traditional images of cultural salience.

Violence comes to be seen as a tool for abolishing the old and accelerating the new. Nonetheless, in each of these cases the resources to actually affect substantive change were scarce. Out of desperation, yet imbued with a sacred sense of destiny, they resorted to the use of an instrument that could render the anticipated denouement: terrorism.

Notes

Introduction

1. W. Scott Morton, *Japan*, 3rd ed. (New York: McGraw-Hill, 1994), 12.
2. Raymond Hammer, *Japan's Religious Ferment* (New York: Oxford University Press, 1962), 34.
3. Sabine MacCormack, *Religion in the Andes: Vision and Imagination in Early Colonial Peru* (Princeton, NJ: Princeton University Press, 1991), 102–103.
4. See Susan Naquin, *Millenarian Rebellion in China: The Eight Trigrams Uprisings of 1813* (New Haven: Yale University Press, 1976) and Jonathan Spence, *God's Chinese Son: The Taiping Heavenly Kingdom of Hong Xiuquan* (New York: W.W. Norton, 1996).
5. Norman Cohn, *Cosmos, Chaos and the World to Come: The Ancient Roots of Apocalyptic Faith* (New Haven, CT: Yale University Press, 1993).
6. See Bernard McGinn, *Antichrist: Two Thousand Years of the Human Fascination with Evil* (New York: HarperCollins, 1994), 10–16, on the origins of Jewish apocalyptic literature.
7. Vittorio Lanternari, *The Religions of the Oppressed: A Study of Modern Messianic Cults* (New York: Mentor Books, 1965).
8. Revelation 20:4–6.
9. Abdulaziz Abdulhessein Sachedina, *Islamic Messianism: The Idea of the Mahdi in Twelver Shi'ism* (Albany: State University of New York Press, 1981).
10. Revelation 20:4–6.
11. See Norman Cohn, *The Pursuit of the Millennium: Revolutionary Millenarians and Mystical Anarchists of the Middle Ages*, 3rd ed. (New York: Oxford University Press, 1970); Michael Barkun, *Disaster and the Millennium* (New Haven: Yale University Press, 1974); James F. Rinehart, *Revolution and the Millennium: China, Mexico, and Iran* (Westport, CT: Praeger, 1997).
12. For an investigation of outbreaks of millenarian expectations in Africa, see Guenther Lewy, *Religion and Revolution* (New York: Oxford University Press, 1974); Lanternari, *The Religions of the Oppressed*; T. O. Ranger, "Connexions between Primary Resistance Movements and Modern Mass Nationalism in East and Central Africa," *Journal of African History*, Vol. 9 (1968), 437–453. In Asia, see Michael Adas,

Prophets of Rebellion: Millenarian Protests against the European Colonial Order (Chapel Hill: University of North Carolina Press, 1979); Carmen Blacker, "Millenarian Aspects of the New Religions in Japan," in Donald H. Shively, ed., *Tradition and Modernization in Japanese Culture* (Princeton: Princeton University Press, 1971); Spence, *God's Chinese Son.* In Melanesia, see Peter Worsley, *The Trumpet Shall Sound: A Study of "Cargo Cults" in Melanesia*, 2nd ed. (New York: Schocken, 1968); F. E. Williams, *The Vailala Madness and Other Essays*, ed. Eric Schwimmer (Honolulu: The University of Hawaii Press, 1977). In the Americas, see Victoria Reifler Bricker, *The Indian Christ, the Indian King: The Historical Substrate of Maya Myth and Ritual* (Austin: University of Texas Press, 1981); Enrique Florescano, *Memory Myth, and Time in Mexico: From Aztecs to Independence*, trans. Albert G. Bork with the assistance of Kathryn R. Bork (Austin: University of Texas Press, 1994); Jacques Lafaye, *Quetzalcoatl and Guadalupe: The Formation of Mexican National Consciousness, 1531–1815* (Chicago: University of Chicago Press, 1976); James Mooney, *The Ghost Dance Religion and the Sioux Oubreak of 1890*, abridged by Anthony F. C. Wallace (1896; reprint Chicago: University of Chicago Press, 1965); Scott Peterson, *Native American Prophecies* (New York: Paragon, 1990); Robert Wasserstrom, *Class and Society in Central Chiapas* (Berkeley: University of California Press, 1983).

13. See Lanternari, *The Religions of the Oppressed.*
14. Cohn, *Pursuit of the Millennium.* 15–16; Rinehart, *Revolution and the Millennium*, 3.
15. Examples of this self-destructing character of many millenarian movements abound in numerous sensational cases: e.g., Heaven's Gate, The People's Temple led by Jim Jones, the Solar Temple, and the Branch Davidians in the 1993 tragedy.
16. Clark R. McCauley and Mary E. Segal, "Social Psychology of Terrorist Groups," in Clyde Hendrick, ed., *Group Processes and Intergroup Relations: Volume 9, Review of Personality and Social Psychology* (Newbury Park, CA: Sage Publications, 1987), 232.
17. David W. Brannan, Philip F. Esler, and N. T. Anders Strindberg, "Talking to 'Terrorists': Towards an Independent Analytical Framework for the Study of Violent Substate Activism," *Studies in Conflict & Terrorism*, Vol. 24 (2001), 3–24.
18. See, as an example, Benjamin Netanyahu, *Fighting Terrorism: How Democracies Can Defeat Domestic and International Terrorists* (New York: Farrar Straus Giroux, 1995).
19. See Elliott Aronson, *The Social Animal*, 8th ed. (New York: W. H. Freeman, 1999).
20. Khalid Duran, "Middle Eastern Terrorism: Its Characteristics and Driving Forces," in Lawrence Howard, ed., *Terrorism: Roots, Impact, and Responses* (New York: Praeger, 1992).

21. In a comprehensive poll of residents of predominately Muslim countries conducted by the Gallup organization in December 2001 and January 2002, 53% of the respondents had an unfavorable opinion of the United States. Most said that they thought that the United States was "aggressive" and "biased" against Islamic values and described it as "ruthless and arrogant" in its foreign policy. Indeed, 15% of the respondents said that the 9/11 attacks were "morally justified." The poll surveyed a total of 9,924 residents of Pakistan, Iran, Indonesia, Turkey, Lebanon, Morocco, Kuwait, Jordan, and Saudi Arabia. See, "Poll: Muslims Call U.S. 'Ruthless, Arrogant,' " available at www.cnn.com/2002/US/02/26/gallup.muslims.
22. "Pakistani Officials Question Two Top al-Qaeda Operatives," Transcript of *CNN Sunday Morning*, aired September 15, 2002, 7:34 a.m. ET.
23. Luigi Bonanate has argued that the term terrorism represents a unique convergence of linguistics and political analysis that creates a "fundamental ambiguity." "In [terrorism] the descriptive and the prescriptive aspects merge inextricably, so that in describing as 'terrorist' the behavior of a certain political group, an evaluation is at the same time suggested; reciprocally when an action is considered 'terrorist,' it is presumed that its structure has also been described." See Luigi Bonanate, "Some Unanticipated Consequences of Terrorism," *Journal of Peace Research*, Vol. 16, No. 3 (1979), 197.
24. Jeanne N. Knutson, "Social and Psychodynamic Pressures toward a Negative Identity: The Case of and American Revolutionary Terrorist," in Yonah Alexander and John M. Gleason, eds., *Behavioral and Quantitative Perspectives on Terrorism* (New York: Pergamon Press, 1981), 105.
25. Indeed, Hyams argues that "many governments make use of preventive terrorism in order to maintain themselves in power despite the will of a majority, or a large minority, of their citizens." See Edward Hyams, *Terrorists and Terrorism* (New York: St. Martin's, 1974), 9.
26. For example, in a comprehensive, 90-page report on terrorist threats to the United States in the aftermath of 9/11, prepared by the National Institute of Public Policy, only one paragraph was devoted to the role of apocalyptic or millenarian variables in the origins and processes of terrorist movements. See Steven Lambakis, James Kiras, and Kristin Kolet, *Understanding "Asymmetric" Threats to the United States* (Fairfax, VA: National Institute for Public Policy, September 2002).

Chapter 1 Terrorism and Prophecy

1. Richard M. Pearlstein, *The Mind of the Political Terrorist* (Wilmington, DE: SR Books, 1991), 1.
2. R. Thackrah, "Terrorism: A Definitional Problem," in Paul Wilkinson and Alasdair M. Stewart, eds., *Contemporary Research on Terrorism* (Aberdeen: Aberdeen University Press, 1987), 24.

3. See Resolution E, *Final Act of the United Nations' Diplomatic Conference of Plenipotentiaries on the Establishment of an International Criminal Court*, UN Doc. A/Conf. 18/10, July 17, 1998, available at www.un.org. This document states: "regretting that no generally acceptable definition of the crimes of terrorism and drug crimes could be agreed upon for the inclusion within the jurisdiction of the court . . ."
4. David C. Rapoport, "Fear and Trembling: Terrorism in Three Religious Traditions," *The American Political Science Review*, Vol. 78, No. 3 (September 1984), 658–677.
5. As examples, Prime Minister Aldo Moro was kidnapped and assassinated by the Red Brigade in the spring of 1978 and Egyptian president Anwar Sadat was shot and killed by al-Jihad gunmen during a military parade on October 6, 1981.
6. For example, the United Nations General Assembly, despite the fact that it has made serious attempts at doing so, has failed to agree on a definition of international terrorism. Abraham Sofaer, "Terrorism and International Law," *Foreign Affairs*, Vol. 64, No. 5 (Summer 1986), 901–922. See also, Harris O. Schoenberg, *A Mandate for Terror: The United Nations and the PLO* (New York: Shapolsky Book, 1989) and Frederick J. Hacker, *Crusaders, Criminals, Crazies: Terror and Terrorism in Our Time* (New York: W.W. Norton, 1976).
7. A similar and more comprehensive content analysis has been conducted by Schmid, Jongman, et al., in which frequencies of definitional elements in 109 definitions of terrorism were analyzed. As one might predict the most common element was "violence, force" identified in 83.5% of definitions, followed by "(psychological) effects and (anticipated) reactions," in 41.5%, "victim-target differentiation" in 37.5%, "method of combat, strategy, tactic" in 30.5%. In the end, such analyses demonstrate the remarkable lack of consistency in defining terrorism. See Alex P. Schmid, Albert J. Jongman, et al., *Political Terrorism: A New Guide to Actors, Authors, Concepts, Data Bases, Theories, and Literature* (New Brunswick: Transaction Books, 1988), 5–6.
8. Thackrah, "Terrorism: A Definitional Problem," 24.
9. Ibid., 26.
10. Ibid., 25. Thackrah refers here to Walter Laqueur, "Terrorism—A Balance Sheet," *Harper's Magazine*, March and November 1976, reprinted in Walter Laqueur, *The Terrorism Reader* (Philadelphia: Temple University Press, 1978).
11. Thackrah, "Terrorism: A Definitional Problem," 26.
12. Bruce Hoffman, *Inside Terrorism* (London: Victor Gollancz, 1998), 14–15.
13. Thackrah, "Terrorism: A Definitional Problem," 30–31.
14. Ibid., 32.
15. This should be differentiated from the categorizations of Hyams, who defines Direct Terrorism as "terrorism against members of the

government" and Indirect Terrorism as "terrorism directed indiscriminately against the government's constituents so as to destroy their confidence in that government." See Hyams, *Terrorists and Terrorism*, 9–10.

16. Thackrah, "Terrorism: A Definitional Problem," 32.
17. Ibid., 232.
18. Quoted in Lynne Lamberg, "Psychiatrist Explores Apocalyptic Violence in Heaven's Gate and Aum Shinrikyo Cults," *Journal of the American Medical Association*, Vol. 278, No. 3 (1997), 191–193.
19. One of the classic examples of this is found in Gustave LeBon, *The Crowd: A Study of the Popular Mind* (1896; reprint Whitefish, MT: Kessinger Publishing, 2003).
20. See, Stanley Williams Moore, *Marx on the Choice between Socialism and Communism* (Cambridge, MA: Harvard University Press, 1980).
21. See Hal Draper, *Karl Marx's Theory of Revolution: The State and Bureaucracy* (New York: Monthly Review Press, 1979).
22. See Emile Durkheim, *The Division of Labor in Society*, trans. George Simpson (1893; reprint New York: Macmillan, 1933) and LeBon, *The Crowd.*
23. Charles Tilly, *From Mobilization to Revolution* (Reading, MA: Addison-Wesley, 1978).
24. Martha Crenshaw, "Thoughts on Relating Terrorism to Historical Contexts," in Crenshaw, ed., *Terrorism in Context* (University Park, PA: The Pennsylvania State University Press, 1995), 3–4.
25. Martha Crenshaw, "The Logic of Terrorism: Terrorist Behavior as a Product of Strategic Choice," in Walter Reich, ed., *Origins of Terrorism: Psychologies, Ideologies, Theologies, States of Mind* (Cambridge: Cambridge University Press, 1990), 10–11.
26. Martin A. Miller, "The Intellectual Origins of Modern Terrorism in Europe," in Crenshaw, *Terrorism in Context*, 62.
27. Martha Crenshaw, "Questions to Be Answered, Research to Be Done, Knowledge to Be Applied," in Reich, *Origins of Terrorism*, 250.
28. Martha Crenshaw, "The Causes of Terrorism," *Comparative Politics*, Vol. 13, No. 4 (1981), 390.
29. Donatella della Porta, "Left Wing Terrorism in Italy," in Crenshaw, *Terrorism in Context*, 154–157.
30. Crenshaw, "Thoughts on Relating Terrorism to Historical Contexts," 6.
31. For an example, see Joseph Margolin, "Psychological Perspectives in Terrorism," in Yonah Alexander and Seymour Maxwell Finger, eds., *Terrorism: Interdisciplinary Perspectives* (New York: John Jay, 1977), 270–282.
32. Ted Robert Gurr, *Why Men Rebel* (Princeton: Princeton University Press, 1970).
33. Maxwell Taylor, *The Fanatics: A Behavioural Approach to Political Violence* (London: Brassey's, 1991).
34. Margolin, "Psychological Perspectives in Terrorism," 273–274.
35. Gurr, *Why Men Rebel*, 24.

36. See David E. Long, *The Anatomy of Terrorism* (New York: Free Press, 1990). He argues that if you "ask any audience" about terrorist behavior the overwhelming sentiment will characterize the terrorist as "crazy." See also Margolin, "Psychological Perspectives in Terrorism," 272, on the pervasive nature of this idea.
37. Jerrold M. Post, "Terrorist Psycho-Logic: Terrorist Behavior as a Product of Psychological Forces," in Reich, *Origins of Terrorism*, 25.
38. Ken Heskin, "The Psychology of Terrorism in Ireland," in Yonah Alexander and Alan O'Day, eds., *Terrorism in Ireland* (New York: St. Martin's, 1984), 88–105. For similar conclusions, see McCauley and Segal, "Social Psychology of Terrorist Groups"; Maxwell Taylor and Ethel Quayle, *Terrorist Lives* (London: Brassey's, 1994).
39. Ruth Elliott and William H. Lockhart, "Characteristics of Scheduled Offenders and Juvenile Delinquents," in Jeremy and Joan Harbison, eds., *A Society in Stress: Children and Young People in Northern Ireland* (London: Open Books, 1980), 90–99.
40. Taylor, *The Fanatics*, 33–34.
41. Ibid., 47.
42. Long, *The Anatomy of Terrorism*, 16.
43. David Rapoport defines terrorism as "extranormal or extramoral violence, a type which goes beyond the conventions or boundaries particular societies establish to regulate coercion. Such conventions identify justifications, establish limits and immunities and through these conventions one is able to distinguish between the appropriate and inappropriate social responses to criminal as opposed to belligerent activities." See David Rapoport, "Why Does Religious Messianism Produce Terror?" in Paul Wilkinson and Alasdair M Stewart, eds., *Contemporary Research on Terrorism* (Aberdeen: Aberdeen University Press, 1987), 73.
44. Martha Crenshaw, "How Terrorists Think: What Psychology Can Contribute to Understanding Terrorism," in Howard, *Terrorism*, 71–80.
45. Cohn, *Pursuit of the Millennium*, 21. This paradigm, he asserts, "is the most significant antecedent of the legacy of attraction to millenarianism in the modern world."
46. Ibid., chapter 2: "The Tradition of Religious Dissent," 37–52. See also, McGinn, *Antichrist*, 185.
47. Cohn, *Pursuit of the Millennium*, 70. For additional interpretations of millenarian speculation and its functional role in the late Middle Ages and early modern period, see also Marjorie Reeves, *The Influence of Prophecy in the Later Middle Ages: A Study of Joachimism* (Oxford: Clarendon Press, 1969); Bernard McGinn, *Visions of the End: Apocalyptic Traditions in the Middle Ages* (New York: Columbia University Press, 1979); Howard Kaminsky, *A History of the Hussite Revolution* (Berkeley: University of California Press, 1967); and F. C. Heyman, *John Zizka and the Hussite Revolution* (Princeton: Princeton University Press, 1955).

48. Cohn, *Pursuit of the Millennium*, 53.
49. Ibid., 16, 40, 110, 158, 224. A notable and not inconsequential exception to this may be found in the "Franciscan Spirituals," who thrived in thirteenth-century Italy.
50. Ibid., 59–60.
51. Ibid., 64.
52. Peter A. Lupsha, "Explanations of Political Violence: Some Psychological Theories versus Indignation," *Politics and Society*, Vol. 2 (1971), 89–104.
53. Ibid., 96.
54. Ibid., 102–105. "The concept of indignation is linked directly to the cultural-philosophical underpinnings of society . . . and, for that reason, [it] seems particularly appropriate for explaining violence, as its logic locates it in that intersection of the psychological and the ethical where ideas of rightness and legitimacy originate" (102).
55. Adas, *Prophets of Rebellion.*
56. Eric J. Hobsbawm, *Primitive Rebels: Studies in Archaic Forms of Social Movement in the 19th and 20th Centuries* (New York: Praeger, 1963).
57. Barkun, *Disaster and the Millennium*, 1974.
58. Samuel Huntington, "The Clash of Civilizations?" *Foreign Affairs*, Vol. 72, No. 3 (1993).
59. See Walter Laqueur, "Postmodern Terrorism," *Foreign Affairs*, Vol. 75, No. 5 (September/October 1996). He asserts that "the past few decades have witnessed the birth of dozens of aggressive movements espousing varieties of nationalism, religious fundamentalism, fascism, and apocalyptic millenarianism . . . Extremist millenarians would like to give history a push, helping to create world-ending havoc replete with universal war, famine, pestilence, and other scourges . . . Those who subscribe to such beliefs number in the hundreds of thousands and perhaps millions."
60. James Gilligan, *Violence* (New York: Vintage, 1996), 11.
61. See J. F. C. Fuller, *Military History of the Western World, Vol. 1: From the Earliest Times to the Battle of Lopanto* (New York: De Capo Press, 1954); Steve Runciman, *A History of the Crusades* (1951; reprint, Cambridge: Cambridge University Press, 1995).
62. Marc Galanter, *Cults, Faith, Healing, and Coercion* (New York: Oxford University Press, 1989), 119–124.
63. Eugene V. Gallagher, " 'Theology Is Life and Death': David Koresh on Violence, Persecution, and the Millennium," in Catherine Wessinger, ed., *Millennialism, Persecution, and Violence: Historical Cases* (Syracuse: Syracuse University Press, 2000), 82–100.
64. Catherine Wessinger, *How the Millennium Comes Violently: From Jonestown to Heaven's Gate* (New York: Seven Bridges Press, 2000).
65. Clark R. McCauley, "The Psychology of Terrorism," *Social Science Research Council Essay Series*, available at www.ssrc.org/sept11/essays/mccauley.htm. See also, Erich Fromm, *The Sane Society* (New York: Henry Holt, 1955), 36–38.

66. W. W. Meisner, *Thy Kingdom Come: Psychoanalytic Perspectives on the Messiah and the Millennium* (Kansas City: Sheed & Ward, 1995), 242–243.
67. David Garfield and Leston Havens, "Paranoid Phenomena and Pathological Narcissim," *American Journal of Psychotherapy*, Vol. 45, No. 2 (1991), 160.
68. Roderick M. Kramer, "Paranoid Cognition in Social Systems: Thinking and Acting in the Shadow of Doubt," *Personality and Social Psychology Review*, Vol. 2, No. 4 (1998), 253.
69. Ibid., 254.
70. For example, in the 1960s, historian Richard Hofstadter identified a "Paranoid Style in American Politics," as a descriptor for an increasing number on the radical Right who believed that there existed a large, sinister, and effective "international conspiratorial network designed to perpetrate acts of the most fiendish character" against the United States. More specifically, Hofstadter sought to draw attention to those factors that fed the McCarthy Era and the Cold War. He concluded that the behavior of this large, politically active group exhibited a pervasive sense of anxiety manifested in feelings of persecution and was "overheated, oversuspicious, overaggressive, grandiose and apocalyptic." See, Richard Hofstadter, *The Paranoid Style of American Politics and Other Essays* (New York: Alfred A. Knopf, 1965). For a more recent study of the phenomenon, see Michael Barkun, *A Culture of Conspiracy: Apocalyptic Vision in Contemporary America* (Berkeley: University of California Press, 2003).
71. Anthony F. C. Wallace, "Revitalization Movements," *American Anthropologist*, Vol. 58 (1956), 626. See also, Anthony F. C. Wallace, *The Death and Rebirth of the Seneca* (New York: Vintage, 1972) and Joel W. Martin, *Sacred Revolt: The Muskogees' Struggle for a New World* (Boston: Beacon Press, 1991).
72. Rapoport, "Why Does Religious Messianism Produce Terror?" 84–85.
73. Taylor, *The Fanatics*, 82.
74. Nehemia Friedland, "Becoming a Terrorist: Social and Individual Antecedents," in Howard, *Terrorism*, 86.
75. Peter Du Preez, *The Politics of Identity: Ideology and the Human Image* (Oxford: Basil Blackwell, 1980), 45–46.

Chapter 2 The Rise of Millenarian Terror

1. Laszlo, Ervin, Robert Artigiani, Allan Combs, and Vilmos Csanyi, *Changing Visions-Human Cognitive Maps: Past, Present, and Future* (Westport, CT: Praeger, 1996), 61.
2. Wallace, "Revitalization Movements," 265.
3. Laszlo et al., *Changing Visions*, 63.
4. Ibid., 59.

5. Rodney Stark, "A Theory of Revelations," *Journal for the Scientific Study of Religion*, Vol. 38, No. 2 (June 1999), 293.
6. Ibid., 294. He argues, "many common, ordinary, even mundane mental phenomena can be experienced as contact with the divine."
7. Anthony F. C. Wallace characterized millenarianism as a form of revitalization movement "defined as a deliberate, organized, conscious effort by members of society to construct a more satisfying culture"; "Revitalization Movements," 265.
8. Steve J. Stern, *Peru's Indian Peoples and the Challenge of the Spanish Conquest: Huamanga to 1640*, 2nd ed. (Madison: University of Wisconsin Press, 1993), 13–14.
9. Francis X. Grollig, *Incaic and Modern Peru* (New Haven, CT: Human Area Files, 1979), 15.
10. Richard L. Burger, *Chavin and the Origins of Andean Civilization* (New York: Thames and Hudson, 1992), 195.
11. MacCormack, *Religion in the Andes*, 1991. See also, Stern, *Peru's Indian Peoples.*
12. Peter G. Roe, "The Josho Hahuanbo Are All Wet and Undercooked: Shipibo Views of the Whiteman and the Incas in Myth, Legend and History," in Jonathan D. Hill, ed., *Rethinking History and Myth: Indigenous South American Perspectives on the Past* (Urbana, IL: University of Illinois Press, 1988), 111.
13. Ibid., 112.
14. Ibid., 112.
15. Ibid., 128.
16. Bernabe Cobo, *Inca Religion and Customs*, trans. and ed. Roland Hamilton (Austin, TX: University of Texas Press, 1990), xvi.
17. Of course, the similarities of this millenarian myth to that of the Biblical account of Noah, the Great Flood, the destruction of evil, and world renewal are all unmistakable.
18. Constance Classen, *Inca Cosmology and the Human Body* (Salt Lake City: University of Utah Press, 1993), 26.
19. Nathan Wachtel, *The Vision of the Vanquished: The Spanish Conquest of Peru through Indian Eyes, 1530–1570*, trans. Ben and Sian Reynolds (New York: Barnes & Noble, 1977), 16.
20. Sarah Lund Skar, *Lives Together—Worlds Apart: Quechua Colonization in Jungle and City* (Oslo, Norway: Scandinavian University Press, 1994), 242.
21. Ibid., 242. See also, Peter F. Klaren, *Peru: Society and Nationhood in the Andes* (New York: Oxford University Press, 2000), 117.
22. Michael F. Brown, "Beyond Resistance: A Comparative Study of Utopian Renewal in Amazonia," *Ethnohistory*, Vol. 38, No. 4 (Fall 1991), 391. He cites Alfred Métraux, "Migrations historiques des Tupi-Guarani," *Journal de la Société des Américanistes de Paris*, n.s., Vol. 19 (1927), 1–45.

23. See Serge Gruzinski, *Man-Gods in the Mexican Highlands*, translated from the French by Eileen Corrigan (Stanford: Stanford University Press, 1989).
24. Brown, "Beyond Resistance," 392. He cites Héléne Clastres, *Terra Sem Mal: O profetismo Tupi-Guarani* (Sao Paulo: Brasiliense, 1978), 60.
25. Judith Shapiro, "From Tupa to the Land without Evil: The Christianization of Tupi-Guarani Cosmology," *American Ethnologist*, Vol. 14 (1987), 131.
26. Michael J. Sallnow, *Pilgrims of the Andes: Regional Cults in Cusco* (Washington, DC: Smithsonian Institution Press, 1987), 128.
27. Mary Dillon and Thomas Abercrombie, "The Destroying Christ: An Aymara Myth of Conquest," in Hill, *Rethinking History and Myth*, 50.
28. Simon Strong, *Shining Path: Terror and Revolution in Peru* (New York: Times Books, 1992), 38.
29. Ibid., 38. See also, José Carlos Mariategui, *Seven Interpretive Essays on Peruvian Reality*, trans. Marjory Urquidi (Austin: University of Texas Press, 1971), 125.
30. Strong, *Shining Path*, 39.
31. Stern, *Peru's Indian Peoples*, 51.
32. Wachtel, *The Vision of the Vanquished*, 179.
33. Stern, *Peru's Indian Peoples*, 51.
34. Klaren, *Peru*, 58. See also, Stern, *Peru's Indian Peoples*, 55.
35. Sallnow, *Pilgrims of the Andes*, 59.
36. Quoted in Klaren, *Peru*, 57.
37. Stern, *Peru's Indian Peoples*, 51–53.
38. Wachtel, *The Vision of the Vanquished*, 180.
39. Klaren, *Peru*, 58.
40. Strong, *Shining Path*, 39.
41. Wachtel, *The Vision of the Vanquished*, 183.
42. Stefano Varese, "The Ethnopolitics of Indian Resistance in Latin America," *Latin American Perspectives*, Vol. 23, No. 2 (Spring 1996), 58.
43. Strong, *Shining Path*, 4. See also Benjamin Keen and Mark Wasserman, *A History of Latin America*, 3rd ed. (Boston: Houghton Mifflin, 1988), 133.
44. See Richard Morse, "The Heritage of Latin America," in Louis Hartz, ed., *The Founding of New Societies: Studies in the History of the United States, Latin America, Canada, and Australia* (New York: Harcourt, Brace and World, 1964), 201–236.
45. Alberto Flores Galindo, "The Rebellion of Tupac Amaru," in Daniel Castro, ed., *Revolution and Revolutionaries: Guerilla Movements in Latin America* (Wilmington, DE: Scholarly Resources, 1999), 3–4.
46. Keen and Wasserman, *A History of Latin America*, 133. The quotas were increased from 15 loads per day out of the mines to 30 loads per day over this period.

47. Galindo, "The Rebellion of Tupac Amaru," 4. See also, Charles F. Walker, *Smoldering Ashes: Cuzco and the Creation of Republican Peru, 1780–1840* (Durham, NC: Duke University Press, 1999), 23. The alcabala, a sales tax paid on most goods traded by non-Indians, rose from 2% to 4% in 1772 and to 6% in 1776. More importantly, Visitor General José Antonio de Areche arrived in 1777 and "enforced the tax's vigorous collection."
48. There is some evidence that Juan Santos Atahualpa had traveled to both Europe and Africa. See Brown, "Beyond Resistance," 393 and Varese, "The Ethnopolitics of Indian Resistance in Latin America," 61.
49. A number of Black slaves lived in the mission settlements. Brown, "Beyond Resistance," 393.
50. Keen and Wasserman, *A History of Latin America*, 122–123.
51. Galindo, "The Rebellion of Tupac Amaru," 1.
52. Walker, *Smoldering Ashes*, 1.
53. Keen and Wasserman, *A History of Latin America*, 133–134.
54. Klaren, *Peru*, 116.
55. Alberto Flores Galindo, *Buscando un Inca*, 4th ed. (Lima: Editorial Horizonte, 1994), 106. Quoted in Walker, *Smoldering Ashes*, 25.
56. Walker, *Smoldering Ashes*, 20–25.
57. Klaren, *Peru*, 112.
58. Walker, *Smoldering Ashes*, 42; Klaren, *Peru*, 118.
59. Walker, *Smoldering Ashes*, 1. "Tupac Amaru was forced to watch the execution of his comrades and family members, including his wife and key confidante, Micaela Bastidas, whose tongue was cut out before she was strangled. Executioners then tortured José Gabriel at length and tied him to four horses to be quartered. When his limbs did not separate from his torso, he was beheaded. The arms, legs, and heads of José Gabriel and Micaela were displayed throughout the viceroyalty."
60. Quoted in David D. Gow, "The Roles of Christ and Inkarri in Andean Religion," *Journal of Latin American Lore*, Vol. 6 (1980), 283.
61. Brown, "Beyond Resistance," 394.
62. See Ted C. Lewellen, "Deviant Religion and Cultural Evolution: The Aymara Case," *Journal for the Scientific Study of Religion*, Vol. 18, No. 3 (1979), 243–251; Brown, "Beyond Resistance," 394; and John H. Bodley, "A Transformative Movement among the Campa of Eastern Peru," *Anthropos*, Vol. 67 (1972), 220–228.
63. Frederick Pike, *The Politics of the Miraculous in Peru: Haya de la Torre and the Spiritualist Tradition* (Lincoln: University of Nebraska Press, 1986), 14.
64. The population of Peru in 1920 was 4.828 million and in 1973 it was 14.628 million. Population Statistics, University of Utrecht, available at www.library.uu.nl/wesp/populstat/americas/peru.htm.
65. Strong, *Shining Path*, 47–48.
66. Pike, *The Politics of the Miraculous in Peru*, 16.

67. Fiona Wilson, "Indians and Mestizos: Identity and Urban Popular Culture in Andean Peru," *Journal of Southern African Studies*, Vol. 26, No. 2 (June 2000).
68. Strong, *Shining Path*, 51.
69. "Israelite Religion," available at http:/purace.unicauca.edu.co/balboa/israelitas.htm.
70. "The Illuminated One," Ilustracion Peruana Caretas, available at www.caretas.com.pe/1379/iluminado.htm.
71. Skar, *Lives Together*, 246.
72. Ibid., 247–248.
73. Brown, "Beyond Resistance," 394.
74. Ibid., 399. He cites Jaime Regan, "Mesianismo Cocama: Un movimiento de resistencia en la Amazonia Peruana," *América Indigena*, Vol. 48 (1988), 132. "The Cocama, many of whom have joined the movement, speak a Tupian language. Apparently various groups of Orden Cruzada pilgrims have set off in search of what they call the Tierra Santa, 'Holy Land,' a terrestrial paradise."
75. Deborah Poole and Gerardo Renique, *Peru: Time of Fear* (London: Latin America Bureau Ltd., 1992), 105–106.
76. Ibid., 106.
77. Mariategui, *Seven Interpretive Essays*, 164.
78. Ibid., 22.
79. According to Buddhist doctrine, the Maitreya "is believed to reside in the Tusita heaven, the fourth of six heavens in the world of desire, from which he will descend to the earth at the appropriate time in order to save living beings." Joseph M. Kitagawa, *On Understanding Japanese Religion* (Princeton: Princeton University Press, 1987), 233.
80. As early as the twelfth century, the concept of the *Mappo*, a Buddhist apocalyptic notion, was recorded in Japanese religion. It was considered to be a "dreadful era of decay and degeneration." Japanese emperors during the traditional period often encouraged a "heightened religious awakening among the common people" in anticipation of the *Mappo*. "The belief in *Mappo* provided a strong impetus to a Buddhist pietism which offered a new soteriological option to the Japanese religious universe. For example, the advocates of Pure Land Pietism, such as Honen (1133–1212) and Shinran (1173–1262), were persuaded that in the period of Mappo, those who believe in the saving power of Buddha Amida could gain rebirth in Amida's Pure Land." Ibid., 76.
81. Alan Sponberg and Helen Hardacre, eds., *Maitreya: The Future Buddha* (Cambridge: Cambridge University Press, 1988).
82. H. Neill McFarland, *The Rush Hour of the Gods: A Study of New Religious Movements in Japan* (New York: Macmillan, 1967), 179.
83. Emily Groszos Ooms, *Women and Millenarian Protest in Meiji Japan: Deguchi Nao and Omotokyo* (Ithaca, NY: Cornell University Press East Asia Program, 1993), 80.

84. Royall Tyler, "The Tokugawa Peace and Popular Religion: Suzuki Shosan, Kakugyo Tobutsu, and Jikigyo Miroku," in Peter Nosco, ed., *Confucianism and Tokugawa Culture* (Princeton: Princeton University Press, 1984), 92–119.
85. McFarland, *The Rush Hour of the Gods*, 29.
86. Ooms, *Women and Millenarian Protest in Meiji Japan*, 81.
87. McFarland, *The Rush Hour of the Gods*, 11.
88. Hugh Borton, "Peasant Uprisings in Japan of the Tokugawa Period," *The Transactions of the Asiatic Society of Japan*, Vol. 16 (1938), 39.
89. McFarland, *The Rush Hour of the Gods*, 57.
90. Ibid.
91. Irwin Scheiner, "The Mindful Peasant: Sketches for a Study of Rebellion," *The Journal of Asian Studies*, Vol. 32, No. 4 (August 1973), 584–587.
92. McFarland, *The Rush Hour of the Gods*, 11.
93. Shibusawa Keizo, ed., *Japanese Life and Culture in the Meiji Era*, trans. Charles S. Terry, Centenary Culture Council Series, Vol. 5 (Tokyo: Obunsha, 1958), 325.
94. McFarland, *The Rush Hour of the Gods*, 11–12.
95. Ibid., 12.
96. Blacker, "Millenarian Aspects of the New Religions in Japan," 574–575. To relieve pain and aid the afflicted, it was not uncommon for an early-nineteenth-century Japanese family to call in a *yamabushi* or spiritual healer to "recite spells over the patient" so that he or she would gain some relief. In the case of Miki and her son, the yamabushi that was hired employed the reciting of a series of "sutras and mantras designed to force the malevolent spirit causing the sickness to leave the patient and enter into a medium, through whose mouth it would announce its identity and its reason for molesting its patient."
97. Ibid., 575.
98. McFarland, *The Rush Hour of the Gods*, 58.
99. Blacker, "Millenarian Aspects of the New Religions in Japan," 584. See also, Patrick Smith, *Japan: A Reinterpretation* (New York: Vintage, 1997), 82.
100. Blacker, "Millenarian Aspects of the New Religions in Japan," 585.
101. Ibid., 577.
102. Yamashita Akiko, "The 'Eschatology' of Japanese New and New New Religions From Tenri-kyo to Kofuku no Kagaku," *Inter-Religio*, Bulletin No. 33 (Summer 1998), 8.
103. Quoted in Blacker, "Millenarian Aspects of the New Religions in Japan," 578.
104. McFarland, *The Rush Hour of the Gods*, 60.
105. Ibid., 61.
106. Blacker, "Millenarian Aspects of the New Religions in Japan," 579–580.

107. McFarland, *The Rush Hour of the Gods*, 64–65.
108. D. W. Brackett, *Holy Terror: Armageddon in Tokyo* (New York: Weatherhill, 1996), 51.
109. Blacker, "Millenarian Aspects of the New Religions in Japan," 585 and 596.
110. McFarland, *The Rush Hour of the Gods*, 42.
111. David E. Kaplan and Andrew Marshall, *The Cult at the End of the World* (New York: Crown Publishers, 1996), 10.
112. Mark R. Mullins, "Ideology and Utopianism in Wartime Japan: An Essay on the Subversiveness of Christian Eschatology," *Japanese Journal of Religious Studies*, Vol. 21 (1994).
113. Blacker, "Millenarian Aspects of the New Religions in Japan," 567–568. The "Religious Bodies Law" of 1945 allowed a "religious body" to exist in an attempt to encourage freedom of religion in Japan. Similar to American laws, these religious groups were exempt from taxes. As a result, many of the se groups can be classified as simply an attempt by some individuals to pursue a business enterprise whose income was tax free. In 1951 the law was amended in an attempt to eliminate this loophole and eliminate fraud. As a result, by 1958 the number of New Religions in Japan had decreased to 171. Nonetheless, by 1964 the number had rose again to 378.
114. Ibid., 586.
115. Jikosan declared herself to be the reincarnation of the Japanese sun goddess, Amaterasu. The present difficulties that had fallen on Japan were a direct result of the people abandoning her worship. See Blacker, "Millenarian Aspects of the New Religions in Japan," 586.
116. Ibid., 585–586.
117. Tsunesaburo Makiguchi and Josei Toda led a group of nearly 60 individuals who founded Soka Kyoiku Gakkai in 1937. During World War II many of these individuals were imprisoned because of the movement's opposition to state Shinto. Makiguchi died in prison in 1944. Nonetheless, Toda, who was released from prison in July 1945 was instrumental in reorganizing the society under its present name of Soka Gakkai in February 1946. By July 1968 it was estimated that the number of households associated with the movement was in excess of 6.5 million. See James Allen Dator, *Soka Gakkai, Builders of the Third Civilization* (Seattle: University of Washington Press, 1969), 3–4.
118. Kaplan and Marshall, *The Cult at the End of the World*, 10. See also, Blacker, "Millenarian Aspects of the New Religions in Japan," 588.
119. Shakyamuni is considered to be the individual who was responsible for bringing the world the doctrine of the Buddha.
120. Blacker, "Millenarian Aspects of the New Religions in Japan," 588.
121. Quoted in ibid., 589.
122. Dator, *Soka Gakkai*, 10.
123. Ibid., 11.

124. Technically, Soka Gakkai is not a religion, it is considered by its members to be a "society of Buddhist laymen devoted to the service of Nichiren Sho-shu." See McFarland, *The Rush Hour of the Gods*, 201.
125. Ibid., 199.
126. Ibid., 195.
127. Shaukat Ali, *Millenarian and Messianic Tendencies in Islamic History* (Lahore, Pakistan: Publishers United Ltd., 1993), iv.
128. Ibid., iv.
129. Ibid.
130. Ibid., v.
131. Moojan Momen, *An Introduction to Shi'I Islam: The History and Documents of Twelver Shi'ism* (New Haven: Yale University Press, 1985), 165.
132. Mohammad Ali Amir-Moezzi, *The Divine Guide in Early Shifsm: The Sources of Esotericism in Islam*, translated from the French by David Streight (Albany: State University of New York Press, 1994), 125.
133. Although the imagery and language of the Book of Revelation indicates the presence of violence and destruction at the end time, their specific relationship to the Messiah remains ambiguous.
134. Shaukat Ali, *Millenarian and Messianic Tendencies in Islamic History*, 15.
135. Ibid., 20.
136. Amir-Moezzi, *The Divine Guide in Early Shifsm*, 125–126.
137. Momen, *An Introduction to Shi'I Islam*, 166. For Sunni sources he refers to Ibn Maja, *Sunan*, Bab Khuruj al-Mahdi, p. 1366, No. 4082; Abu Dawud, *Sunan*, Kitab al-Mahdi, Vol. 2, p. 422. "Shi'i sources for this are numerous; see, for example, al-Mufid, *al-Irshad*, p. 341 (Tr. 548)."
138. Momen, *An Introduction to Shi'i Islam*, 166–167.
139. Shaukat Ali, *Millenarian and Messianic Tendencies in Islamic History*, 17.
140. The passion plays, which commemorate the story of Husayn, and the processions of the ninth and tenth of the religious month of Moharram were held to observe the events of Karbala. Apart from being a symbol of martyred innocence, Husayn is popularly venerated in Iran in his role of hajat-deh (need-giver), who "grants prayers and brings succor when addressed with proper demonstrations of self abasement and helplessness." Mary Heglund, "Two Images of Husain: Accommodation and Revolution in an Iranian Village," in Nikki R. Keddie, ed., *Religion and Politics in Iran* (New Haven: Yale University Press, 1983), 218–235. The 'Ashura ceremonies, which are held annually, celebrate the "martyrdom" of Husayn, who is considered by Shi'as to be the Third Imam. He died on the tenth day of Moharram in 680 CE. Husayn and 72 companions were ambushed and slaughtered by the oppressive, tyrannical Ummayad ruler Yazid

in the City of Karbala. See also Amal Saad-Ghorayeb, *Hizbullah: Politics & Religion* (Sterling, VA: Pluto Press, 2002), 11.

141. R. K. Ramazani, "Shi'ism in the Persian Gulf," in Juan R. I. Cole and Nikki Keddie, eds., *Shi'ism and Social Protest* (New Haven: Yale University Press, 1986), 32.
142. Seyyed Hossein Nasr, *Islam: Religion, History, and Civilization* (San Francisco: HarperCollins, 2003), 178.
143. Sachedina, *Islamic Messianism*, 3–7.
144. Ibid., 5.
145. Ibid., 5. On the other hand, many other followers of Muhammad felt that the elders of the community should choose his successor from among the men of the Prophet's tribe of Quraysh. Those who followed this notion became known as the "people of the custom and community," or Sunni.
146. Nasr, *Islam*, 12.
147. For an overview of the revolutionary potential of Shi'ite millenarian beliefs, see Said Amir Arjomand, "Millennial Beliefs, Hierocratic Authority, and Revolution in Shi'ite Iran," in Said Amir Arjomand, ed., *The Political Dimensions of Religion* (Albany: State University of New York Press, 1993), 219–239.
148. Hamid Enayat and Mangol Bayat, "Ayatollah Sayyid Ruhullah Khumayni and Wilayat-I Faqih," in Seyyed Hossein Nasr, Hamid Dabashi, and Seyyed Vali Reza Nasr, eds., *Expectation of the Millennium: Shi'ism in History* (Albany: State University of New York Press, 1989), 348.
149. Ibid., 348.
150. Karl Heinrich Gobel, "Imamate," trans. Hamid Dabashi, in Nasr et al., *Expectation of the Millennium*, 6.
151. David Pinault, *The Shiites: Ritual and Popular Piety in a Muslim Community* (New York: St. Martin's, 1992), 53.
152. Ibid., 53–54.
153. Fouad Ajami, *The Vanished Imam: Musa Sadr and the Shia of Lebanon* (Ithaca, NY: Cornell University Press, 1986), 22.
154. Youssef M. Choueiri, *Islamic Fundamentalism* (Boston: Twayne Publishers, 1990), 25–28; See also, Sachedina, *Islamic Messianism*, 6–11.
155. Ajami, *The Vanished Imam*, 23.
156. Pinault, *The Shiites*, 53.
157. Mohammad Mohaddessin, *Islamic Fundamentalism: The New Global Threat* (Washington, DC: Seven Locks Press, 1993), 2.
158. Ibid., v.
159. "The Twelfth Imam," available at www.shia.org. The reference is *Sahih Tirmidhi*, Verse 2, p. 86.
160. See Yann Richard, *Shi'ite Islam*, trans. Antonia Nevill (Cambridge, MA: Blackwell, 1995), chapter 2.
161. Nasr, *Islam*, 73–74.

162. Said Amir Arjomand, *The Shadow of God and the Hidden Imam: Religion, Political Order, and Societal Change in Shi'ite Iran From the Beginning to 1890* (Chicago: University of Chicago Press, 1984), 197.
163. In the period 1844–1845, expectations abounded within the Shi'ite world that the "promised one (Mahdi) would appear. In Shaykhi circles . . . these speculations received particular emphasis." See Juan R. I. Cole and Moojan Momen, "Mafia, Mob and Shiism in Iraq: The Rebellion of Ottoman Karbala 1824–1843," *Past and Present*, No. 112 (August 1986), 133–134.
164. E. G. Browne, "The Babis of Persia," in Moojan Momen, ed., *Selections from the Writings of E. G. Browne on the Babi and Baha'i Religions* (Oxford: George Ronald, 1987), 196. First published in the *Journal of the Royal Asiatic Society* (1889).
165. Nikki R. Keddie, "Religion and Irreligion in Early Iranian Nationalism," *Comparative Studies in Society and History*, Vol. 4, No. 3 (1962), 267. See also, P. Smith, *Japan*, 9–11.
166. Ibid., 12.
167. Browne, "The Babis of Persia," 190–191.
168. Quoted in Muhammed Zarandi Nabil, *The Dawnbreakers: Nabil's Narrative of the Early Days of the Baha'i Revelation* (Wilmette, IL: Baha'i Publishing Trust, 1932), 253.
169. Edward Granville Browne, British scholar and professor of Arabic Studies at Oxford University, spent much of his life living in, studying, and writing about Persia and, specifically, the Babi movement. Nonetheless, his works have been discredited by religious scholars; specifically, the followers of the prophet Baha'u'llah—the Baha'i's—a faith that traces its theological roots to the Babi movement. Baha'i writers argue that, "unfortunately, Professor Browne did not rightly judge all that he observed, and his writings have tended to fortify critics and enemies of the Baha'i faith." See H. M. Balyuzi, *Edward Granville Browne and the Baha'i Faith* (London: George Ronald, 1970).
170. Browne, "The Babis of Persia," 208–209.
171. Dennis MacEoin, "The Babi Concept of Holy War," *Religion*, Vol. 12 (1982), 93–129. The messianic expectations of the Bab contributed to his call for jihad and were clearly linked to his role as the Imam, "the victorious leader of the holy war of the last days."
172. Keddie, "Religion and Irreligion in Early Iranian Nationalism," 267–268.
173. P. Smith, *Japan*, 17.
174. Nasr, *Islam*, 139.
175. Ibid., 141.
176. Ruh Allah Khomeini, *Islam and Revolution*, trans. and ed. Hamid Algar (Berkeley, CA: Mizan Press, 1981), 27. The majority of this text is a translation of Khomeini's *Islamic Government*. A book that

originated in a series of lectures given by Khomeini at Najaf between January 21 and February 8, 1970. In this book Khomeini details the theoretical bases of his religio-political philosophy, the need for an Islamic government, the specific form of such a government, and a program for the establishment of an Islamic government in Iran.

177. Khomeini, *Islam and Revolution*, 32.
178. Quoted in Said Amir Arjomand, "Traditionalism in Twentieth-century Iran," in Said Amir Arjomand, ed., *From Nationalism to Revolutionary Islam* (Albany: State University of New York Press, 1984), 221.
179. Ibid., 61. The *Majles* is the National Parliamentary Assembly of Iran.
180. For a more thorough treatment of the development of Khomeini's ideas of political authority in the modern Shi'a community and how they contributed greatly to the Iranian Revolution, see Rinehart, *Revolution and the Millennium*, 137–142.
181. Khomeini, *Islam and Revolution*, 202.
182. Ibid., 55–56, 62.
183. Ibid., 61.
184. Ibid., 61–62.
185. This has also been translated as the "Sovereignty of the Jurist."
186. The concept of political authority resting in the hands of one high-ranking, religious scholar was not new in Shi'a scholarship and theology. And it was certainly not created by Khomeini. Such a concept is steeped in Iranian tradition and culture. It was first expressed in written form, and in a religio-political context, over 100 years before by the Mullah Ahmad Naraqi. Khomeini was now reactivating it, with some modifications, "as a plausible theory of theocratic monism that was to assume the character of a miraculously revealed panacea to reverse imitative Westernization and to cure the strains of the rapidly emerging industrial society." See, Arjomand, *The Shadow of God and the Hidden Imam*, 268–269. Nonetheless, it was Khomeini who must be given credit for adapting the concept to late-twentieth-century conditions and fully implementing it in the Islamic Republic of Iran.
187. Khumayni, Ayatollah Sayyid Ruhullah Musawi, "Ayatollah Sayyid Ruhullah Musawi Khumayni and Wilayat-I Faqih," in Nasr et al., *Expectation of the Millennium*, 356. Mohaddessin defines the velayat-e faqih as "the guardianship of the religious jurist." "The essence of the theory, developed and applied by Khomieni, is that one man with a thorough knowledge law is designated as vali-e faqih, heir to the Prophet Muhammad and the Imams. He also acts as vice regent to the Mahdi, the messianic Twelfth Imam of Shi'ite Islam. The vali wields absolute authority and sovereignty over the affairs of the entire Muslim nation. No public or private matter concerning a Muslim or anyone else living in the Islamic world is beyond the vali's jurisdiction" (17). See also Shahrough Akhavi. *Religion and Politics in Contemporary Iran: Clergy–State Relations in the Pahlavi Period* (Albany: State

University of New York Press, 1980). He defines velayat as "allegiance to the rule of the Imams; their rule on the basis of their ability to interpret the holy law, especially its esoteric meanings" (xiii).

188. Ervand Abrahamian, *The Iranian Mojahedin* (New Haven: Yale University Press, 1989), 22.
189. Khomeini, *Islam and Revolution*, 63.
190. Saad-Ghorayeb, *Hizbullah*, 59.
191. Khomeini, *Islam and Revolution*, 102.
192. Saab-Ghorayeb, *Hizbullah*, 64.
193. Abrahamian, *The Iranian Mojahedin*, 21–23. Rather than preaching the "quietism" suggested by many other members of the ulama, Khomeini pressed the Shi'a faithful to "protest actively against tyranny, bad government, and oppression. And instead of tolerating the institution of monarchy as a lesser evil to that of complete social anarchy . . . he argued that Shi'ism and monarchism were incompatible and that the only form of rule acceptable was that of Islamic government."
194. Nasr, *Islam*, 13.
195. Hala Jaber, *Hezbollah: Born with a Vengeance* (New York: Columbia University Press, 1997), 9.
196. Kamal Salibi, *A House of Many Mansions: The History of Lebanon Reconsidered* (Berkeley: University of California Press, 1988), 17.
197. Ibid., 18.
198. Jaber, *Hezbollah*, 9.
199. Ibid., 10.
200. Ibid., 10.
201. Saad-Ghorayeb, *Hizbullah*, 7.
202. Magnus Ranstorp, *Hizb'allah in Lebanon: The Politics of the Western Hostage Crisis* (New York: St. Martin's Press, 1997), 25.
203. Whereas the Shi'a-dominated region in the south possessed about 20 percent of the population of Lebanon, it received only a 0.7% share of the expenditures of the 1974 national budget. See Hasan Sharif, "South Lebanon: Its History and Geopolitics," in Samih Farsoun and Elaine Hagopian, eds., *South Lebanon* (Washington, DC: Association of Arab-American University Graduates, 1978), 10–11.
204. Graham E. Fuller and Rend Rahim Francke, *The Arab Shi'a: The Forgatten Muslims* (New York: St. Martin's, 1999), 46. See also, Saad-Ghorayeb, *Hizbullah*, 8.
205. Fuller and Francke, *The Arab Shi'a*, 10.
206. See Barkun, *Disaster and the Millennium*.

Chapter 3 The Mediating Role of the Prophet

1. Ann Ruth Willner, *The Spellbinders: Charismatic Political Leadership* (New Haven: Yale University Press, 1984), 13–14.
2. Taylor, *The Fanatics*, 142–143.

3. Howard Gardner, with the collaboration of Emma Laskin, *Leading Minds: An Anatomy of Leadership* (New York: Basic Books, 2001), 14.
4. Gary Wills, *Certain Trumpets: The Call of Leaders* (New York: Simon and Schuster, 1994).
5. Leslie Pratch and Jordan Jacobowitz, "The Psychology of Leadership in Rapidly Changing Conditions: A Structural Psychological Approach," *Genetic, Social & General Psychology Monographs*, Vol. 123, No. 2 (May 1997), 169–197.
6. Wallace, "Revitalization Movements," 627.
7. Rinehart, *Revolution and the Millennium*, 118.
8. Weston La Barre, *The Ghost Dance: The Origins of Religion* (Garden City, NY: Doubleday, 1970).
9. W. W. Meissner, *Thy Kingdom Come: Psychoanalytic Perspectives on the Messiah and the Millennium* (Kansas City: Sheed & Ward, 1995), 283–286.
10. William H. Friedland, "For a Sociological Concept of Charisma," *Social Forces*, Vol. 43 (October 1964), 18–26.
11. Ann Ruth Willner and Dorothy Willner, "The Rise and Role of Charismatic Leaders," *Annals of the American Academy of Political and Social Science*, Vol. 358 (March 1965), 82–84.
12. See Rinehart, *Revolution and the Millennium*, 117–120.
13. Strong, *Shining Path*, 4–5.
14. Ibid., 5. Strong asserts that Guzman, "in the 1952 school magazine . . . wrote a report on dividing students into groups to study culture, sports, religion, journalism, and economics: 'at the head of each group there will be a leader,' he specified. 'The group leader will appoint four assistants . . . there will be a central committee made up of nine members.' "
15. Ibid., 8. In 1960, Guzman worked as a census taker in Peru following a devastating earthquake in the Arequipa. Strong argues that this experience had a dramatic effect on Guzman, by exposing him to the misery and difficulties of Peru's poor.
16. Guzman completed two doctoral theses, both written in 1961, at the National University of San Augustin. The first was entitled "The Kantian Theory of Space." The second, for a doctorate in law, was an interpretation of South American history from a Marxist perspective. Ibid., 8–9.
17. Ibid., 10.
18. David Scott Palmer, "Rebellion in Rural Peru: The Origins and Evolution of Sendero Luminoso," *Comparative Politics*, Vol. 18, No. 2 (January 1986), 127.
19. Strong, *Shining Path*, 10.
20. Palmer, "Rebellion in Rural Peru," 133. He asserts, "although founded in 1540, the city of Ayacucho . . . was not connected to the rest of the country by road until 1924."
21. Strong, *Shining Path*, 11–12.

22. Ibid., 14–15.
23. Gustavo Gorriti, *The Shining Path: A History of the Millenarian War in Peru*, translated, with an introduction by Robin Kirk (Chapel Hill: University of North Carolina Press, 1999), 180.
24. Gabriela Tarazona-Sevillano and John B. Reuter, *Sendero Luminoso and the Threat of Narcoterrorism* (New York: Praeger, 1990), 5.
25. Ibid., 6.
26. Gorriti, *The Shining Path*, 18.
27. Gordon McCormick, "The Shining Path and Peruvian Terrorism," *RAND Paper Series*, Number P-7297 (Santa Monica, CA: RAND Corporation, 1987), 11.
28. Palmer, "Rebellion in Rural Peru," 128.
29. Quoted in Strong, *Shining Path*, 7.
30. Led by Khrushchev, they were increasingly advocating a moderation of the Marxist commitment to the use of revolutionary violence and a program of "Peaceful Co-existence" with the West.
31. Martin Koppel, *Peru's Shining Path: Anatomy of a Reactionary Sect* (New York: Pathfinder, 1993), 11.
32. Strong, *Shining Path*, 16, 19. There are other accounts that Guzman made three different trips to China—1964, 1967, and 1975. See Cynthia McClintock, *Revolutionary Movements in Latin America: El Salvador's FMLN and Peru's Shining Path* (Washington: United States Institute of Peace, 1998), 65.
33. Strong, *Shining Path*, 57.
34. Colin Harding, "The Rise of Sendero Luminoso," in Rory Miller, ed., *Region and Class in Modern Peruvian History* (Liverpool: University of Liverpool, Institute for Latin American Studies, 1987), 186.
35. Gorriti, *The Shining Path*, 64.
36. Strong, *Shining Path*, 22.
37. David Scott Palmer, "Peru's Persistent Problems," *Current History* (January 1990), 128–129.
38. Thomas Harvey, "Sendero Luminoso: The Rise of a Revolutionary Movement," *Fletcher Forum* (Summer 1992), 165. See also, Strong, *Shining Path*, 48–57.
39. Palmer, "Rebellion in Rural Peru," 141; Carlos Ivan Degregori, "After the Fall of Abimael Guzman: The Limits of Sendero Luminoso," in Maxwell A. Cameron and Philip Mauceri, eds., *The Peruvian Labyrinth: Polity, Society, Economy* (University Park: The Pennsylvania State University Press, 1997), 179–191.
40. Poole and Renique, *Peru: Time of Fear*, 39.
41. Degregori, "After the Fall of Abimael Guzman," 181.
42. Jefrey Gamarra, "Conflict, Post-Conflict and Religion: Andean Responses to New Religious Movements," *Journal of Southern Africa Studies*, Vol. 26, No. 2 (June 2000), 275.
43. Strong, *Shining Path*, 64.

44. *Interview with Chairman Gonzolo*, Conducted by the Editors of *El Diario* (Berkeley, CA: The Committee to Support the Revolution in Peru, 1991), 3–4.
45. Quoted in Strong, *Shining Path*, 61.
46. Quoted in Poole and Renique, *Peru: Time of Fear*, 50–51.
47. Varese, "The Ethnopolitics of Indian Resistance in Latin America," 65. "From that initial symbolic action, though many [anthropologists] have been reluctant to acknowledge it, undeniable elements of Quechua Indian culture became increasingly evident in Shining Path activities."
48. Strong, *Shining Path*, 65.
49. Quoted in ibid., 66.
50. Ibid., 66.
51. Degregori, "After the Fall of Abimael Guzman," 188. See also Strong, *Shining Path*, 23. He asserts, "Dubbed everything from horseman of the apocalypse to philosopher-king, the man whose war has cost the lives of twenty thousand people, mostly poor people in the crusade for a communist utopia."
52. Poole and Renique, *Peru: Time of Fear*, 43. See also, Gorriti, *The Shining Path*, 25.
53. Tarazona-Sevillano and Reuter, *Sendero Luminoso*, 22.
54. Gorriti, *The Shining Path*, 15; McClintock, *Revolutionary Movements in Latin America*, 64.
55. "People of the Shining Path," *Dispatches*, British Broadcasting Corporation, 40 min. video cassette (Berkeley, CA: Committee to Support the Revolution in Peru, 1992). In the film, this speech is delivered by a young Sendero female to a group of members at a party rally in the rural highlands of Peru.
56. Strong, *Shining Path*, 67.
57. Gorriti, *The Shining Path*, 185–186.
58. Ibid., 232. In a text prepared at Conference II, Guzman is asserted to be the great interpreter of the writings of Mariategui. "Because of [Chairman] Gonzalo, we know Mariategui's military thought, because he systematized it in light of Marxism–Leninism–Maoism." Gorriti cites *El Pensamiento Militar del Partido*, December 1982, 4–5.
59. Ibid., 186.
60. "Why Is the World Interested in Peru?" The New Flag, The People's War in Peru, available at http://www.blythe.org/peru-pcp/intro/intro1.htm.
61. "Statement of the Political Prisoners and War Prisoners of Peru," translated by Peru's People's Movement, The New Flag, The People's War in Peru, available at http://www.blythe.org/peru-pcp/intro1tcc. htm.
62. Gamarra, "Conflict, Post-Conflict and Religion," 275.
63. *El Diario Interview with Chairman Gonzolo*, 57–58.
64. In the criminal investigation and trials that took place in the aftermath of the attack by Aum Shinrikyo, Asahara was referred to by his birth

name Matsumoto Chizuo. See Ian Reader, *Religious Violence in Contemporary Japan: The Case of Aum Shinrikyo* (Honolulu: University of Hawaii Press, 2000), xv.

65. Shimazono Susumu, "The Evolution of Aum Shinrikyo as a Religious Movement," in Robert J. Kisala and Mark R. Mullins, eds., *Religion and Social Crisis in Japan: Understanding Japanese Society through the Aum Affair* (New York: Palgrave, 2001), 22.
66. Reader, *Religious Violence in Contemporary Japan*, 7.
67. Kaplan and Marshall, *The Cult at the End of the World*, 8. See also, Reader, *Religious Violence in Contemporary Japan*, 44.
68. Reader, *Religious Violence in Contemporary Japan*, 44.
69. Kaplan and Marshall, *The Cult at the End of the World*, 9.
70. Ibid., 9. "One tonic, called Almighty Medicine, was simply tangerine peel in alcohol solution."
71. Ibid., 9.
72. Reader, *Religious Violence in Contemporary Japan*, 45.
73. Quoted in Kaplan and Marshall, *The Cult at the End of the World*, 9.
74. Reader, *Religious Violence in Contemporary Japan*, 47.
75. Susumu, "The Evolution of Aum Shinrikyo as a Religious Movement," 23.
76. Manuel Castells, Shujiro Yazawa, and Emma Kiselyova, "Insurgents against the Global Order: A Comparative Analysis of the Zapatistas in Mexico, the American Militia and Japan's Aum Shinrikyo," *Berkeley Journal of Sociology*, Vol. 40 (1996), 42.
77. Susumu, "The Evolution of Aum Shinrikyo as a Religious Movement," 23.
78. Brackett, *Holy Terror*, 62.
79. Ibid., 62.
80. Ibid., 63.
81. Ibid., 63.
82. Susumu, "The Evolution of Aum Shinrikyo as a Religious Movement," 24. He cites such Asahara texts as *Psychic Power: A Hidden Method of Development*, written in 1986.
83. Brackett, *Holy Terror*, 63.
84. Ibid., 64. See also, Reader, *Religious Violence in Contemporary Japan*, 53.
85. Susumu, "The Evolution of Aum Shinrikyo as a Religious Movement," 26.
86. Ibid., 26. He cites Tanaka Kimiaki, *Chomikkyo: Jirin tantora [Ultra esoteric religion: Jirin tantra]* (Tokyo: Toho Shuppan, 1994).
87. See Susumu, "The Evolution of Aum Shinrikyo as a Religious Movement," 26; Lamberg, "Psychiatrist Explores Apocalyptic Violence," 191–193.
88. Susumu, "The Evolution of Aum Shinrikyo as a Religious Movement," 28.
89. Quoted in ibid., 32–33. See also Brackett, *Holy Terror*, 66.
90. Reader, *Religious Violence in Contemporary Japan*, 57.

91. Quoted in Susumu, "The Evolution of Aum Shinrikyo as a Religious Movement," 33.
92. Brackett, *Holy Terror*, 75.
93. Ibid., 15.
94. "From Mysticism to Murder: Lawrence Shainberg Interviews Robert Jay Lifton on Aum Shinrikyo," *Tricycle: The Buddhist Review* (Winter 1997).
95. Kaplan and Marshall, *The Cult at the End of the World*, 32.
96. Haruki Murakami, *Underground: The Tokyo Gas Attack and the Japanese Psyche*, translated from the Japanese by Alfred Birnbaum and Philip Gabriel (New York: Vintage International, 2001), 232.
97. Quoted in Brackett, *Holy Terror*, 69.
98. Susumu, "The Evolution of Aum Shinrikyo as a Religious Movement," 40.
99. "From Mysticism to Murder."
100. Quoted in Robert Jay Lifton, *Destroying the World to Save It: Aum Shinrikyo, Apocalyptic Violence and the New Global Terrorism* (New York: Henry Holt, 1999), 66–67.
101. Ibid., 67–68.
102. David. C. Rapoport, "Sacred Terror: A Contemporary Example from Islam," in Reich, *Origins of Terrorism*, 121.
103. Lifton, *Destroying the World to Save It*, 204.
104. Augustus Richard Norton, *Amal and the Shi'a: Struggle for the Soul of Lebanon* (Austin, TX: University of Texas Press, 1987), 40.
105. Fuller and Francke, *The Arab Shi'a*, 204. See also, John L. Esposito, *Unholy War: Terror in the Name of Islam* (New York: Oxford University Press, 2002), 66.
106. Norton, *Amal and the Shi'a*, 40.
107. Ajami, *The Vanished Imam*, 82–83. "In the early 1960s, newly available statistics put before the Lebanese the inequalities of their country. In an economy which was heavily skewed in favor of the service sectors—banking, trade, and tourism—the top 4 percent of the country's population claimed 32 percent of the national income, while the bottom 50 percent took in only 18 percent of the income." These and other statistics on social change come from Tawfiq Beydoun, *Ithr al NIzam al Iqtisadi ala Tasruf al Musthalik fi Lubnan* (The Impact of the Economic System on the Consumer in Lebanon) (Beirut: Lebanese University, 1970).
108. Ibid., 23.
109. Ibid., 24.
110. Ibid., 86.
111. Jaber, *Hezbollah*, 11–12.
112. Ajami, *The Vanished Imam*, 89.
113. Quoted in Ajami, *The Vanished Imam*, 91.
114. In 1963, Khomeini was arrested and deported from Iran, first to Turkey and later to Iraq, for his antigovernment activities. This

period of exile (which lasted 16 years) was an experience that contributed to the radicalization of Khomeini's ideas on government and religion. Khomeini spent 14 of these years at Najaf. See Rinehart, *Revolution and the Millennium*, 138.

115. Ranstorp, *Hizb'allah in Lebanon*, 27. See also, Jaber, *Hezbollah*, 20.
116. Quoted in Jaber, *Hezbollah*, 54.
117. Ajami, *The Vanished Imam*. See also, Jaber, *Hezbollah*, 13.
118. Ajami, *The Vanished Imam*, 190.
119. Ibid., 24.
120. Ajami, *The Vanished Imam*, 200.
121. Jaber, *Hezbollah*, 12.
122. Saad-Ghorayeb, *Hizbullah*, 10. See also, Ajami, *The Vanished Imam*, 179–180.
123. Walid Khalidi, *Conflict and Violence in Lebanon: Confrontation in the Middle East* (Cambridge: Harvard Center for International Affairs, 1979), 127–128.
124. This became known as "Operation Peace for Galilee," as designated by Israel's minister of Defense, Ariel Sharon.
125. Jaber, *Hezbollah*, 11.
126. Saad-Ghorayeb, *Hizbullah*, 11.
127. Fuller and Francke, *The Arab Shi'a*, 1.
128. Ibid.
129. Ajami, *The Vanished Imam*, 191.
130. Jaber, *Hezbollah*, 48.
131. Ibid., 19–20.
132. Ibid., 51.
133. Ranstorp, *Hizb'allah in Lebanon*, 26–27.
134. Jaber, *Hezbollah*, 52.
135. Martin Kramer, *Hezbollah's Vision of the West* (Washington: The Washington Institute for Near East Policy Papers, No. 16, 1989), 9.
136. Quoted in Ajami, *The Vanished Imam*, 196.
137. Ajami, *The Vanished Imam*, 196.
138. Quoted in Saad-Ghorayeb, *Hizbullah*, 65. He attributes these remarks to Ammar al-Mussawi, "Interview: Ammar al-Mussawi," Interview by Giles Trendle, *Lebanon Report*, Vol. 5, No. 12 (December 1994), 10; Al-Sayyid 'Abbas al-Musawi, Ba'albakk, Amiru-Zakira, 10 Muharram 1410, 212; Al-Sayyid Hassan Nasru'llah, "Jerusalem Day" southern suburbs of Beirut, al-Manar Television, January 15 and 24, 1999.
139. Saad-Ghorayeb, *Hizbullah*, 66.
140. Quoted in Kramer, *Hezbollah's Vision of the West*, 11.
141. Ibid., 9–10.
142. Quoted in Martin Kramer, "Redeeming Jerusalem: The Pan-Islamic Premise of Hizballah," in David Menashri, ed., *The Iranian Revolution and the Muslim World* (Boulder, CO: Westview Press, 1990), 113.
143. Jaber, *Hezbollah*, 51.

144. Jaber, *Hezbollah*, 52.
145. Ibid., 65. The Party of God does not consider itself to have "members." Because it deems itself a pan-Islamic movement, "whose ideology spreads beyond the domestic confines of a conventional political party, its followers or adherents are considered to be the masses."
146. Ibid., 66.
147. Ibid., 65.
148. Martin Kramer, "The Oracle of Hizbullah: Sayyid Muhammad Husayn Fadlallah," in R. Scott Appleby, ed., *Spokesman for the Despised: Fundamentalist Leaders of the Middle East* (Chicago: University of Chicago Press, 1997), 83–181.
149. Ibid.
150. Ibid.
151. Ibid.
152. Quoted in ibid.; Kramer cites a Fadlallah interview in *Monday Morning*, October 15, 1984.
153. Ibid.
154. Ajami, *The Vanished Imam*, 214.
155. Quoted in Ajami, *The Vanished Imam*, 214–215.
156. Ajami, *The Vanished Imam*, 216.
157. Kramer, *Hezbollah's Vision of the West*, 15.
158. Ajami, *The Vanished Imam*, 217.

Chapter 4 Alienation and the Quest for Renewal

1. F. P. Kilpatrick, "Problems of Perception in Extreme Situations," *Human Organization*, Vol. 16 (Summer 1957), 20–22.
2. Georg W. F. Hegel, *Phenomenology of Spirit* (New York: Oxford University Press, 1979).
3. Zvi Rosen, *Bruno Bauer and Karl Marx: The Influence of Bruno Bauer on Marx's Thought* (The Hague: Nijhoff, 1977).
4. Ludwig Feuerbach, *Principles of the Philosophy of the Future* (Indianapolis: Hackett Publishers, 1986).
5. Karl Marx, "Economic and Philosophic Manuscripts of 1844," in Robert C. Tucker, ed., *The Marx-Engels Reader*, 2nd ed. (New York: W.W. Norton, 1978), 97–98.
6. Ibid., 72, 74, 78.
7. Emile Durkheim, *Suicide: A Study in Sociology* (1897; reprint Glencoe, IL: Free Press, 1951).
8. Melvin Seeman, "On the Meaning of Alienation," *American Sociological Review*, Vol. 24 (1959), 42–62.
9. Ibid., 44.
10. Robert K. Merton, *Mass Persuasion* (New York: Harper, 1946), 143.
11. See Wallace, "Revitalization Movements," 264–281.

12. Hoffman, *Inside Terrorism*, 94.
13. Rapoport, "Fear and Trembling," 659.
14. Mark Juergensmeyer, "The Logic of Political Violence," *The Journal of Strategic Studies*, Vol. 10, No. 4 (December 1987), 185.
15. Rapoport, "Why Does Religious Messianism Produce Terror?," 74.
16. Ibid., 74.
17. David Rapoport, "The Politics of Atrocity," in Alexander and Seymour, *Terrorism*, 56.
18. Palmer, "Peru's Persistent Problems," 5.
19. M. Tammen, "Drug War vs. Land Reform in Peru," *USA Today Magazine*, Vol. 120, No. 2560 (January 1992), 50.
20. Keen and Wasserman, *A History of Latin America*, 420.
21. Ibid.
22. Tammen, "Drug War vs. Land Reform in Peru," 50.
23. Palmer, "Peru's Persistent Problems," 14.
24. Ibid., 13.
25. McClintock, *Revolutionary Movements in Latin America*, 188.
26. Ibid., 193.
27. Degregori, "The Origins and Logic of Shining Path," 70.
28. Paul Goodwin Berg, Jr., "The Legitimacy of Political Violence?" presented at the Area Studies Symposium, University of Massachusetts, Amherst, April 1987, International Studies Program, University of Massachusetts, Amherst.
29. Poole and Renique, *Peru: Time of Fear*, 40.
30. Ibid.
31. Tarazona-Sevillano and Reuter, *Sendero Luminoso*, 197.
32. "Revolution in Peru" (Berkeley, CA: Committee to Support that Revolution in Peru, 1985), 10.
33. Tarazona-Sevillano and Reuter, *Sendero Luminoso*, 194.
34. Ibid., 202.
35. Ibid., 191.
36. McClintock, *Revolutionary Movements in Latin America*, 273.
37. Koppel, *Peru's Shining Path*, 14.
38. *El Diario Interview with Chairman Gonzolo*, 15,31.
39. Ibid., 52–53.
40. Quoted in Gorriti, *The Shining Path*, 34–35.
41. Gorriti, *The Shining Path*, 68.
42. Ibid.
43. Ibid., 65.
44. "Flickers from the Past: How Big a Threat Is the Shining Path?" *The Economist*, Vol. 368, No. 8333 (July 19, 2003), 28.
45. Shimazono Susumu, "The Evolution of Aum Shinrikyo as a Religious Movement," 19.
46. James Allen Dator, "Soka Gakkai: A Sociological Interpretation," *Contemporary Religions in Japan*, Vol. 6, No. 3 (1965), 213.
47. McFarland, *The Rush Hour of the Gods*, 52–53.

48. McFarland, *The Rush Hour of the Gods*, 53–54. He asserts that the "incidence of personal and social tragedy stemming from the misappropriation of freedom continues to be very high. What is the solution? Says one Japanese: 'a rigid discipline formerly applied from outside must now be applied from within.' " He quotes Inouye Syuzi, "Japan in Search of a Soul," *Japan Quarterly*, Vol. 4, No. 1 (January–March 1957), 100.
49. Castells et al., 45.
50. Shimazono Susumu, "The Evolution of Aum Shinrikyo as a Religious Movement," 21.
51. Rei Kimura, *Aum Shinrikyo: Japan's Unholy Sect* (North Charlestown, SC: BookSurge Publishing, 2002), 12–13.
52. Daniel Metraux, *Aum Shinrikyo and Japanese Youth* (Lanham, MD: University Press of America, 1999), 6.
53. Reader, *Religious Violence in Contemporary Japan*, 102–103.
54. Ibid., 71.
55. Metraux, *Aum Shinrikyo and Japanese Youth*, 5–6.
56. Reader, *Religious Violence in Contemporary Japan*, 101.
57. Ibid., 46.
58. Metraux, *Aum Shinrikyo and Japanese Youth*, 1.
59. Reader, *Religious Violence in Contemporary Japan*, 49. Reader compares the New Religion in Japan during this period to the rise of new age religions in the West.
60. Murakami, *Underground*, 227–229.
61. Reader, *Religious Violence in Contemporary Japan*, 103.
62. Murakami, *Underground*, 304. These comments came from his personal interviews with Aum members. In this case, Miyuki Kanda, who, at the age of 16, left high school and joined Aum along with her two older brothers.
63. Metraux, *Aum Shinrikyo and Japanese Youth*, 21.
64. Ibid., 21.
65. Murakami, *Underground*, 252–253.
66. Reader, *Religious Violence in Contemporary Japan*, 51.
67. Metraux, *Aum Shinrikyo and Japanese Youth*, 5. He asserts, "When a religious movement such as Aum promised them special powers, an accepting community, and hope for happiness, a number of these youths responded positively. Religious movements such as Aum Shinrikyo appealed to the mystical, occult mentality that occupied the minds of increasing numbers of Japanese in the 1980s and 1990s. Younger Japanese rejected the pragmatic utilitarian values of mainstream Japanese society in favor of a more humanistic worldview that sought a better understanding of the true meaning of life. Youth looking for salvation and recovery of soul joined Aum because it promised them a prefabricated and easy solution to their quest."
68. Ibid., 6–7.
69. Lifton, *Destroying the World to Save It*, 50–52 and 268.

70. Murakami, *Underground*, 275–276.
71. Ibid., 256.
72. Ibid., 306.
73. Ian Reader, *A Poisonous Cocktail: Aum Shinrikyo's Path to Violence* (Copenhagen: Nordic Institute of Asian Studies, 1996), 23.
74. "From Mysticism to Murder."
75. Murakami, *Underground*, 258.
76. Ibid., 263.
77. Ibid.
78. Murakami, *Underground*, 259.
79. Elizabeth Picard, "The Lebanese Shi'a and Political Violence," Discussion paper, United Nations Research Institute for Social Development, Geneva, April, 1993, 7.
80. Ibid., 7–8.
81. Fuller and Francke, *The Arab Shi'a*, 46.
82. Momen, *An Introduction to Shi'i Islam*, 39, 183.
83. Jaber, *Hezbollah*, 85.
84. Ibid., 85–86.
85. Ajami, *The Vanished Imam*, 142.
86. Quoted in Ibid., 143. He cites *Al Haya*t, February 1, 1974, as the source of this transcript of the speech.
87. Ibid., 144.
88. Helena Cobban, "The Growth of Shi'i Power in Lebanon," in Cole and Keddie, *Shi'ism and Social Protest*, 143–144.
89. Ajami, *The Vanished Imam*, 145; see also Cobban, "The Growth of Shi'i Power in Lebanon," 142–144.
90. Saad-Ghorayeb, *Hizbullah*, 34.
91. A. Nizar Hamzeh, "Lebanon's Hizbullah: From Islamic Revolution to Parliamentary Accommodation," *Third World Quarterly*, Vol. 14, No. 2 (1993).
92. "Hezbollah: Identity and Goals," available at www.hizbollah.com.
93. Kramer, *Hezbollah's Vision of the West*, 105–106.
94. See the website www. Hizbollah.org.
95. Jaber, *Hezbollah*, 55.
96. Ibid., 57.
97. Ibid., 22.
98. Quoted in Ibid., 23.
99. Ibid., 76.
100. Ibid., 76–77.
101. In 2000, it was estimated that there were about 1,500 fighters in the Hezbollah organization. About two-third of these were considered to be part-time soldiers. See Norton, "Amal and the Shi'a," 5.
102. Augustus Richard Norton, "Hizballah and the Israeli Withdrawal from Southern Lebanon," *Journal of Palestinian Studies*, Vol. 30, No. 1 (Autumn 2000), 5.

103. Jaber, *Hezbollah*, 26.
104. Brian Whitaker, "Hizbollah: Israel Is an Illegitimate Entity," *The Guardian*, March 4, 2001.
105. Quoted in Jaber, *Hezbollah*, 56–57.
106. Jaber, *Hezbollah*, 84.
107. Quoted in Jaber, *Hezbollah*, 86–87.
108. Jaber, *Hezbollah*, 89.
109. Whitaker, "Hizbollah: Israel Is an Illegitimate Entity."
110. Jaber, *Hezbollah*, 146.
111. Ibid., 147.
112. Ibid., 147.
113. Zafar Bangash, "Leadership, Commitment and Courage-The Basis of Hizbullah's Victory over the Zionists," *Crescent International*, August 1–15, 2000.
114. Ibid.
115. Ibid.
116. Jaber, *Hezbollah*, 148.
117. See Hamzeh, "Lebanon's Hizbullah."
118. Esposito, *Unholy War*, 147. He asserts: "Though many Islamic associations and NGOs are nonpolitical and nonviolent, others like Lebanon's Hizbollah and Hamas in Palestine have combined extensive and effective educational and social services with political action and militant jihad."

Chapter 5 Identity and Millenarian Violence

1. S. Epstein, "The Self Concept: A Review and the Proposal of an Integrated Theory of Personality," in Ervin Staub, ed., *Personality: Basic Aspects and Current Research* (Englewood Cliffs, NJ: Prentice Hall, 1980), 233.
2. R. Janoff-Bulman, "The Aftermath of Victimization: Rebuilding Shattered Assumptions," in C. R. Figley, ed., *Trauma and Its Wake* (New York: Brunner/Mazel, 1985).
3. Rinehart, *Revolution and the Millennium*, 161.
4. Janoff-Bulman, "The Aftermath of Victimization," 24.
5. Kenneth Hoover, *The Power of Identity: Politics in a New Key* (Chatham, NJ: Chatham House Publishers, 1997), xi.
6. Ibid., 19.
7. William Bloom, *Personal Identity, National Identity and International Relations* (New York: Cambridge University Press, 1990), 23.
8. Erik H. Erikson, *Childhood and Society* (New York: W.W. Norton, 1963).
9. Erik H. Erikson, *Identity and the Life Cycle* (New York: W.W. Norton, 1994), 147.

10. Erik H. Erikson, *Identity: Youth and Crisis* (New York: W.W. Norton, 1968), 133.
11. Bloom, *Personal Identity*, 38–39.
12. Clark R. McCauley, "The Psychology of Group Identification and the Power of Ethnic Nationalism," in Daniel Chirot and Martin E. P. Seligman, eds., *Ethnopolitical Warfare: Causes, Consequences, and Possible Solutions* (New York: American Psychological Association, 2001), 343.
13. Indeed, Benedict Anderson has defined the concept of nationalism as an "imagined community." See *Imagined Communities: Reflections on the Origin and Spread of Nationalism* (New York: Verso, 1991).
14. Else Frenkel-Brunswik, Daniel J. Levinson, Theodor W. Adorno, and R. Nevitt Sanford, *The Authoritarian Personality* (1950; reprint, New York: W.W. Norton, 1993).
15. Paul Wallace, "Political Violence and Terrorism in India: The Crisis of Identity," in Crenshaw, *Terrorism in Context*, 353.
16. Barkun, *Disaster and the Millennium*, 45.
17. McCauley and Segal, "Social Psychology of Terrorist Groups," 235.
18. Martha Crenshaw, "An Organizational Approach to the Analysis of Political Terrorism," *Orbis* 29.
19. Hoover, *The Power of Identity*, 123.
20. Strong, *Shining Path*, 60.
21. Koppel, *Peru's Shining Path*, 14.
22. McClintock, *Revolutionary Movements in Latin America*, 271.
23. Robin Kirk, *The Monkey's Paw: New Chronicles from Peru* (Amherst: University of Massachusetts Press, 1997), 63.
24. McClintock, *Revolutionary Movements in Latin America*, 272.
25. Tarazona-Sevillano and Reuter, *Sendero Luminoso*, 45–46.
26. Gorriti, *The Shining Path*, 110.
27. Ibid., 99.
28. Ibid., 104.
29. Ibid., 105.
30. Strong, *Shining Path*, 66–67.
31. Gorriti, *The Shining Path*, xi.
32. "From Mysticism to Murder."
33. Ibid.
34. Reader, *A Poisonous Cocktail*, 23.
35. Kaplan and Marshall, *The Cult at the End of the World*, 3.
36. Murakami, *Underground*, 104.
37. Brackett, *Holy Terror*, 7.
38. Metraux, *Aum Shinrikyo and Japanese Youth*, 6.
39. Reader, *A Poisonous Cocktail*, 25. He asserts that in order to achieve a sense of self-esteem that their commitment to Aum provided, most initiates seem to have placed all of their valued, yet limited possession of a sense of self in Asahara himself. See also, Murakami, *Underground*, 230–231.

40. Metraux, *Aum Shinrikyo and Japanese Youth*, v. Metraux asserts that according to Aum membership lists discovered by police in 1995, 47.5% of *shukke* were in their twenties and 75.4% were in their twenties and thirties.
41. Kaplan and Marshall, *The Cult at the End of the World*, 3.
42. Reader, *Religious Violence in Japan*, 9–10.
43. Brackett, *Holy Terror*, 102.
44. Ibid., 103–104.
45. Cobban, "The Growth of Shi'i Power in Lebanon," 138.
46. Juan Cole, *Sacred Space and Holy War: The Politics, Culture and History of Shi'ite Islam* (London: I. B. Tauris, 2002), 16–30.
47. Cobban, "The Growth of Shi'i Power in Lebanon," 139.
48. Ajami, *The Vanished Imam*, 61–62.
49. Fuller and Francke, *The Arab Shi'a*, 34.
50. Ibid., 45.
51. Ibid., 17.
52. Kramer, *Hezbollah's Vision of the West*, 25.
53. Whitaker, "Hizbollah: Israel Is an Illegitimate Entity."
54. "Hezbollah: Identity and Goals."
55. Ibid.
56. Ajami, *The Vanished Imam*, 201. This expression is attributed to Shaykh Muhammad Mahdi Shams al Din, the clerical deputy to Musa al-Sadr on the Higher Shi'a Council.
57. Richard, *Shi'ite Islam*, 97.
58. Whitaker, "Hizbollah: Israel Is an Illegitimate Entity," 12.
59. Bangash, "Leadership, Commitment and Courage."
60. Quoted in Ajami, *The Vanished Imam*, 202. He cites *An Nahar*, October 18, 1983.
61. Ajami, *The Vanished Imam*, 202. Bangash, "Leadership, Commitment and Courage."
62. Jaber, *Hezbollah*, 18–19.
63. Ajami, *The Vanished Imam*, 203.
64. Ibid.
65. "An Open Letter: The Hizballah Program," www.ict.org.il/articles/Hiz_letter.htm.
66. Saad-Ghorayeb, *Hizbullah*, 16–17. See also, David George, "Pax Islamica: An Alternative New World Order?" in Youssef Choueiri, ed., *Islamic Fundamentalism* No. 2 (Boston: Twayne, 1990), 82.
67. Saad-Ghorayeb, *Hizbullah*, 19.
68. Jaber, *Hezbollah*, 58.
69. "An Open Letter: The Hizballah Program,"
70. Kramer, *Hezbollah's Vision of the West*, 27.
71. Ibid., 29. He cites a speech by Shaykh Ibrahim Qusayr of Dayr Qanun al-Nahr, Al-Ahd, February 28, 1986. The occasion was a visit by Iran's charge d'affaires, Mahmud Nurani, to Beirut.
72. Saad-Ghorayeb, *Hizbullah*, 77.

73. Martin Kramer, "Redeeming Jerusalem," 118.
74. Ibid., 119. See also Saad-Ghorayeb, *Hizbullah*, 76–78. He asserts that Hezbollah "seeks to instill in all Muslims an Islamic identity which would override all of their national affiliations, and which would be conducive to the creation of an '*umma mujahida*' (combative community) capable of defeating Israel. Only once such an *umma* emerges will the establishment of a 'greater Islamic state'—of which Lebanon would be an indivisible part—become reality."
75. Kramer, "Redeeming Jerusalem," 119.
76. Saad-Ghorayeb, *Hizbullah*, 72.
77. Ibid., 74.

Bibliography

Abrahamian, Ervand. *The Iranian Mojahedin*. New Haven: Yale University Press, 1989.

Adas, Michael. *Prophets of Rebellion: Millenarian Protest Movements against the European Colonial Order*. Chapel Hill: University of North Carolina Press, 1979.

Ajami, Fouad. *The Vanished Imam: Musa Sadr and the Shia of Lebanon*. Ithaca, NY: Cornell University Press, 1986.

Akhavi, Sharough. *Religion and Politics in Contemporary Iran: Clergy State Relations in the Pahlavi Period*. Albany: State University of New York Press, 1980.

Ali, Shaukat. *Millenarian and Messianic Tendencies in Islamic History*. Lahore, Pakistan: Publishers United Ltd., 1993.

Amal Saad-Ghorayeb. *Hizbu'llah: Politics & Religion*. Sterling, VA: Pluto Press, 2002.

Amir-Moezzi, Mohammad Ali. *The Divine Guide in Early Shi'ism: The Sources of Esotericism in Islam*. Translated by David Streight. Albany: State University of New York Press, 1994.

"An Open Letter: The Hizballah Program." www.ict.org.il/articles/Hiz_letter.htm.

Anderson, Benedict. *Imagined Communities: Reflections on the Origin and Spread of Nationalism*. New York: Verso, 1991.

Arjomand, Said Amir. *The Shadow of God and the Hidden Imam: Religion, Political Order, and Societal Change in Shi'ite Iran from the Beginning to 1890*. Chicago: University of Chicago Press, 1984.

———. "Traditionalism in Twentieth-Century Iran." In *From Nationalism to Revolutionary Islam*. Ed. Said Amir Arjomand. Albany: State University of New York Press. 1984.

———. "Millennial Beliefs, Hierocratic Authority, and Revolution in Shi'ite Iran." In *The Political Dimensions of Religion*. Ed. Said Amir Arjomand. Albany: State University of New York Press, 1993, 219–239.

Aronson, Elliott. *The Social Animal*. 8th ed. New York: W.H. Freeman and Company, 1999.

Balyuzi, H. M. *Edward Granville Browne and the Baha'i Faith*. London: George Ronald, 1970.

Bangash, Zafar. "Leadership, Commitment and Courage—The Basis of Hizbullah's Victory Over the Zionists." *Crescent International* August 1–15, 2000.

Bangura, Yusuf. "The Search for Identity: Ethnicity, Religion and Political Violence." Occasional Paper No. 6. World Summit for Social Development. Geneva: United Nations Institute for Social Development, 1994, 24.

Barkun, Michael. *Disaster and the Millennium*. Syracuse: Syracuse University Press, 1986.

———. *A Culture of Conspiracy: Apocalyptic Visions in Contemporary America*. Berkeley: University of California Press, 2003.

Berg, Paul Goodwin, Jr. "The Legitimacy of Political Violence?" Presented at the Area Studies Symposium, University of Massachusetts, Amherst, April 1987. International Area Studies Program, University of Massachusetts, Amherst.

Blacker, Carmen. "Millenarian Aspects of the New Religions in Japan." In *Tradition and Modernization in Japanese Culture*. Ed. Donald H. Shively. Princeton: Princeton University Press, 1971, 563–600.

Bloom, William. *Personal Identity, National Identity, and International Relations*. New York: Cambridge University Press, 1990.

Bodley, John H. "A Transformative Movement among the Campa of Eastern Peru." *Anthropos* Vol. 67 (1972).

Bonanate, Luigi. "Some Unanticipated Consequences of Terrorism." *Journal of Peace Research* Vol. 16, No. 3 (1979), 197–211.

Borton, Hugh. "Peasant Uprisings in Japan of the Tokugawa Period." *The Transactions of the Asiatic Society of Japan* Vol. 16 (1938).

Brackett, D. W. *Holy Terror: Armageddon in Tokyo*. New York: Weatherhill, 1996.

Brannan, David W., Philip F. Esler, and N. T. Anders Strindberg. "Talking to 'Terrorists': Towards an Independent Analytical Framework for the Study of Violent Substate Activism." *Studies in Conflict & Terrorism* Vol. 24 (2001), 3–24.

Bricker, Victoria Reifler. *The Indian Christ, the Indian King: The Historical Substrate of Maya Myth and Ritual*. Austin: University of Texas Press, 1981.

Brown, Michael F. "Beyond Resistance: A Comparative Study of Utopian Renewal in Amazonia." *Ethnohistory* Vol. 38, No. 4 (Fall 1991).

Browne, E. G. "The Babis of Persia." In *Selections from the Writings of E. G. Browne on the Babi and Baha'i Religions*. Ed. Moojan Momen. Oxford: George Ronald, 1987, 196. First published in the *Journal of the Royal Asiatic Society* (1889).

Burger, Richard L. *Chavin and the Origins of Andean Civilization*. New York: Thames and Hudson, 1992.

Canadian Security Intelligence Service. "Terrorism and the Rule of Law: Dangerous Compromise in Colombia." *Commentary No 13* (October 1991).

Castells, Manuel, Shujiro Yazawa, and Emma Kiselyova. "Insurgents against the Global Order: A Comparative Analysis of the Zapatistas in Mexico, the American Militia and Japan's Aum Shinrikyo. *Berkeley Journal of Sociology*,

Vol. 40, Department of Sociology, University of California at Berkeley, 1995–1996.

Choueiri, Youssef M. *Islamic Fundamentalism.* Boston: Twayne Publishers, 1990.

Classen, Constance. *Inca Cosmology and the Human Body.* Salt Lake City: University of Utah Press, 1993.

Cobban, Helena. “The Growth of Shi’i Power in Lebanon.” In *Shi’ism and Social Protest.* Ed. Juan R. I. Cole and Nikki R. Keddie. New Haven: Yale University Press, 1986.

Cobo, Bernabe. *Inca Religion and Customs.* Trans. and Ed. Roland Hamilton. Austin: University of Texas Press, 1990.

Cohn, Norman. *The Pursuit of the Millennium: Revolutionary Millenarians and Mystical Anarchists of the Middle Ages.* 2nd ed. New York: Oxford University Press, 1970.

———. *Cosmos, Chaos, and the World to Come: The Ancient Roots of Apocalyptic Faith.* New Haven, CT: Yale University Press, 1993.

Cole, Juan. *Sacred Space and Holy War: The Politics, Culture, and History of Shi’ite Islam.* London: I.B. Tauris, 2002.

Cole, Juan R. I. and Moojan Momen. “Mafia, Mob and Shiism in Iraq: The Rebellion of Ottoman Karbala 1824–1843.” *Past and Present* No. 112 (August 1986), 112–143.

Crenshaw, Martha. “The Causes of Terrorism.” *Comparative Politics* No. 13 (1981), 379–399.

———. “An Organizational Approach to the Analysis of Political Terrorism.” *Orbis* Vol. 29 (1985), 465–489.

———. “The Psychology of Political Terrorism.” In *Political Psychology: Contemporary Problems and Issues.* Ed. Margaret G. Herrmann. San Francisco: Jossey-Bass, 1986, 379–413.

———. “The Logic of Terrorism: Terrorist Behavior as a Product of Strategic Choice.” In *Origins of Terrorism: Psychologies, Ideologies, Theologies, States of Mind.* Ed. Walter Reich. Cambridge: Cambridge University Press, 1990, 7–24.

———. “Questions to Be Answered, Research to Be Done, Knowledge to Be Applied.” In *Origins of Terrorism: Psychologies, Ideologies, Theologies, States of Mind.* Ed. Walter Reich. Cambridge: Cambridge University Press, 1990, 247–260.

———. “How Terrorists Think: What Psychology Can Contribute to Understanding Terrorism.” In *Terrorism: Roots, Impact, Responses.* Ed. Lawrence Howard. New York: Praeger, 1992, 71–79.

———. “Thoughts on Relating Terrorism to Historical Contexts.” In *Terrorism in Context.* Ed. Martha Crenshaw. University Park, PA: The University of Pennsylvania Press, 1995.

Dator, James Allen. “Soka Gakkai: A Sociological Interpretation.” *Contemporary Religions in Japan* Vol. 6, No. 3 (1965).

———. *Soka Gakkai, Builders of the Third Civilization.* Seattle: University of Washington Press, 1969.

Degregori, Carlos Ivan. "The Origins and Logic of Shining Path: Two Views." In *The Shining Path of Peru*. Ed. David Scott Palmer. New York: St. Martin's, 1994.

Della Porta, Donatella. "Left Wing Terrorism in Italy." In *Terrorism in Context*. Ed. Martha Crenshaw. University Park, PA: The Pennsylvania State University Press, 1995, 105–159.

Develop the People's War to Serve the World Revolution. Berkeley, CA: The Committee to Support the Revolution in Peru, 1988.

Dillon, Mary and Thomas Abercrombie. "The Destroying Christ: An Aymara Myth of Conquest." In *Rethinking History and Myth: Indigenous South American Perspectives on the Past*. Ed. Jonathan D. Hill. Urbana, IL: University of Illinois Press, 1988.

Draper, Hal. *Karl Marx's Theory of Revolution: The State and Bureaucracy*. New York: Monthly Review Press, 1979.

Duran, Khalid. "Middle Eastern Terrorism: Its Characteristics and Driving Forces." In *Terrorism: Roots, Impact, and Responses*. Ed. Lawrence Howard. New York: Praeger, 1992, 47–69.

Durkheim, Emile. *The Division of Labor in Society*. Trans. George Simpson. 1893 Reprint. New York: Macmillan, 1933.

———. *Suicide: A Study in Sociology*. 1897 Reprint. Glencoe, IL: Free Press, 1951.

Elliott, Ruth and William H. Lockhart. "Characteristics of Scheduled Offenders and Juvenile Delinquents." In *A Society Under Stress: Children and Young People in Northern Ireland*. Ed. Jeremy and Joan Harbison. London: Open Books, 1980.

Enayat, Hamid and Mangol Bayat, "Ayatollah Sayyid Ruhullah Khumayni and Wilayat-I Faqih," In *Expectation of the Millennium: Shi'ism in History*. Ed. Seyyed Hossein Nasr, Hamid Dabashi, and Seyyed Vali Reza Nasr. Albany: State University of New York Press, 1989.

Epstein, S. "The Self-Concept: A Review and the Proposal of an Integrated Theory of Personality." In *Personality: Basic Aspects and Current Research*. Ed. Ervin Staub. Englewood Cliffs, NJ: Prentice-Hall, 1980.

Erikson, Erik H. *Childhood and Society*. New York: W.W. Norton, 1963.

———. *Identity: Youth and Crisis*. New York: W.W. Norton, 1968.

———. *Identity and the Life Cycle*. New York: W.W. Norton, 1994.

Esposito, John L. *Islam and Politics*. Syracuse, NY: Syracuse University Press, 1984.

———. *Unholy War: Terror in the Name of Islam*. New York: Oxford University Press, 2002.

Feuerbach, Ludwig. *Principles of the Philosophy of the Future*. Indianapolis: Hackett Publishers, 1986.

Final Act of the United Nations' Diplomatic Conference of Plenipotentiaries on the Establishment of an International Criminal Court. United Nations Document A/Conf. 18/10, July 17, 1998. www.un.org.

"Flickers from the Past: How Big a Threat Is the Shining Path?" *The Economist* Vol. 368, No. 8333 (July 19, 2003), 28.

Florescano, Enrique. *Memory, Myth, and Time in Mexico: From the Aztecs to Independence.* Trans. Albert G. Bork with the assistance of Kathryn R. Bork. Austin: University of Texas Press, 1994.

Frenkel-Brunswik, Else, Daniel J. Levinson, Theodor W. Adorno, and R. Nevitt Sanford. *The Authoritarian Personality.* 1950 Reprint. New York: W.W. Norton, 1993.

Friedland, Nehemia. "Becoming a Terrorist: Social and Individual Antecedents." In *Terrorism: Roots, Impact, and Responses.* Ed. Lawrence Howard. New York: Praeger, 1992, 81–93.

Friedland, William H. "For a Sociological Concept of Charisma." *Social Forces* Vol. 43 (October 1964), 18–26.

"From Mysticism to Murder: Lawrence Shainberg Interviews Robert Jay Lifton on Aum Shinrikyo." *Tricycle: The Buddhist Review* (Winter 1997).

Fromm, Erich. *The Sane Society.* New York: Henry Holt and Company, 1955.

Fuller, Graham E. and Rend Rahim Francke. *The Arab Shi'a: The Forgotten Muslims.* New York: St. Martin's Press, 1999.

Fuller, J. F. C. *Military History of the Western World.* Volume One. New York: De Capo Press, 1954.

Galanter, Marc. *Cults, Faith, Healing and Coercion.* New York: Oxford University Press, 1989.

Galindo, Alberto Flores. "The Rebellion of Tupac Amaru." In *Revolution and Revolutionaries: Guerilla Movements in Latin America.* Ed. Daniel Castro. Wilmington, DE: Scholarly Resources, 1999.

Gallagher, Eugene V. " 'Theology Is Life and Death': David Koresh on Violence, Persecution, and the Millennium." In *Millennialism, Persecution, and Violence: Historical Cases.* Ed. Catherine Wessinger. Syracuse: Syracuse University Press, 2000.

Gamarra, Jefrey. "Conflict, Post-Conflict and Religion: Andean Responses to New Religious Movements." *Journal of Southern African Studies* Vol. 26, No. 2 (June 2000), 271–287.

Gardner, Howard, in collaboration with Emma Laskin. *Leading Minds: An Anatomy of Leadership.* New York: Basic Books, 1995.

Garfield, David and Leston Havens. "Paranoid Phenomena and Pathological Narcissism." *American Journal of Psychotherapy* Vol. 45, No. 2 (April 1991).

George, David. "Pax Islamica: An Alternative New World Order?" In *Islamic Fundamentalism.* No. 2. Ed. Youssef Choueiri. Boston: Twayne, 1990.

Gilligan, James. *Violence.* New York: Vintage, 1996.

Gobel, Karl-Heinrich. "Imamate." In *Expectation of the Millennium: Shi'ism in History.* Trans. Hamid Dabashi. Ed. Seyyed Hossein Nasr, Hamid Dabashi, and Seyyed Vali Reza Nasr. Albany: State University of New York Press, 1989, 2–6.

Gorriti, Gustavo. *The Shining Path: A History of the Millenarian War in Peru.* Translated from the Spanish, with an introduction by Robin Kirk. 1990 Reprint. Chapel Hill: University of North Carolina Press, 1999.

Gow, David. "The Roles of Christ and Inkarri in Andean Religion." *Journal of Latin American Lore* Vol. 6 (1980), 279–296.

Grollig, Frances X. *Incaic and Modern Peru.* New Haven, CT: Human Relations Area Files, 1979.

Gruzinski, Serge. *Man-Gods in the Mexican Highlands.* Translated from the French by Eileen Corrigan. Stanford: Stanford University Press, 1989.

Gurr, Ted Robert. *Why Men Rebel.* Princeton: Princeton University Press, 1970.

Hacker, Frederick J. *Crusaders, Criminals, Crazies: Terror and Terrorism in Our Time.* New York: W.W. Norton, 1976.

Halawi, Majed. *A Lebanon Defied: Musa al-Sadr and the Shi'a Community.* Boulder, CO: Westview Press, 1992.

Hammer, Raymond. *Japan's Religious Ferment.* New York: Oxford University Press, 1962.

Hamzeh, A. Nizar. "Lebanon's Hizbullah: From Islamic Revolution to Parliamentary Accommodation." *Third World Quarterly* Vol. 14, No. 2 (1993).

Harding, Colin. "The Rise of Sendero Luminoso." In *Region and Class in Modern Peruvian History.* Ed. Rory Miller. Liverpool, 1987.

Harvey, Thomas. "Sendero Luminoso: The Rise of a Revolutionary Movement." *Fletcher Forum* (Summer 1992).

Hegel, Georg W. F. *Phenomenology of Spirit.* New York: Oxford University Press, 1979.

Heglund, Mary. "Two Images of Husain: Accommodation and Revolution in an Iranian Village." In *Religion and Politics in Iran.* Ed. Nikki R. Keddie. New Haven: Yale University Press, 1983.

Heskin, Ken. "The Psychology of Terrorism in Northern Ireland." In *Terrorism in Ireland.* Ed. Yonah Alexander and Alan O'Day. New York: St. Martin's, 1984, 88–105.

Heyman, F. C. *John Zizka and the Hussite Revolution.* Princeton: Princeton University Press, 1955.

"Hezbollah: Identity and Goals." www.hizbollah.org.

Hobsbawm, Eric J. *Primitive Rebels: Studies in Archaic Forms of Social Movement in the 19th and 20th Centuries.* New York: Praeger, 1963.

Hoffman, Bruce. *Inside Terrorism.* London: Victor Gollancz, 1998.

Hofstader, Richard. *The Paranoid Style in American Politics and Other Essays.* New York: Alfred A. Knopf, 1965.

Hoover, Kenneth. *The Power of Identity: Politics in a New Key.* Chatham, NJ: Chatham House Publishers, 1997.

Huntington, Samuel. "The Clash of Civilizations?" *Foreign Affairs* Vol. 72, No. 3 (1993).

Hyams, Edward. *Terrorists and Terrorism.* New York: St. Martin's Press, 1974.

"Interview with Chairman Gonzalo." Conducted by the editors of *El Diario.* Berkeley, CA: The Committee to Support the Revolution in Peru, 1991.

"Israelite Religion." http:/purace.unicauca.edu.co/balboa/israelitas.htm.

Jaber, Hala. *Hezbollah: Born with a Vengeance.* New York: Columbia University Press, 1997.

Janoff-Bulman, R. "The Aftermath of Victimization: Rebuilding Shattered Assumptions." In *Trauma and Its Wake*. Ed. C. R. Figley. New York: Brunner/Mazel, 1985.

Juergensmeyer, Mark. "The Logic of Religious Violence." *The Journal of Strategic Studies* Vol. 10, No. 4 (December 1987), 172–193.

———. *The New Cold War: Religious Nationalism Confronts the Secular State*. Berkeley: University of California Press, 1993.

Kaminsky, Howard. *A History of the Hussite Revolution*. Berkeley: University of California Press, 1967.

Kaplan, David E. and Andrew Marshall. *The Cult at the End of the World*. New York: Crown Publishers, 1996.

Keddie, Nikki R. "Religion and Irreligion in Early Iranian Nationalism." *Comparative Studies in Society and History* Vol. 4, No. 3 (1962).

Keen, Benjamin and Mark Wasserman. *A History of Latin America*. 3rd ed. Boston: Houghton Mifflin, 1988.

Khalidi, Walid. *Conflict and Violence in Lebanon: Confrontation in the Middle East*. Cambridge: Harvard Center for International Affairs, 1979.

Khomeini, Ruh Allah. *Islam and Revolution*. Trans. and Ed. Hamid Algar. Berkeley, CA: Mizan Press, 1981.

Khumayni, Ayatollah Sayyid Ruhullah Musawi. "Ayatollah Sayyid Ruhullah Musawi Khumayni and Wilayat-I Faqih." In *Expectations of the Millennium: Shi'ism in History*. Ed. Seyyed Hossein Nasr, Hamid Dabashi, and Seyyed Vali Reza Nasr. Albany: State University of New York Press, 1989.

Kilpatrick, F. P. "Problems of Perception in Extreme Situations." *Human Organization* Vol. 16 (Summer 1957).

Kimura, Rei. *Aum Shinrikyo: Japan's Unholy Sect*. North Charlestown, SC: BookSurge Publishing, 2002.

Kirk, Robin. *The Monkey's Paw: New Chronicles from Peru*. Amherst: University of Massachusetts Press, 1997.

Kisala, Robert J. and Mark R. Mullins, eds. *Religion and Social Crisis in Japan: Understanding Japanese Society through the Aum Affair*. New York: Palgrave, 2001.

Kitagawa, Joseph M. *On Understanding Japanese Religion*. Princeton: Princeton University Press, 1987.

Klaren, Peter F. *Peru: Society and Nationhood in the Andes*. New York: Oxford University Press, 2000.

Knutson, Jeanne N. "Social and Psychodynamic Pressures toward a Negative Identity: The Case of an American Revolutionary Terrorist." In *Behavioral and Quantitative Perspectives on Terrorism*. Ed. Yonah Alexander and John M. Gleason. New York: Pergamon Press, 1981.

Koppel, Martin. *Peru's Shining Path: Anatomy of a Reactionary Sect*. New York: Pathfinder, 1993.

Kramer, Martin. *Hezbollah's Vision of the West*. Washington: Washington Institute for Near East Policy Papers, Number Sixteen, 1989.

Kramer, Martin. "The Moral Logic of Hizballah." In *Origins of Terrorism: Psychologies, Ideologies, Theologies, States of Mind.* Ed. Walter Reich. Cambridge: Cambridge University Press, 1990, 131–167.

———. "The Oracle of Hizbullah: Sayyid Muhammad Husayn Fadlallah." In *Spokesmen for the Despised: Fundamentalist Leaders of the Middle East.* Ed. R. Scott Appleby. Chicago: University of Chicago Press, 1997, 83–181.

———. "Redeeming Jerusalem: The Pan-Islamic Premise of Hizballah." In *The Iranian Revolution and the Muslim World.* Ed. David Menashri. Boulder, CO: Westview Press, 1990, 105–130.

Kramer, Roderick. "Paranoid Cognition in Social Systems: Thinking and Acting in the Shadow of Doubt." *Personality and Social Psychology Review* Vol. 2, No. 4 (1998).

La Barre, Weston. *The Ghost Dance: The Origins of Religion.* Garden City, NY: Doubleday, 1970.

Lafaye, Jacques. *Quetzalcoatl and Guadalupe: The Formation of Mexican National Consciousness, 1513–1815.* Chicago: University of Chicago Press, 1976.

Lambakis, Steven, James Kiras, and Kristen Kolet. "Understanding 'Asymmetric' Threats to the United States." Fairfax, VA: National Institute for Public Policy, September 2002.

Lamberg, Lynne "Psychiatrist Explores Apocalyptic Violence in Heaven's Gate and Aum Shinrikyo Cults," *Journal of the American Medical Association* Vol. 278, No. 3 (1997), 191–193.

Lanternari, Vittorio. *The Religions of the Oppressed: A Study of Modern Messianic Cults.* New York: Mentor Books, 1965.

Laqueur, Walter. "Postmodern Terrorism." *Foreign Affairs* Vol. 75, No. 5 (September/October 1996), 24–36.

Laszlo, Ervin, Robert Artigiani, Allan Combs, and Vilmos Csanyi. *Changing Visions—Human Cognitive Maps: Past, Present, and Future.* Westport, CT: Praeger, 1996.

LeBon, Gustave. *The Crowd: A Study of the Popular Mind.* 1896 Reprint. Whitefish, MT: Kessinger Publishing Company, 2003.

Lewellen, Ted C. "Deviant Religion and Cultural Evolution: The Aymara Case." *Journal for the Scientific Study of Religions* Vol. 18, No. 3 (1979).

Lewy, Guenther. *Religion and Revolution.* New York: Oxford University Press, 1974.

Lifton, Robert Jay. *Destroying the World to Save It: Aum Shinrikyo, Apocalyptic Violence, and the New Global Terrorism.* New York: Henry Holt, 1999.

Long, David E. *The Anatomy of Terrorism.* New York: Free Press, 1990.

Lupsha, Peter. "Explanation of Political Violence: Some Psychological Theories Versus Indignation." *Politics and Society* Vol. 2 (1971), 88–104.

MacCormack, Sabine. *Religion in the Andes: Vision and Imagination in Early Colonial Peru.* Princeton: Princeton University Press, 1991.

MacEoin, Dennis. "The Babi Concept of Holy War." *Religion* Vol. 12 (1982), 93–129.

Margolin, Joseph. "Psychological Perspectives in Terrorism." In *Terrorism: Interdisciplinary Perspectives.* Ed. Yonah Alexander and Seymour Maxwell Finger. New York: John Jay, 1977, 270–282.

Mariategui, José Carlos. *Seven Interpretive Essays on Peruvian Reality.* Austin: University of Texas Press, 1971.

Martin, Joel W. *Sacred Revolt: The Muskogees' Struggle for a New World.* Boston: Beacon Press, 1991.

Marty, Martin and R. Scott Appleby, eds. *Religion, Ethnicity, and Self-Identity.* Hanover, NH: University Press of New England, 1997.

Marx, Karl. "Economic and Philosophic Manuscripts of 1844." In *The Marx–Engels Reader.* 2nd ed. Ed. Robert C. Tucker. New York: W.W. Norton, 1978, 97–98.

McCauley, Clark R. "The Psychology of Terrorism." Social Science Research Council Essay Series. www.ssrc.org/sept11/essays/mccauley.htm.

McCauley, Clark R. and Mary E. Segal. "Social Psychology of Terrorist Groups." In *Group Processes and Intergroup Relations: Volume 9, Review of Personality and Social Psychology.* Ed. Clyde Hendrick. Newbury Park, CA: Sage Publications, 1987, 231–256.

———. "The Psychology of Group Identification and the Power of Ethnic Nationalism." In *Ethnopolitical Warfare: Causes, Consequences, and Possible Solutions.* Ed. Daniel Chirot and Martin E. P. Seligman. New York: American Psychological Association, 2001.

McClintock, Cynthia. *Revolutionary Movements in Latin America: El Salvador's FMLN and Peru's Shining Path.* Washington: United States Institute of Peace, 1998.

McCormick, Gordon. "The Shining Path and Peruvian Terrorism," *Rand Paper Series,* Number P-7297. Santa Monica, CA: RAND Corporation, 1987.

McFarland, H. Neill. *The Rush Hour of the Gods: A Study of New Religious Movements in Japan.* New York: Macmillan, 1967.

McGinn, Bernard. *Visions of the End: Apocalyptic Traditions in the Middle Ages.* New York: Columbia University Press, 1979.

———. *Antichrist: Two Thousand Years of the Human Fascination with Evil.* San Francisco: Harper, 1994.

Meissner, W. W. *Thy Kingdom Come: Psychoanalytic Perspectives on the Messiah and the Millennium.* Kansas City: Sheed & Ward, 1995.

Merton, Robert K. *Mass Persuasion.* New York: Harper, 1946.

Metraux, Daniel. *Aum Shinrikyo and Japanese Youth.* Lanham MD: University Press of America, 1999.

Miller, Martin A. "The Intellectual Origins of Modern Terrorism in Europe." In *Terrorism in Context.* Ed. Martha Crenshaw. University Park, PA: The Pennsylvania State University Press, 1995, 27–62.

Mills, C. Wright. *The Causes of World War Three.* London: Secker and Warburg, 1958.

Mohaddessin, Mohammad. *Islamic Fundamentalism: The New Global Threat.* Washington, DC: Seven Locks Press, 1993.

Momen, Moojan. *An Introduction to Shi'i Islam: The History and Doctrines of Twelver Shi'ism.* New Haven: Yale University Press, 1985.

Mooney, James. *The Ghost Dance Religion and the Sioux Outbreak of 1890.* Abridged by Anthony F. C. Wallace. 1896 Reprint. Chicago: University of Chicago Press, 1965.

Moore, Stanley Williams. *Marx on the Choice between Socialism and Communism.* Cambridge, MA: Harvard University Press, 1980.

Morse, Richard. "The Heritage of Latin America." In *The Founding of New Societies: Studies in the History of the United States, Latin America, Canada, and Australia.* Ed. Louis Hartz. New York: Harcourt, Brace and World, 1964.

Morton, W. Scott. *Japan: Its History and Culture.* 3rd ed. New York: McGraw-Hill, 1994.

Mullins, Mark. "Ideology and Utopianism in Wartime Japan: An Essay on the Subversiveness of Christian Eschatology." *Japanese Journal of Religious Studies* Vol. 21 (1994).

Mullins, Michael. "Aum Shinrikyo as an Apocalyptic Movement." In *Millennium, Messiahs, and Mayhem: Contemporary Apocalyptic Movements.* Ed. Thomas Robbins and Susan J. Palmer. New York: Routledge, 1997, 313–324.

Murakami, Haruki. *Underground: The Tokyo Gas Attack and the Japanese Psyche.* Translated from the Japanese by Alfred Birnbaum and Philip Gabriel. New York: Vintage International, 2001.

Nabil, Muhammed Zarandi. *The Dawnbreakers: Nabil's Narrative of the Early Days of the Baha'i Revelation.* Wilmette, IL: Baha'i Publishing Trust, 1932.

Naquin, Susan. *Millenarian Rebellion in China: The Eight Trigrams Uprisings of 1813.* New Haven, CT: Yale University Press, 1976.

Nasr, Seyyed Hossein. *Islam: Religion, History, and Civilization.* San Francisco: HarperCollins, 2003.

Netanyahu, Benjamin. *Fighting Terrorism: How Democracies Can Defeat Domestic and International Terrorists.* New York: Farrar Straus Giroux, 1995.

Norton, Augustus Richard. *Amal and the Shi'a: Struggle for the Soul of Lebanon.* Austin, TX: University of Texas Press, 1987.

———. "Hizballah and the Israeli Withdrawal from Southern Lebanon." *Journal of Palestinian Studies* Vol. 30, No. 1 (Autumn 2000).

Office of the Coordinator for Counterterrorism. *Patterns of Global Terrorism 1996.* US Department of State Publications, 10433. Washington, DC: State Department Publications, April 1997.

Ooms, Emily Groszos. *Women and Millenarian Protest in Meiji Japan: Deguchi Nao and Omotokyo.* Ithaca, NY: Cornell University East Asia Program, 1993.

"Pakistani Officials Question Two Top al-Qaeda Operatives." Transcript of *CNN Sunday Morning.* Aired September 15, 2002, 7:34 ET.

Palmer, David Scott. "Rebellion in Rural Peru: The Origins and Evolution of Sendero Luminoso." *Comparative Politics* Vol. 18, No. 2 (January 1986), 127–146.

———. "Peru's Persistent Problems." *Current History* (January 1990).

Pearlstein, Richard M. *The Mind of the Political Terrorist.* Wilmington, DE: SR Books, 1991.

"People of the Shining Path." *Dispatches.* Produced by British Broadcasting Corporation. Videocassette, 40 minutes. Berkeley, CA: Committee to Support the Revolution in Peru, 1992.

Peterson, Scott. *Native American Prophecies.* New York: Paragon, 1990.

Picard, Elizabeth. "The Lebanese Shia and Political Violence." Discussion Paper, United Nations Research Institute for Social Development, April 1993.

Pike, Frederick. *The Politics of the Miraculous in Peru: Haya de la Torre and the Spiritualist Tradition.* Lincoln: University of Nebraska Press, 1986.

Pinault, David. *The Shiites: Ritual and Popular Piety in a Muslim Community.* New York: St. Martin's, 1992.

"Poll: Muslims Call U.S. 'Ruthless, Arrogant,' " www.cnn.com/2002/US/02/26/gallup.muslims.

Poole, Deborah and Gerardo Renique. *Peru: Time of Fear.* London: Latin American Bureau, 1992.

Population Statistics, University of Utrecht. www.library.uu.nl/wesp/populstat/americas/peru.htm.

Post, Jerold M. "Rewarding Fire with Fire? Effects of Retaliation on Terrorist Group Dynamics." In *Contemporary Trends in World Terrorism.* Ed. Anat Kurz. New York: Praeger, 1987, 103–115.

———. "Terrorist Psycho-Logic: Terrorist Behavior as a Product of Psychological Forces." In *Origins of Terrorism: Psychologies, Ideologies, Theologies, States of Mind.* Ed. Walter Reich. Cambridge: Cambridge University Press, 1990, 25–40.

Pratch, Leslie and Jordan Jacobowitz. "The Psychology of Leadership in Rapidly Changing Conditions: A Structural Psychological Approach." *Genetic, Social, and General Psychology Monographs* Vol. 123, No. 2 (May 1997), 169–197.

Du Preez, Peter. *The Politics of Identity: Ideology and the Human Image.* Oxford: Basil Blackwell, 1980.

Ramazani, R. K. "Shi'ism in the Persian Gulf." In *Shi'ism and Social Protest.* Ed. Juan R. I. Cole and Nikki Keddie. New Haven: Yale University Press, 1986.

Ranger, T. O. "Connexions between 'Primary Resistance' Movements and Modern Mass Nationalism in East and Central Africa." *Journal of African History* Vol. 9 (1968), 437–453, 631–641.

Ranstorp, Magnus. *Hizb'allah in Lebanon: The Politics of the Western Hostage Crisis.* New York: St. Martin's Press, 1997.

Rapoport, David C. "The Politics of Atrocity." In *Terrorism: Interdisciplinary Perspectives.* Ed. Yonah Alexander and Seymour Finger. New York: John Jay, 1977, 46–61.

———. "Fear and Trembling: Terrorism in Three Religious Traditions." *The American Political Science Review* Vol. 78, No. 3 (September 1984), 658–677.

Rapoport, David C. "Why Does Religious Messianism Produce Terror?" In *Contemporary Research on Terrorism*. Ed. Paul Wilkinson and Alasdair M. Stewart. Aberdeen: Aberdeen University Press, 1987, 72–88.

———. "Sacred Terror: A Contemporary Example from Islam." In *Origins of Terrorism: Psychologies, Ideologies, Theologies, States of Mind*. Ed. Walter Reich. Cambridge: Cambridge University Press, 1990, 103–130.

Reader, Ian. *Religion in Contemporary Japan*. Honolulu: University of Hawaii Press, 1991.

———. *A Poisonous Cocktail: Aum Shinrikyo's Path to Violence*. Copenhagen: Nordic Institute of Asian Studies, 1996.

———. *Religious Violence in Contemporary Japan: The Case of Aum Shinrikyo*. Honolulu: University of Hawaii Press, 2000.

Reeves, Marjorie. *The Influence of Prophecy in the Later Middle Ages: A Study of Joachimism*. Oxford: Clarendon Press, 1969.

Resolution E, *Final Act of the United Nations' Diplomatic Conference of Plenipotentiaries on the Establishment of an International Criminal Court*. UN Doc. A/Conf. 18/10, July 17, 1998. www.un.org.

"Revolution in Peru." Berkeley, CA: Committee to Support the Revolution in Peru, 1985.

Richard, Yann. *Shi'ite Islam*. Trans. Antonia Nevill. Cambridge, MA: Blackwell, 1995.

Rinehart, James F. *Revolution and the Millennium: China, Mexico, and Iran*. Westport, CT: Praeger, 1997.

Roe, Peter G. "The Josho Nahuanbo Are All Wet and Undercooked: Shipibo Views of the Whiteman and the Incas in Myth, Legend, and History." In *Rethinking History and Myth: Indigenous South American Perspectives on the Past*. Ed. Jonathan D. Hill. Urbana, IL: University of Illinois Press, 1988, 106–135.

Rosen, Zvi. *Bruno Bauer and Karl Marx: The Influence of Bruno Bauer on Marx's Thought*. The Hague: Nijhoff, 1977.

Rudé, George. *The Crowd in History: A Study of Popular Disturbances in France and England, 1730–1848*. Revised Edition. London: Lawrence and Wishart, 1981.

Runciman, Steven. *A History of the Crusades*. 1951 Reprint. Cambridge: Cambridge University Press, 1995.

Sachedina, Abdulaziz Abdulhussein. *Islamic Messianism: The Idea of the Mahdi in Twelver Shi'ism*. Albany: State University of New York Press, 1981.

Salibi, Kamal. *A House of Many Mansions: The History of Lebanon Reconsidered*. Berkeley: University of California Press, 1988.

Sallnow, Michael J. *Pilgrims of the Andes: Regional Cults in Cusco*. Washington, DC: Smithsonian Institution Press, 1987.

Scheiner, Irwin. "The Mindful Peasant: Sketches for a Study of Rebellion." *The Journal of Asian Studies* Vol. 32, No. 4 (August 1973), 579–591.

Schmid, Alex P., Albert J. Jongman, et al. *Political Terrorism: A New Guide to Actors, Authors, Concepts, Data Bases, Theories, and Literature*. New Brunswick, NJ: Transaction Books, 1988.

Schoenberg, Harris O. *A Mandate for Terror: The United Nations and the PLO.* New York: Shapolsky Books, 1989.

Seeman, Melvin. "On the Meaning of Alienation." *American Sociological Review* Vol. 24 (1959), 42–62.

Shapiro, Judith. "From Tupa to the Land without Evil: The Christianization of Tupi-Guarani Cosmology." *American Ethnologist* Vol. 14 (1987).

Sharif, Hasan. "South Lebanon: Its History and Geopolitics." In *South Lebanon.* Ed. Samih Farsoun and Elaine Hagopian. Washington, DC: Association of Arab-American University Graduates, 1978.

Shibusawa Keizo, ed. *Japanese Life and Culture in the Meiji Era.* Trans. Charles S. Terry. Centenary Culture Council Series, Vol. 5. Tokyo: Obunsha (1958).

Shimazono Susumu. "The Evolution of Aum Shinrikyo as a Religious Movement." In *Religion and Social Crisis in Japan: Understanding Japanese Society through the Aum Affair.* Ed. Robert J. Kisala and Mark R. Mullins. New York: Palgrave, 2001, 19–52.

Skar, Sarah Lund. *Live's Together—World's Apart: Quechua Colonization in Jungle and City.* Oslo: Scandinavian University Press, 1994.

Smith, Patrick. *Japan: A Reinterpretation.* New York: Vintage, 1997.

Smith, Peter. *The Babi and Baha'i Religions: From Messianic Shi'ism to a World Religion.* Cambridge: Cambridge University Press, 1987.

Sofaer, Abraham. "Terrorism and the Law." *Foreign Affairs* Vol. 64, No. 5 (Summer 1986), 901–922.

Spence, Jonathan. *God's Chinese Son: The Taiping Heavenly Kingdom of Hong Xiuquan.* New York: W.W. Norton, 1996.

Sponberg, Alan, and Helen Hardacre, eds. *Maitreya, the Future Buddha.* Cambridge: Cambridge University Press, 1988.

Stark Rodney, "A Theory of Revelations." *Journal for the Scientific Study of Religion* Vol. 38, No. 2 (June 1999).

"Statement of the Political Prisoners and War Prisoners of Peru." Trans. Peru's People's Movement, *The New Flag.* The People's War in Peru Website http://www.blythe.org/peru-pcp/intro1tcc.htm.

Stern, Steve J. *Peru's Indian Peoples and the Challenge of Spanish Conquest: Huamanga to 1640.* 2nd ed. Madison: University of Wisconsin Press, 1993.

———. *Shining and Other Paths: War and Society in Peru, 1980–1995.* Durham: Duke University Press, 1998.

Strong, Simon. *Shining Path: Terror and Revolution in Peru.* New York: Times Books, 1992.

Tammen, M. "Drug War vs. Land Reform in Peru." *USA Today Magazine* Vol. 120, No. 2560 (January 1992).

Tarazona-Sevillano, Gabriela and John B. Reuter. *Sendero Luminoso and the Threat of Narcoterrorism.* New York: Praeger, 1990.

Taylor, Maxwell. *The Fanatics: A Behavioural Approach to Political Violence.* London: Brassey's, 1991.

Taylor, Maxwell and Ethel Quayle. *Terrorist Lives.* London: Brassey's, 1994.

Terrorist Research and Analytical Center, National Security Division, Federal Bureau of Investigation. *Terrorism in the United States 1995.* Washington, DC: US Department of Justice, 1996.

Thackrah, R. "Terrorism: A Definitional Problem." In *Contemporary Research on Terrorism.* Ed. Paul Wilkinson and Alasdair M. Stewart. Aberdeen: Aberdeen University Press, 1987, 24–41.

"The Illuminated One." *Ilustracion Peruana Caretas.* www.caretas.com.pe/1379/iluminado.htm.

"The Twelfth Imam." www.shia.org.

Tilly, Charles. *From Mobilization to Revolution.* Reading, MA: Addison-Wesley, 1978.

Tyler, Royall. "The Tokugawa Peace and Popular Religion: Suzuki Shosan, Kakugyo Tobutsu, and Jikigyo Miroku." In *Confucianism and Tokugawa Culture.* Ed. Peter Nosco. Princeton: Princeton University Press, 1984, 92–119.

United States Central Intelligence Agency. Senior Analytical Manager, DCI Counterterrorist Center, Speech to the World Affairs Council, San Antonio, Texas, October 7, 1996.

United States Departments of the Army and the Air Force. *Military Operations in Low Intensity Conflict.* Field Manual 100–20/Air Force Pamphlet 3–20. Washington, DC, Headquarters, Departments of the Army and Air Force, 1990.

Varese, Stefano. "The Ethnopolitics of Indian Resistance in Latin America." *Latin American Perspectives* Vol. 23, No. 2 (Spring 1996), 58–71.

Wachtel, Nathan. *The Vision of the Vanquished: The Spanish Conquest of Peru through Indian Eyes, 1530–1570.* Trans. Ben and Sian Reynolds. New York: Barnes & Noble, 1977.

Walker, Charles F. *Smoldering Ashes: Cuzco and the Creation of Republican Peru, 1780–1840.* Durham, NC: Duke University Press, 1999.

Wallace, Anthony F. C. "Revitalization Movements." *American Anthropologist* Vol. 58 (1956).

———. *The Death and Rebirth of the Seneca.* New York: Vintage, 1969.

Wallace, Paul. "Political Violence and Terrorism in India." In *Terrorism in Context.* Ed. Martha Crenshaw. University Park, PA: The Pennsylvania State University Press, 1995.

Walsh, James. "Shoko Asahara: The Making of a Messiah." *Time* Vol. 145, No. 14 (1995), 30–32.

Wasserstrom, Robert. *Class and Society in Central Chiapas.* Berkeley: University of California Press, 1983.

Watanabe, Manabu. "Religion and Violence in Japan Today: A Chronological and Doctrinal Analysis of Aum Shinrikyo." *Terrorism and Political Violence* Vol. 10, No. 4 (Winter 1998).

Wessinger, Catherine. *How the Millennium Comes Violently: From Jonestown to Heaven's Gate.* New York: Seven Bridges Press, 2000.

Whitaker, Brian. "Hizbollah: Israel Is an Illegitimate Entity." *The Guardian* March 4, 2001.

"Why a People's War?" *The New Flag*. The People's War in Peru Website. http://www.blythe.org/peru-pcp/intro/intro2.htm.

"Why Is the World Interested in Peru?" *The New Flag*. The People's War in Peru Website. http://www.blythe.org/peru-pcp/intro/intro1.htm.

Williams, F. E. *"The Vailala Madness" and Other Essays*. Ed. Eric Schwimmer. Honolulu: The University of Hawaii Press, 1977.

Willner, Ann Ruth. *The Spellbinders: Charismatic Political Leadership*. New Haven: Yale University Press, 1984.

Willner, Ann Ruth and Dorothy Willner. "The Rise and Role of Charismatic Leaders." *Annals of the American Academy of Political and Social Science* Vol. 358 (March 1965), 82–95.

Wills, Gary. *Certain Trumpets: The Call of Leaders*. New York: Simon and Schuster, 1994.

Wilson, Fiona. "Indians and Mestizos: Identity and Urban Popular Culture in Andean Peru." *Journal of Southern African Studies* Vol. 26, No. 2 (June 2000).

Worsley, Peter. *The Trumpet Shall Sound: A Study of "Cargo Cults" in Melanesia*. 2nd ed. New York: Schocken, 1968.

Yamashita, Akiko. "The 'Eschatology' of Japanese New and New New Religions From Tenri-kyo to Kofuku no Kagaku." *Inter-Religio* Bulletin No. 33 (Summer 1998), 3–21.

Zawodny, J. K. "Infrastructures of Terrorist Organizations." In *Perspectives on Terrorism*. Ed. L. Z. Freedman and Yonah Alexander. Wilmington, DE: Scholarly Resources, 61–70.

INDEX